Ha

William J. Higginson

KODANSHA INTERNATIONAL
Tokyo • New York • London

Distributed in the United States by Kodansha America, Inc., 114 Fifth Avenue, New York, N.Y. 10011, and in the United Kingdom and continental Europe by Kodansha Europe Ltd., 95 Aldwych, London WC2B 4JF. Published by Kodansha International Ltd., 17-14 Otowa 1-chome, Bunkyo-ku, Tokyo 112, and Kodansha America, Inc.

First edition, 1996.
96 97 98 10 9 8 7 6 5 4 3 2 1

ISBN 4-7700-2090-2

Library of Congress Cataloging-in-Publication Data
A catalog record for this book is available from the Library of Congress

Dedicated to

Penny Harter

poet and partner

and

Tadashi "Shōkan" Kondō

and

Kristine Young Kondō

poets and ambassadors

CONTENTS

PREFACE

A few words may be in order on how this book came into being and how these poems were collected. I have been actively studying the use of seasonal topics in the haikai poetries since 1983, when I finished writing *The Haiku Handbook: How to Write, Share, and Teach Haiku*. In the late 1980s this led to my "Seasoned Haiku" column in *Frogpond*, the magazine of the Haiku Society of America, and a good deal of correspondence with poets about the seasonal aspects of their work. In 1990 I planned to conclude this study with a book discussing my discoveries, but soon found that there was no book in English that clearly set out the development of the seasonal theme in the Japanese tradition. Nor was their any comprehensive collection of poems upon which one might base a discussion of the seasonal aspects of haiku around the world. This resulted in what I have come to call "The Haiku Seasons Project"—my own attempt to understand the natural basis for the Japanese haikai tradition, and to apply that understanding to poems written by both Japanese poets and others responding to that tradition.

This book's companion volume, *The Haiku Seasons: Poetry of the Natural World*, presents a brief history of the place of nature and the seasons in traditional Japanese poetry, from the *Manyōshū* over a millennium ago to the dominant form of haiku publication in Japan today, the *haikai saijiki* or poetry almanac. In conclusion, *The Haiku Seasons* proposes the creation of an international saijiki, based on the Japanese model, with poems from many languages, countries, and climates. It includes a number of examples of the kinds of entries and poems that might appear in such a book. And I hope it serves as a bridge between a traditional Japanese understanding of the saijiki and this book, which attempts to be such an international poetry almanac.

While I worked on the haiku seasons project, interest in writing linked poems was growing outside of Japan, and it became apparent that many poets wanted a practical guide to help them handle the seasons in renku. A month-long North American tour of readings by Japanese renku poets and collaborative writing sessions in which

Americans and Canadians joined their Japanese guests in 1992 spurred further interest, and a brief guide to season words prepared for that tour became an important tool for North American poets who went on to write more renku later.

Meanwhile, the history and understanding of haiku and senryu have varied greatly inside and outside of the Japanese poetry community. Haiku and senryu poets writing in Japanese have typically shunned each other, each seeing its work as a—or perhaps the only—true descendant of Bashō's haikai. Poets writing in other languages have often not known a great deal about the differences between the two types of short poems, and sometimes lumped them together without indicating, or knowing, which is which. The alienation of the two groups of poets in Japan and the ignorance of the poets outside Japan have resulted in communication problems. Because of the inclusion of senryu among foreign haiku, Japanese haiku poets have often seen foreign adaptations of haiku as inferior to Japanese haiku. Because foreign haiku poets have known little about senryu, many of them have sought contacts only with the haiku community in Japan.

The rising interest in renku, both in Japan and elsewhere, offers an opportunity to see the haikai world whole. In and immediately after Bashō's day, the same poets participated in renku and wrote and judged haiku and senryu. Today the need for understanding the interdependent relationships among the hokku, or opening stanza of a renku, and the main types of internal stanzas of the same renku, many of which might be classified as haiku or senryu, leads me to the conclusion that only a saijiki that includes and clearly differentiates among "the three faces of haikai"—hokku, haiku, and senryu—will truly serve the needs of the widest range of interested readers and poets. That is the intent of this book.

An international haikai saijiki is an experiment. A great deal of work by many people has gone into producing this small beginning. Poets in widely separated areas have given me much help and encouragement, digging out facts on local events and phenomena. I have acknowledged those who have made major contributions to my work at the end of this preface.

THE NATURE AND ORGANIZATION OF THIS BOOK

Haiku World: An International Poetry Almanac includes over 1,000 poems originally written in 25 languages by more than 600 poets from some 50 countries. The poems are organized under 680 seasonal and nonseasonal topics. To summarize its main features:

1. For the first time in any language, *Haiku World* collects a substantial number of haiku and related poems by Japanese and non-Japanese poets on an equal footing in their most traditional setting, so that this poetry, originating in Japan but now composed and appreciated worldwide, may be seen by all parties as a truly global phenomenon. Thus, *Haiku World* provides a comprehensive overview of the state of the art in the latter decades of the twentieth century.

2. *Haiku World* shows how haiku and related poems written in all languages equally reflect the primary characteristics of the haikai genre. Arranging the poems by traditional topics allows each poem to join the global effort to see and appreciate the human and natural world, to become a part of the great chorus rather than remain isolated as a private solo.

3. *Haiku World* demonstrates the diversity and unity of the various poetries collectively known as haikai—haiku, senryu, and renku—with a broad sampling from all three.

4. *Haiku World* offers a selection of Japanese as well as non-Japanese haikai poems that apply to aspects of life beyond the borders of any specific season by including a nonseasonal section based on the deepest aspects of the tradition and on recent developments in constructing Japanese saijiki.

While *The Haiku Seasons* introduces the development and purposes of the traditional Japanese haikai saijiki and proposes an international collection organized in a similar manner, *Haiku World* has its own "Introduction to the International Haikai Saijiki" describing this book's structure and use. And *Haiku World* includes a full index to topics, season words, and keywords.

The "International Haikai Saijiki" that makes up the bulk of *Haiku World* is a collection of haiku, senryu, and linked-verse-related stanzas, all organized not by poet or language or country, but by topic. There are more than 680 topic entries in the saijiki. Though its organization closely follows that of one of the most authoritative of Japanese saijiki, I strongly recommend that both Japanese and non-Japanese readers carefully peruse the "Introduction to the International Saijiki" before plunging directly into the saijiki itself, since this saijiki includes some features not found in typical Japanese saijiki.

The "Index of Topics, Season Words, and Keywords" includes the 3,600 words and phrases that are discussed in the body of the saijiki. This may seem like a large number, but even the smallest "season guide" commonly found in Japanese haiku poets' shirt pockets and purses—the *Kiyose* edited by the mid-twentieth century master Kyoshi Takahama and revised by his son Toshio—includes about 2,400. The *Hototogisu New Saijiki* edited by Kyoshi's granddaughter, Teiko Inahata, and about the size of a field guide discusses more than 6,000 season words in over 2,100 entries.

The saijiki index shows the season of each word or phrase, as well as its place in the text. Though usually omitted in Japanese saijiki, *Haiku World* also includes an index of poets.

The Haiku Seasons provides the background necessary to appreciate the saijiki in general—and to learn where some of its quirks come from. The introduction to the saijiki in *Haiku World* explains a number of unique features not found in any previous Western-language book that I know of. After that, readers may wish to browse here and there in the main body of the saijiki, or read it straight through, as an anthology and guide to haikai literature around the world. Finally, the index will help readers quickly find the season of any term included in the book, and refer them to specific articles for more information and sample poems. (Note: A bibliography in *The Haiku Seasons* lists all books mentioned in this preface and the introduction to the saijiki.)

THE POEMS AND THEIR PLACEMENT BY SEASONS

The majority of the poems collected in this international saijiki were sent to me by their authors as a result of a call for poems mailed in January 1994.

As a consequence of including many poems sent to me by the poets themselves, almost all of the poets represented in the saijiki are living today. In only a very few cases have I included poems by poets who were not living in 1990. To the best of my knowledge all works included in the saijiki were composed within the last two to three decades, many within the few years prior to publication of this book.

One guiding principle overshadowed all others in selecting poems for inclusion in the saijiki: quality. No poet, no country, no seasonal phenomenon, was included merely because of a desire to include the same. Perhaps three-quarters of the poems in the saijiki were selected purely on the basis of merit from the work submitted in response to the call for poems. The remaining twenty-five percent or so were picked from published sources, or—in a very few cases—specifically commissioned in order to ensure that particular topics were included. In selecting from published sources, I avoided including poems in already widely distributed books known to most English-language haiku poets; virtually nothing here duplicates work in *The Haiku Handbook: How to Write, Share, and Teach Haiku* (Kodansha International) by myself and Penny Harter, or in either edition of Cor van den Heuvel's book, *The Haiku Anthology* (Anchor Doubleday, 1974; Simon & Schuster, 1986). I hope that most readers will find the poems here as fresh and exciting as I have during the process of assembling them.

While I made good use of the seasonal information supplied by many of the poets who sent work for possible inclusion, and most of the poems found their places quite easily, I was faced with some problems regarding seasonal placement. In the simplest instances a poem clearly refers to a phenomenon traditionally included in the Japanese system, and nothing in the poem or the region in which the poem may have been composed contradicts the traditional placement. In another common case, a poem clearly identifies a seasonal phenomenon which may not occur in Japan or has not yet been included in Japanese saijiki, but which correlates well with other phenomena already acknowledged in the system, and so the poem naturally falls into place in a new entry among similar phenomena. These two cases account for the overwhelming majority of the placements in this saijiki. (Since the seasons of haikai begin and end at times of the year different from the now-conventional European understanding of the seasons, some of these "obvious" placements will still mystify those unfamiliar with this aspect of the haikai tradition. *The Haiku Seasons* gives the necessary background.)

In a few instances, however, poems seem to have seasonal meanings for their authors which I and other readers could not discern upon close reading, or poems have obvious seasonal meanings which contradict their authors' statements about seasonal content. In the latter situation, seasonal poems have been placed according to the apparent seasons in the poems. And poems which do not present phenomena commonly associated with a particular season either by fact of nature or by tradition have been placed in the "All Year" section of the saijiki. This nonseasonal section is fully explained in the introduction to the saijiki.

TRANSLATIONS

Many of the poems in the saijiki were originally written in English, the only language in which I can claim much skill. If the original is not in English, both the original and an English translation have been supplied. The many translations were arrived at in one of three ways: The authors supplied me with their own translations, or with translations made by friends, which I then checked and altered, if necessary, to accord with the goals of this book. The poems and translations appeared in publications, and I subsequently revised the translations, if needed. Or I encountered the poems only in their original languages and made translations of my own; this is often the case with poems from Japanese, French, and Spanish.

Virtually all of the translations have been checked with native speakers who are themselves poets; I must take credit for any remaining errors, which will be happily repaired in future printings if I receive corrections. (Address at the end of this preface.)

My goals in making or reworking translations have been, first, to make the poem as clear and accessible in English as in the original; second, to make the translation as much a poem as the original; third, to translate as literally as possible the word or phrase linking the poem to the topic under which it appears in the saijiki. In the past translators of Japanese haiku have not known or paid much attention to the season words themselves, resulting in translations that obscure or even change the season beyond recognition. I hope that this book will help translators to better understand the significance of the seasonal aspect of most traditional haiku, and to identify the specific seasonal content of the poems they are working on. Without understanding the season and its implications for the content of a traditional Japanese poem with a seasonal element, it may well be nearly impossible to produce a translation that accurately projects the experience in the mind of even the casual Japanese reader.

All poems in *Haiku World* are given with the original language on the left and an English translation on the right for languages other than English. In some cases, for example Japanese and Urdu, the original languages appear in transliterated form so that readers of English may have an impression of the sounds of the originals.

A NOTE ON NAMES

For a century and a half the Japanese have been dealing with the fact that names in Asia are usually presented with the family name first, followed by the given name, the opposite of the way they are presented in most of Europe. Their solutions have included printing family names in all capital letters in Western-language publications, as well as putting names in either Eastern or Western order.

The all-capital-letter solution may seem practical to those whose original language has no upper and lower case letters, but shouts the family name at native readers of English and other Western languages. Since the given names of haiku, renku, and senryu poets are often more important than the family names, an approach that emphasizes the family name seems unwarranted. Meanwhile, Japanese writers and publishers have increasingly used Western languages—there are several fine Japanese newspapers in English, for example. And these Japanese Western-language publishers have almost uniformly moved to putting all names in the same order, the Western order with given name first.

In *The Haiku Handbook* I originally chose to follow the Japanese-language practice, and put the surnames of Japanese poets first. This meant that Japanese and Western names were given in the opposite order. For *The Haiku Seasons* and *Haiku World* this seems to make little sense, as many of the Japanese names included appear regularly given-name-first in Western publications, and several are of persons of Japanese ancestry living in countries where their names normally appear given-name-first. All names in *The Haiku Seasons* are presented given-name-first except in the publication acknowledgements and author index at the end of the book. Note also that I have followed the same practice in transliterating Japanese names as with Japanese words, using the romanization found in *Kenkyusha's New Japanese-English Dictionary* in which the final *n* remains *n* before *b*, *m*, and *p*, instead of changing to *m*. Exceptions occur when a Japanese poet personally prefers a different romanization; for example, Tohta Kaneko (instead of Tōta).

ACKNOWLEDGEMENTS

In *The Haiku Seasons* I gratefully acknowledged the many Japanese individuals and institutions that have hosted myself and my wife since the publication of *The Haiku Handbook* in 1985, thus contributing to my understanding of the saijiki. Here I must thank those many people who provided extraordinary service to compiling and understanding the materials that went directly into making this book.

Many of the poets included in *Haiku World* not only sent poems in manuscript, but included copies of their books and detailed notes on the seasonal phenomena involved in their poems as well. I am very grateful to all the poets who responded for their generosity and patience. (An appendix acknowledges the publications where many of the poems included in the saijiki previously appeared.)

In addition, a number of prominent Japanese haiku masters have graciously allowed me to use selections from their works, for which I am deeply grateful.

Several poets and other good people provided me with haiku publications in addition to their own works, gave me extensive information on seasonal phenomena in the form of books or detailed personal accounts, helped greatly with translations, put me in touch with or recommended other poets, or all of the above. These essential collaborators include Elisabeth Alley; Dimitar Anakiev, editor of *Haiku Novine*; Herb Barrett; Janice M. Bostok; Miriana Bozin; Margret Buerschaper, president of the German Haiku Society; Marijan Čekolj, president of the Croatian Haiku Association; David Cobb, secretary of the British Haiku Society; Ion Codrescu, president of the Haiku Society of Constanţa, Romania; Mihaela Codrescu; Susan P. Coen and her daughters Nancy and Stephanie; Carol Conti-Entin; Alfonso Cisneros Cox; Kristen Deming; Jhinabhai Desai; James Dunlap, proprietor of Alla Books; Bart Durham, proprietor of De la Peña Books; Dee Evetts; Thomas Fitzsimmons, publisher of Katydid Books; Ty Hadman; Doris Heitmeyer, secretary of the Haiku Society of America; Karel Hellemans, secretary of the editorial board of *Vuursteen*; Kimiko Horne, member of the *Kaitei* and *Nindō* haiku clubs; Tsunehiko Hoshino; Deon Kesting; Elizabeth Searle Lamb, former editor of *Frogpond*; Tomislav Maretić; Michael McNierney; Bart Messoten, *Vuursteen* editor for Flanders; Manuela Miga; John O'Connor; Nicholas Potter, proprietor of Nicholas Potter Booksellers; Anne Ranasinghe; Wanda Reumer, former president of the Haiku Circle of the

Netherlands; Leo and Elizabeth Romero, proprietors of Books and More Books; the Santa Fe Public Library, particularly the undaunted reference staff including Russell Smith and Elizabeth West; Hiroaki Sato; Humberto Senegal, president of the Colombia Association for Haiku; Bill Sewell, president of the New Zealand Poetry Society; Jeanette Stace, secretary of the New Zealand Poetry Society; Sakuzō Takada; Kiyoko Tokutomi, co-founder of the Yuki Teikei Haiku Society of the United States and Canada; Makoto Ueda, chairman of the Department of Asian Studies, Stanford University; the University of New Mexico Herbarium; Cor van den Heuvel, editor of *The Haiku Anthology*; Michael Dylan Welch, publisher of Press Here books; David Wright, past president of the Yuki Teikei Haiku Society of the United States and Canada; and Ikuyo Yoshimura of the Rainbow English Haiku Society, Gifu.

Willard Johnson, professor in the Department of Religious Studies of San Diego State University and author of *Riding the Ox Home* (one of the more useful books on Buddhism), gave me the extended loan of his library of books on bird lore, East and West.

Meagan Calogeras, Editor at Kodansha International, provided considerable guidance that greatly improved the manuscript of both books at every stage of development. Much of their coherence and lucidity derives from her efforts. Responsibility for any persisting difficulties in readability remains with the author. In addition, the design department at Kodansha International has found ways to present the text that greatly assist in adapting the formats of a Japanese saijiki to the needs of an English-language work.

The Witter Bynner Foundation for Poetry funded a translation project at Santa Fe Preparatory School in the latter half of 1994 which in part supported the author during work on these books; my deep gratitude goes to these institutions, and to Foundation Director Steven Schwartz and Headmaster Stephen M. Machen for their generous assistance.

Paul Hummel, chiropractor, and his staff including Phoebe Hummel, Linda Leonard, Jeff Meyer, Debra Meyer, and Susan Steffy, kept me going physically when it seemed the body would give up before this project got done. And Steve Swart, doctor of oriental medicine, helped me establish a routine to restore general health during the final months of this book's preparation.

Penny Harter, wife and confidante, supported me and this project in more ways than words can tell.

In the coming year I hope to launch an international newsletter devoted to haikai. For information, please write to me at From Here Press, P. O. Box 2740, Santa Fe, NM 87504.

I hope that *The Haiku Seasons* and *Haiku World* promote a deeper understanding of haiku and the closely related poetry of hokku and senryu. This understanding may inform and assist in the creative process, but is not intended to limit or hamper that process. Do not put history, theory, or organization between yourself and Bashō's pine tree, but use these and all such books to help you go out and find the pine tree, so that you may "learn of the pine" sooner, and more richly.

William J. Higginson
Santa Fe, May 1996

INTRODUCTION TO
THE INTERNATIONAL HAIKAI SAIJIKI

Submit to nature, return to nature.

Bashō (1644-1694)

Each Season offers a kind of haiku that cannot be picked at any other time. . . . But I do not see nature as something quiet or in terms of the four seasons alone. I see active movement in it. I see force in it.

Seisensui Ogiwara (1884-1976)
translated by Makoto Ueda

Here is an anthology of hokku, haiku, and senryu arranged by season and category. The first five sections cover the classic seasons of haikai: Spring, Summer, Autumn, Winter, and the New Year. A final section, All Year, includes topics and poems which connect with nature, but which do not name anything either traditionally or obviously connected with the seasons.

For an overview of the saijiki in general, its history and organization, please read Chapter 5 of this book's companion volume, *The Haiku Seasons*. The chapter includes a fuller explanation of the relationship between the seasons and the calendar, which will help you to understand what follows. Chapter 6 of *The Haiku Seasons*, focused on how to build and use an international saijiki and even how to make your own, may also be particularly helpful.

THE CALENDAR AND THE SEASONS

The traditional seasons of Japanese haikai follow the old Chinese solar calendar, with spring beginning midway between the winter solstice and spring equinox. Thus, each season peaks at its solstice or equinox. (Compare this with the astronomical definition of the seasons as each beginning on its respective solstice or equinox.) Seasons are further divided into early, middle, and late periods.

To give an idea of the whole system, here is a chart of the seasons of traditional Japanese poetry with corresponding dates in the Gregorian calendar for both temperate zones.

TRADITIONAL JAPANESE SEASONS AND THE GREGORIAN CALENDAR

(See Notes following.)

NORTH TEMPERATE	SEASONAL PERIOD	SOUTH TEMPERATE
4 Feb–5 Mar (Feb)	Early Spring	8 Aug–7 Sep (Aug)
6 Mar–4 Apr (Mar)	Mid Spring	8 Sep–7 Oct (Sep)
5 Apr–5 May (Apr)	Late Spring	8 Oct–6 Nov (Oct)
6 May–5 Jun (May)	Early Summer	7 Nov–6 Dec (Nov)
6 Jun–6 Jul (Jun)	Mid Summer	7 Dec–4 Jan (Dec)
7 Jul–7 Aug (Jul)	Late Summer	5 Jan–3 Feb (Jan)
8 Aug–7 Sep (Aug)	Early Autumn	4 Feb–5 Mar (Feb)
8 Sep–7 Oct (Sep)	Mid Autumn	6 Mar–4 Apr (Mar)
8 Oct–6 Nov (Oct)	Late Autumn	5 Apr–5 May (Apr)
7 Nov–6 Dec (Nov)	Early Winter	6 May–5 Jun (May)
7 Dec–4 Jan (Dec)	Mid Winter	6 Jun–6 Jul (Jun)
5 Jan–3 Feb (Jan)	Late Winter	7 Jul–7 Aug (Jul)

Notes:

1. Dates shown for the north temperate zone correspond to the named periods according to the Japanese tradition. Exact dates for any given period may vary by one day from year to year—with the variation in solstice or equinox.

2. The months and dates listed for the south temperate zone are constructed on the model of those for the north temperate zone, with the dates flipped appropriately.

3. The months shown in parentheses are nominally accepted for each period by traditional haikai poets. These work quite well for all but the border-season "Observances" (festivals and holidays), which, if they fall very early in the month, belong in the preceding seasonal period. (See the example in note 4.)

4. Any holiday observed on a fixed date stays on its date, and flips to the opposite season in the opposite hemisphere. For example, April Fools' Day (1 April) is in mid spring in the northern temperate zone, mid autumn southern.

5. Note the difference between the pair of terms "mid summer" and "mid winter" and the pair "midsummer" and "midwinter". The former haikai terms always refer to the month-long periods in the middle of the seasons, while the latter longstanding English words designate the respective solstices and the few days immediately surrounding them. Thus, "midsummer" means the summer solstice and the few days surrounding it that comprise the middle of "mid summer". To facilitate understanding the distinction, I suggest pronouncing the single words with an accent on "mid-", and accenting both "mid" and the initial syllable of the season evenly in the two-word phrases. (These are the standard English pronunciations.)

Chapter 5 of *The Haiku Seasons* explains the changes in the saijiki when Japan adopted the Gregorian calendar in the late nineteenth century. The modern saijiki includes the New Year as a separate season, with its own holiday activities and associated phenomena. The New Year and mid winter overlap in time. For example, a poem on "the first dream" of the year will appear under that topic in the New Year, while another on the topic "ice fishing" finds its place in Winter, though the same poet may have written both on the same day.

TROPICAL SEASONS

The tropics present a special problem for the saijiki. People living near the equator have a very different sense of seasons, since the rhythms of nature are controlled by fluctuations in rainfall rather than by shifts in temperature.

For example, residents of Central America may call their dry season *verano* (Spanish for "summer") and the wet season *invierno* ("winter"). In this winter, which runs from about mid February or March through mid October, "because of plentiful rain, the earth is brilliantly green, [with] birds singing and nesting, crops growing in the fields"—according to Alexander F. Skutch, in *A Naturalist on a Tropical Farm* (University of California Press, 1980). In the same region summer may extend from late October or November well into February or March, and features hot, dry weather without the lush growth of winter.

In the tropics as anywhere else, there are many things that happen only at certain times of the year, including the arrivals and departures of migratory birds (several species on opposite schedules from those seen in temperate zones), the blooming of certain trees and plants, and so on. A valuable guide to seasonal phenomena of western Costa Rica will be found in Skutch's book, which includes a substantial chapter called "A Tropical Year" organized month-by-month. But, as he points out, this calendar is specific to the west coast of Costa Rica, and will not work in other parts of central and northern South America, let alone in other tropical regions.

Sri Lanka and southern India, for example, may have four seasons, two wet and two dry, varying from year to year. The main wet season, nominally from May through October, is called "Monsoon Season" or the "Southwest Monsoons" after the source of prevailing winds which particularly affect the western coasts. On the eastern coasts, the "Northeast Trade Winds" blow from November to May, with a "Northeast Monsoon"—rainy season—from December to February or March. Usually between these rainy seasons two relatively dry periods intervene, a "cool season" from late September to December, and a "hot season" from February to May. As in Central America, a good deal of bird and blossom activity is typical of particular times of year.

The seasons in both Central America and South Asia depend more on local elevation and orientation to the seas and prevailing winds—which control rainfall—than on latitude and temperature gradients. The following chart summarizes my rough understanding of these two tropical situations:

SOME TROPICAL SEASONS

MAR APR MAY JUN JUL AUG SEP OCT NOV DEC JAN FEB

Central <-----------------"winter" (wet) ------------------>|<---- "summer" (dry) -->
America primary growing season

South <---- "hot" ---->|< ---- "Monsoon Season" -->|<-- "cool" -->|<--- "NE --->
India (dry) (wet) (dry) Monsoon"

This only suggests the range of possibilities. If a sufficient number of haikai poets becomes active in the tropics, perhaps they will organize a saijiki according to their seasonal consciousness. In this saijiki, which includes relatively few poems specific to the tropics, I have placed tropical poems and topics according to the months in which they fall. Those that reflect a seasonal consciousness quite different from that of the temperate zones have descriptions indicating the sense of the seasons involved. Thus a topic appropriate to March appears in Spring, but clearly notes its locale and seasonal connection.

ORGANIZATION OF THE SECTIONS

The five seasonal sections of the saijiki are divided into the categories listed below. Within each category, entries follow the order indicated, with some variation from season to season.

SEASONAL CATEGORIES

The Season: general climate; reminders of the previous season; solstice or equinox (which is the *middle* of the season); the months; time and length of day; temperature; approaching the end of the season; anticipating the next season.

The Heavens: sky, heavenly bodies, winds, precipitation, storms, other sky phenomena, light and shade.

The Earth: landscape; seascape; fields; forests; streams, rivers, and lakes.

Humanity: clothes; food; home; work and school; sports, recreation, and the arts; illness; travel and communications; moods.

Observances: sacred and secular holidays and festivals; associated decorations, clothing, foods, and activities; death anniversaries (usually of literary persons).
Animals: mammals; amphibians and reptiles; birds; fishes; mollusks; insects.
Plants: blossoming trees; foliage of trees and shrubs; garden flowers; fruits and vegetables; wildflowers and other wild vegetation; seaweed; fungi.

In the all-year (nonseasonal) section I have included topics similar to those listed in the *English Saijiki* edited by Naritoshi Narita, and Tohta Kaneko's *Modern Haiku Saijiki*, in an order that closely parallels the seasonal sections. Some of the categories have different titles, but the entries contain much the same kind of information as that found in the seasonal sections, in the same order. A poem that seems mainly about one of these nonseasonal topics but contains a recognized seasonal reference is included in the appropriate seasonal section.

ALL-YEAR (NONSEASONAL) CATEGORIES

The Year: the whole year or years. (Most phrases including the word "year" relate to the end of the year—mid winter—or to The New Year; this section includes phenomena that pervade or characterize a whole year and that do not reflect only the shift from one year to another.)
The Heavens: same as seasonal sections.
The Earth: same as seasonal sections, with the addition of place names.
Humanity: the body; youth and age; clothes; food; home; work and school; sports, recreation, and the arts; illness; travel and communications; moods.
Customs and Religion: relationships; sacred and secular events and rituals outside of dated holidays (birthdays, coming of age, marriage and wedding anniversaries, funerals); religion; sacred places (except that place names are included above in The Earth category).
Animals: same as seasonal sections.
Plants: same as seasonal sections.

Events such as birthdays may create some confusion. The birthdays of major national or religious figures, for example **BUDDHA'S BIRTHDAY**, are celebrated publicly, and obviously fall in the appropriate season. But the birthdays of private individuals will not have a seasonal meaning for those outside their immediate families and associates. So **birthday cake** relates to the all-year topic **BIRTHDAY**, and a poem about it will appear here—unless the poem also contains a seasonal reference. (In actual practice, if a poem clearly indicates whose birthday it refers to, and is shared only with those who know that person, then the poem is seasonal for that audience. Should the poem then be published for a wider audience, however, in effect it becomes nonseasonal.)

HOW TO FIND AN ENTRY

Organized as above, a saijiki places related and similar phenomena near one another in their respective seasons. As a result it is relatively easy to find a specific phenomenon once you have become familiar with the arrangement. The organization also allows browsing to learn more about similar phenomena in that category and season. Cross references lead to related entries in different seasons and categories.

It does take a while to learn the organization of a saijiki, however. And more often than not, I go to a saijiki to confirm my recollection of what season a specific phenomenon falls in. The Saijiki Index, which comes at the very end and includes all seasonal topics, season words, all-year topics, and keywords in this book, will quickly lead you to the pages where they are discussed. As in a Japanese saijiki, the index also indicates the season of each term. If this is all you need you may not have to look beyond the index—though I advise checking the entry to make sure it refers to the phenomenon you have in mind. This is especially true for the names of plants and birds, as many common names for them refer to more than one genus or species. (In many entries I have included scientific names to aid in identification.) Also, many common Japanese season words have homonyms which are also season words, for example *kagerō* (heat shimmer, all spring), *kagerō* (spider silk, all summer) and *kagerō* (day-fly, early autumn), or *tsuyu* (rainy season, mid summer) and *tsuyu* (dew, all autumn). English and other languages have similar problems; consider "kite" (the toy, all spring) and "kite" (the bird, all year). In such cases, the index carries a separate entry for each homonym. Finally, it is wise to remember that the index contains entries in several languages; a word that appears to be English in the index may actually be from another language and carry a different meaning from the English word of the same spelling.

If you are like me you probably will want to read the entry anyway, either to refresh your memory as to why it falls in that season or to see if there is some other helpful information in the entry. And it may be a good idea to read a poem or two on a topic that interests you, for an example often helps us understand a term better than any discussion.

THE ENTRIES AND EXAMPLE POEMS

Each category is divided into entries by topics in bold capital letters. If a given topic also appears in the *Japan Great Saijiki*, the *English Saijiki*, Tohta's *Modern Haiku Saijiki*, or some other prominent Japanese saijiki its Japanese translation appears in italics immediately following the English topic. (Note that I use the romanization similar to that found in *Kenkyusha's New Japanese-English Dictionary*, which mainly follows the conventions of the Hepburn Romanization, except that the consonant *n* falling before the consonants *b*, *m*, and *p* is represented by the letter *n*, not *m*; thus: *tonbo* [dragonfly], not *tombo*.) The absence of romanized Japanese here indicates the first appearance of the topic in a saijiki, to the best of my knowledge. These new topics usually reflect the seasonal consciousness of poets outside of Japan and appear here on the basis of established usage or natural occurrence in their regions.

Many authorities recognize some words and phrases as "seasonal topics" (*kidai*) and others as "season words" (*kigo*). Seasonal topics designate phenomena associated with a particular season, either by natural occurrence, or by tradition. Most topics refer to obviously seasonal phenomena: the blooming times of various plants; the appearances of one or another migratory bird, fish, or insect in a given locale; an annual festival or holiday; certain human activities; and weather patterns characteristic of a specific time of year. Other topics have become associated with specific times of year because of common human perceptions recognized in literature for generations. In this saijiki all topics appear in bold capital letters at the heads of entries and in references to other topics within entries.

In addition, many seasonal topics can be expressed in more than one way, and some of these additional season words (often phrases rather than single words) may also appear in an entry. In most writing about haikai the term "season word" includes the notions of both seasonal topic and season word, unless a particular poem is being discussed. Then the careful critic will distinguish between the seasonal topic of the poem and the season word in the poem itself that refers to that topic. A seasonal topic becomes a season word when the same word or phrase is used in a poem. In the entries season words that are not also topics appear in text in bold lowercase letters.

Note that not all critics agree on which terms are seasonal topics and which are season words. For example, one may designate **rising moon** as a season word under the topic **MOON**, while another will call **RISING MOON** itself a seasonal topic. In the *Japan Great Saijiki*—which is a collaboration among many poets and scholars—"rising moon" appears both in the entry for "moon" and as another entry by itself. In such cases I generally allow each term a separate entry.

The nonseasonal topics and keywords in the all-year section of this saijiki relate to each other in much the same way as do seasonal topics and season words.

Each entry introduces poems illustrating the way the topic has been used. When a poem from a language other than English or Japanese appears as an example, that poem's season word or keyword in its language is included in the entry, with the language noted.

Other italicized words or phrases in an entry may be either the Japanese or scientific (Latin) names of animals and plants; context usually makes clear which. Scientific names of families appear in roman type, genera and species in italics; families and genera are capitalized. A designation such as *Jacaranda sp.* means "species of the genus *Jacaranda*"; that is, the indicated common name refers to more than one representative of the genus. For the spellings of English common names I usually follow recent nature guides. These may differ slightly from spellings found in some dictionaries, especially as to hyphenation. In the common names of animals and plants only proper names are capitalized, such as American robin.

Some topics are singular, some plural. The Japanese language offers no guidance on this matter, since it usually provides no clue as to number. But observation and tradition usually supply a common-sense solution: Generally we look at one river at a time, but many cherry blossoms, and my choices reflect this. A poet writing in a European language must, of course, write of one or more-than-one, and such usage has influenced my decisions in this regard.

Next, after the seasonal topic and its translation at the head of an entry in a seasonal section, parentheses enclose one of the following words: all, early, mid, late. These indicate the part of the season to which the topic applies. "All" refers to the entire season, the others to the designated third. A footnote on each left-hand page shows the months nominally associated with the parts of each season—such as "Early spring, February/August"—with the north temperate month preceding that for the south temperate zone. (This does not apply to the New-Year or All-Year sections.)

The table near the beginning of this introduction called "Traditional Japanese Seasons and the Gregorian Calendar" gives a more precise view of early, mid, and late seasons. But it is important to remember that these traditional assignments are simply a convenient way to organize our observations of seasonal phenomena and poems about them. Astronomical seasons may stay the same, but perceived seasons can and do vary considerably from year to year, even in the same place. Also, the range of geography and climate found in Japan alone almost defies attempts to create a consistent timeline for many phenomena. Blinding oneself to the actual phenomena of a given place and time because of some loyalty to the saijiki will only interfere with both creating poems and appreciation of the phenomena themselves. But events in the natural world do generally follow a certain sequence, and many things occur at about the same time, though the time may vary a bit from year to year and place to place. The appearance of a certain bird or insect may well coincide with the blooming of a particular plant or the arrival of a particular weather pattern, for example, however early or late that may come in a given year.

The seasonal placement of topics in a saijiki should make sense in terms of the usual experience of a majority of the poets involved and the haikai tradition. In most cases where phenomena have been traditionally recognized in Japan, the season corresponds reasonably well for poets outside of Japan. If a particular phenomenon occurs at different times in different parts of the globe, I have usually placed it in the traditional Japanese position in the saijiki and indicated the variation.

The main text of an entry tells something about the topic. It may explain the seasonal association, if not immediately obvious, or give literary, cultural, or scientific background, or all of these. Often an entry includes other names for the topic, or identifies closely related phenomena traditionally associated with it—both of which constitute additional season words or keywords under that topic. The notation "Also called:" indicates terms which mean the same thing as the topic itself; "Also:" introduces related terms traditionally included under the same topic.

Space in a single volume of this size does not allow the inclusion of all the many topics that have been recognized in traditional saijiki, or that might be proposed for saijiki outside of Japan. In order to increase the usefulness of this saijiki, however, I have often included references to related topics in a given entry, with indications of their seasons. Sometimes these are cross-references to other entries in this saijiki, but often they refer to entries that might have been included but are not. Since all topics, season words, and keywords are indexed, this expands the total number of topics covered well beyond the number of separate entries.

I specifically encourage poets to think beyond the few examples of season words or keywords offered in this saijiki. While most Japanese haiku poets of the twentieth century have traditionally included an already accepted set-phrase in a poem on a seasonal topic, I feel that a better approach would be to ensure that persons accustomed to reading haiku and related poems will clearly understand a poem's seasonal association, regardless of the specific words used to convey it. Accordingly, in most entries I have included a representative rather than exhaustive list of such terms.

Each entry ends with one or more poems demonstrating the topic in use. The poems appear in their original languages on the left, non-English originals in italics. An original not in the Roman alphabet is given in Roman transliteration rather than the original orthography, so that English-speakers may have an impression of its sound. English translations appear to the right; in a few cases where space would not allow presentation side-by-side, the English may be below the original. Poets' names follow, in the normal English order: given name or pen name, then family name. (A few poets have requested that only their pen names be used.) Poets' locales follow their names. For those residing in the United States or Canada, the state or province appears in the usual postal two-letter abbreviation; for others the country is listed. One caution in this connection: Poets travel and move at least as much as other people, and the poem may well have been composed somewhere other than the place where the poet now lives.

To the right of the poet's name and place each poem is identified as either hokku [h], haiku [k], or senryu [s], according to the source of the poem or my own understanding of these three different kinds of poems. Some border-line examples are marked [k/s] for "haiku or senryu", meaning that one might read the poem either way, depending on context, personal background, mood, and so on. A footnote on right-hand pages reminds readers what these designations mean. (See Chapter 4 of *The Haiku Seasons* for the distinctions among the three types.) Note that in general usage outside of this book the distinction between "hokku" and "haiku" is usually ignored, and most readers will be comfortable thinking of both [h] and [k] as indicating haiku. For linked-verse poets, however, the distinction is important, and for all readers these designations may help sort out the differences among hokku, haiku, and senryu, all parts of the larger haikai genre.

If some aspect of a poem other than its seasonal topic seems to need explanation, a brief note may be included in the entry text associated with it.

The following sample entry demonstrates most of these features.

SAMPLE ENTRY

SNAIL, *katatsumuri*, *slak*—Afrikaans, *caracol*—Spanish, *puž*—Serbian (all). Refers to land snails normally seen in summer gardens and fields, comprising the order Stylommatophora. The order also includes the **SLUG** (*namekuji*), a separate all-summer topic. Snails are legendary for carrying their cumbersome shells with them and for moving slowly.

the snail who doesn't move
—next time you look for him
he's somewhere else

Fred Schofield, England [k/s]

Skielik alleen	Suddenly alone
die gaste het vertrek—	the guests having departed—
Slak teen die ruit	Snail at the window

Hélène Kesting, South Africa [k]

El caracol lleva	The snail carries
su casa.	its house.
La nuestra se quedó.	Ours stayed behind.

Berta G. Montalvo, FL [s]

Na vlati trave	On a grass blade
Odsjaji puževog traga	Reflected in a snail's trail
Sunce zalazi	The setting sun

Svetlana Mladenović, Yugoslavia [k]

As in Japanese saijiki, entries in *Haiku World* differ greatly in thoroughness. Several factors contribute to this. Many topics are quite familiar, and require little comment, such as common articles of clothing. Several topics have special meaning for those involved in haikai, and therefore require fuller explanations, for example, **CAT'S LOVE**. Some topics are not well known outside their cultural milieux, including most holidays. A number of topics have wide recognition but have not yet been presented in a consistent and satisfying way in English; I think of the whole group of topics relating to haze, mist, and so on. And finally, not least important, is the personal preference of the person writing the entries. Conscious that no similar book has yet appeared in English, I may have erred on the side of prolixity here and there, but mainly I have tried to write each topic entry so that it provides the information I would want to know, were I to begin writing a poem about its subject.

In collaborative saijiki like the *Japan Great Saijiki* there is as much variation from entry to entry because of personal style as there is because of the diversity of materials. As I have become more and more immersed in such treasure troves, I have learned to appreciate the clarity and directness of certain writers over others, and often look to the end of an entry to see who wrote it so that I may know whether to expect a clear presentation of the facts or a rambling series of semi-relevant observations. In my own writing I have tried to emulate those Japanese authors whose saijiki entries have most pleased me.

MORE ON ENTRIES

As you start using a saijiki many phenomena and human activities may seem unnaturally confined in rigid time periods. Are there no mushrooms outside of autumn? But as familiarity deepens the great flexibility of the system becomes apparent. While the most inclusive term, **MUSHROOM**, has become traditionally associated with autumn—when a majority of noticeable and edible mushrooms are abundant—you will also find the names of specific mushrooms or types listed in the seasons when they in fact normally appear. Similarly, **INSECTS**, traditionally autumnal and including the season word **voices of insects**, does not limit specific insects, even those that sing such as cicadas, to autumn. In fact, **CICADAS** is a summer topic, probably because various species begin their raucous cries in May, June, or July; most quiet down by the end of August. (By contrast, **CRICKETS** are autumnal, because, although some types begin singing in spring and others may continue into winter, they crescendo in autumn.) In another instance, **FLY** being a summer topic does not prevent a **WINTER FLY** from showing up, and indeed a poem on the latter may have more force.

In a typical Japanese saijiki there are numerous entries in each season that have exact parallels in other seasons. For example, the topic the **COMING OF SUMMER** (*rikka*), included in this saijiki, parallels the **COMING OF SPRING** (*risshun*), **COMING OF AUTUMN** (*risshū*), and **COMING OF WINTER** (*rittō*), all of which appear in standard Japanese saijiki. In other cases, such as "fly" (above) and "moon", the unmodified term is always associated with a particular season, but when it appears at a different time of year the name of the appropriate season can be included, as in **SUMMER MOON** (*natsu no tsuki*).

If a nonseasonal topic becomes seasonal by means of adding the name of the season there may be two options regarding location in the saijiki. One would be to simply place a poem on such a topic under the name of the season itself—usually the first entry for that season. But, for example, what of "summer dusk"? **AUTUMN DUSK** (*aki no kure*) is already included in traditional saijiki as a separate topic in addition to **AUTUMN EVENING** (*aki no yoi*), probably for the simple reason that we are more conscious of this time in autumn, as it comes earlier and earlier with each day. But Japanese saijiki generally do not include the term that would correspond to "summer dusk"—*natsu no kure*. In this case it seems more appropriate to include **SUMMER DUSK** as a topic in the section of the saijiki that deals with time of day than to place it under just the name of the season.

One note for writers: Some poets outside of Japan have seen the inclusion of the name of a season in a haiku as an easy and superficial way to meet the seasonal requirement, and therefore to be avoided.

Two observations argue against this view of the name of the season in a poem as undesirable. First, there are many seasonal topics already in wide use which include the name of the season. Second, the name of the season alone is not one of the weaker topics, but one of the more challenging. A poem may seem to become seasonal with the inclusion of the name of the season, but such a poem must then express some quality deeply felt in the season itself. Otherwise the name of the season will have no real effect, and, like any other ineffectual word in a poem, should be omitted. (Of course, if a phenomenon is already associated with a particular season, the name of that season should not be added to it in a poem. "Spring frog" and "autumn moon", for example, are redundant.)

POEMS WITH TWO SEASON WORDS

In Japanese as well as English and other languages, one occasionally encounters a poem with two season words. Should that happen, there are three possibilities, resulting in the following placement in this saijiki. Whichever season word dominates the seasonal understanding of a poem, and thus its placement in the saijiki, is said to be *the* season word of that poem. (I draw examples from the old masters to show that this is not just a modern phenomenon.)

Same season: When both season words relate to topics in the same season, the poem goes under the topic most central to its meaning if there is no conflict between the topics as to the time period within the season. If a time conflict does exist, it will be resolved in favor of the more limited time period. Sample poem:

uguisu o	with a warbler
tama ni nemuru ka	for a soul is it sleeping?
taoyanagi	graceful willow

Bashō

BUSH WARBLER (*uguisu*) is an all spring topic, but **WILLOW** (*yanagi*) is specific to late spring, so the poem belongs under the latter topic. This poem is mainly about the willow, so the placement seems doubly appropriate. Bashō changes Chuang-tzu's famous butterfly-dreaming man into a warbler-dreaming tree.

Different seasons, one dominates: When season words relate to topics in different seasons, usually one or the other obviously governs, and the poem will be placed under that topic in its season. Sample:

ōgi nite	with a fan
sake kumu kage ya	I drink *sake* in the shade . . .
chiru sakura	falling cherry blossoms

Here Bashō mimics a noh actor; when the play calls for drinking *sake* (rice wine, pronounced "sah-kay"), the actor mimes the motions using a closed folding fan as a prop. Since **FALLING CHERRY BLOSSOMS** (*chiru sakura*) is not only a topic appropriate to spring but actually happens in spring, the poem is definitely placed in spring. A **FAN** (*ōgi*), normally a summer seasonal topic, can easily be present at other seasons.

harahara to	ploppity-plop
arare furisuguru	the snow pellets come down
tsubaki kana	on these camellias

Buson

SNOW PELLETS or graupel (*arare*—often translated as "hail") may fall any time of year, but has long been recognized as a winter seasonal topic. When it is coupled with a topic strongly associated with springtime, such as **CAMELLIAS** (*tsubaki*), the poem in question must also find itself in spring. With the camellias, Buson does not have to say "spring snow pellets" (*haru no arare*), though that is a seasonal topic in its own right. NOTE: These camellias are most likely red.

Different seasons, neither dominates: When season words relate to topics in different seasons and there is no way to say definitively that the experience belongs in one or the other, the poem will be placed under the most appropriate topic in the all-year section. Sample:

tsuki hana ya	moon and blossoms . . .
yonjūkunen no	forty-nine years of
muda aruki	pointless walking

Issa (1762-1826)

Though **MOON** is an autumnal topic and **BLOSSOMS** belongs to spring, here Issa uses "moon and blossoms" to mean poetry. Rather than preaching to others about art, Issa is mumbling to himself that his life has amounted to nothing but worrying about "moon and blossoms"—a pointless task. Since the theme of the poem relates to "years" it belongs in the all-year section, under the topic **YEAR or YEARS**.

Note that most apparent conflicts between a season word and a word or phrase in a poem that might place the poem under a topic in the all-year section of the saijiki resolve in favor of the appropriate seasonal topic.

PROBLEMS IN MAKING AN INTERNATIONAL SAIJIKI

The three brief essays that interrupt the body of the saijiki deal with special problem areas that I encountered while organizing the topics and poems.

The first, "Butterflies Through the Year" concerns a common misunderstanding about some popular saijiki topics. For example, broadly generic terms such as "butterfly" (spring), "insects" (autumn), and "mushroom" (autumn) have led some beginning poets to believe that one may write of these phenomena only in these seasons. In fact, "summer butterfly", "autumn butterfly", and even "winter butterfly" are also popular topics. As the essay makes plain, each of these topics conjures up specific images in the minds of experienced haiku readers. Similar situations exist for "insects" and "mushrooms".

"On Haze, Mist, Fog" takes up the problem of varying translations for a variety of closely related phenomena, all of which are seasonal topics. To sort out a number of poems on these topics, I had to carefully examine the meanings of several Japanese words and their possible English counterparts. The solutions arrived at here must be taken as tentative and subject to revision by myself or others in the future. But I hope that the entries and poems I have placed under them make some kind of provisional sense for the moment.

"Words in International Haikai" presents a problem that will increasingly trouble haikai poets and readers as we move into an era of instantaneous worldwide personal communication and greater interest in the seasonal aspect of haikai. Succinctly put, one cannot know when what one writes in one's own language, literally translated into another, happens to be an idiomatic expression in the receiving language for something quite alien to one's intent. This may be especially true for season words, which often take on special meanings in haikai contexts that they do not have in everyday commerce. I predict that translators will have to give increasing attention to the nuances of season words as haikai becomes a more and more international genre.

These essays will give readers some notion of the intricacies of a potentially borderless haikai culture. Haikai poems and articles are already speeding around the globe by facsimile and electronic mail, and I am sure that this traffic will increase substantially over the next few years. May our ability to sensibly understand and appreciate the poems keep pace.

WHAT IS A SAIJIKI FOR?

The best way to familiarize yourself with a saijiki is to use it. Carry it with you on walks, and check its entries against the things you see. Do the same when you travel. How does your experience compare with the experience of others? Place it on a table near where you work or relax, and pick it up now and then just to browse through the pages looking for an interesting passage, an intriguing poem. If you have trouble understanding an entry, review the section above called "The Entries and Example Poems", but try not to get bogged down in technicalities.

There are important reasons for the existence of this kind of book. First, the organization of a saijiki makes it possible to use one as a handy reference, a guide to the seasons and seasonal phenomena, and a quick way to find poems on a favorite topic. Many Japanese haikai poets use a saijiki to better understand the world around them, as well as how other poets have responded to that world. A saijiki can bring the depth of tradition to the sense of possibility offered by immediate experience.

Second, a saijiki's organization of poems by topic rather than by individual authorship conveys a powerful sense of poetry as a group enterprise, a cultural and social phenomenon rather than the quirky product of a single, ego-bound intelligence.

Finally, and most important, a saijiki helps us expand our enjoyment in reading and writing poems in the haikai genre. For as we come to better understand the phenomena captured in hokku, haiku, and senryu we better understand the poems themselves. And for those who write, what besides the saijiki can give us a better sense that our work joins a communion through time and around the globe with other members of the community of poets and lovers of poetry?

For a more thorough discussion of the background, theory, and use of the saijiki, and information on how to make one for yourself or a group, see the companion volume, *The Haiku Seasons*.

THE INTERNATIONAL HAIKAI SAIJIKI

SPRING

The following entries appear under Spring, in the categories indicated.

Note: An asterisk at the end of an entry's text indicates that additional poems and season words on the topic may be found in Chapter 6 of *The Haiku Seasons*.

SPRING—THE SEASON

SPRING, *haru*, *ghūmē*—Gujarati (all). Technically, "spring" in haikai means the period from about 4 February through about 5 May and centering on the vernal equinox, but commonly accepted as February through April (August to October in the southern hemisphere). This accords with a traditional understanding of the season in England: "Spring . . . The first season of the year, or that between winter and summer, . . . in popular use in Great Britain comprising the months of February, March, and April," but may be harder to accept "in U.S. [where spring is popularly] March, April, and May."—*Oxford English Dictionary* (See the section titled "The Calendar and the Seasons" at the beginning of the introduction to the saijiki, above, and also the discussion of "midsummer" and "midwinter" in *The Haiku Seasons*, page 106.)

Poems on the season per se are included here. Generally, the word "spring" adds a sense of warmth, lightness, new life, and optimism to a poem. Note the possible confusion with "spring" meaning a natural **FOUNTAINHEAD** or **wellspring**, a summer topic. Also: **springtime** (*Frühling*—German). Regarding phrases combining "spring" with the names of otherwise nonseasonal phenomena—or phenomena traditionally associated with other seasons—see pages 32–33 in the introduction to the saijiki.

skinny young men
grouped around the car's raised hood
spring

Winona Baker, BC [k]

in a dream I longed
for another landscape—where
spring has no master!

Bill Wyatt, England [k]

hiroshima nī	Carrying Hiroshima dust
raj laī janaman	spring roams
ghūmē wasa nta.	among the populace.

Jhinabhai "Sneharashmi" Desai, India [k]

spring
the cracks in the spade handle
a little deeper

Stephen Hobson, Australia [k]

A ball in springtime
making its way downriver
slowly to the sea

David Burleigh, Japan [k]

Mit klammen Fingern	With numb fingers
meinen ersten Eiskaffee	my first iced coffee—
jetzt ist es Frühling!	now it is springtime!

Annemarie Rödler, Austria [s]

FEBRUARY, *nigatsu* (early). Each month has its own character. February, though early spring, still feels like winter in the northern hemisphere. But if we have the spirit to look for them, there are signs of spring amidst the leftover winter. (In the southern hemisphere February equates to early autumn, and will have the appropriate seasonal associations. Southern-hemisphere poems in which the name of the month dominates the poem are placed in this saijiki according to season, rather than month.) Like the names of seasons, the names of months may be combined with other phenomena to create seasonal topics. Those already traditional have their own entries; others are included here. As with the names of seasons, poems involving the names of months must have a tone or feeling essential to that month.

On Coney Island beach
a snowman scans the sea:
February morning

Donatella Cardillo-Young, NY [k]

LUNAR NEW YEAR, *kyūshōnen* (early). Before Japan adopted the Gregorian calendar for business and civil functions in 1872, all of East and Southeast Asia fixed dates according to the Chinese lunar calendar, which begins on the day of the first new moon after the sun enters Aquarius. Thus the **Chinese New Year** begins on a date ranging from 21 January to 19 February Gregorian. In all cultures of the region, the first few days of the New Year constitute one of the most important holidays, called in Mandarin Chinese *Xin Nian*, in Korean *Suhl*, and in Vietnamese *Tet*. For Southeast Asia, which is in the tropics, this comes during the rainy season. As a result of fighting in and around Saigon and a number of provincial Vietnamese capitals during the Tet holiday in 1968, the word **Tet** is associated with the Vietnam War in American minds.

At Quang Tri, Vietnam

Tet:
both armies
wet

Ty Hadman, Peru [k/s]

SIGNS OF SPRING, *haru meku* (early). The Japanese literally says **springlike**, and was classically used to refer to well-known early signs of spring, such as **GATHERING YOUNG HERBS** (*wakana tsumi*, now a New Year topic). In haikai the topic should not be used together with other already identified early spring seasonal topics, but—like the name of a season or month—should be paired with an otherwise nonseasonal image that takes on a special resonance in early spring. Also: **summoning spring** (*amorce du printemps*—French).

L'amorce du printemps	Summoning spring
Un peloton de cyclistes	A line of cyclists
traverse le dimanche	rides across Sunday

Patrick Blanche, France [k]

MARCH, *sangatsu* (mid). Third month in the Gregorian calendar, in haikai March is roughly equivalent to the north temperate zone's mid spring, when gusty **SPRING WINDS** dominate the season. By March winter has lost all but a toe-hold on the land, and we begin to believe in spring. Sometimes we rush the season: In the following poem **LEMONADE STAND** is clearly a summer seasonal topic. (For the southern hemisphere, this is mid autumn.)

middle of March
the first lemonade stand
has a slow day

Allan Curry, BC [k/s]

LATE SPRING, *banshun* (late). Traditionally 5 April through 4 May; nominally April in the northern hemisphere. In haikai tradition the late season brings a feeling of time moving onward and the next season's imminent arrival, though not as strongly felt as that in **PASSING SPRING**, below. Late spring offers the joy of many blossoming trees and plants.

late spring—
hands of the school clock
skipping

Sylvia Forges-Ryan, CT [k]

APRIL, *shigatsu* (late). April has much the same feeling as **LATE SPRING**, above, in the north temperate zone. See comment on the names of months in general at **FEBRUARY**, above. Also: **April morning**.

April morning
this cold, wet grass—
how much I have traveled

Peggy Heinrich, CT [k]

SPRING MORNING, *haru no asa* (all). Gradually mornings in spring become warmer, as the sun rises earlier and the deep cold of winter loses its grip.

spring morning:
the puppy and I
tumble out of bed

Helen E. Dalton, HI [k]

SPRING NIGHT, *haru no yo*, *prolećno veče*—Serbian (all). Spring nights gradually grow shorter and milder.

Prolećno veče	The spring night—
pod točkovima transportera	a lizard dies under the wheel
umire gušter.	of a troop carrier.

Dimitar Anakiev, Slovenia [k]

WARM, *atataka* (all). While much of spring is still cold, we are sensitive to the least **warmth** (*Wärme*—German).

damp morning:
cash for a journey
warm from the machine

Dee Evetts, NY [k]

Sonnige Wärme	The warmth of the sun
durchflutet mich nur bei dir.	flows through me only with you.
Mein Süden bist du.	You are my South.

Charles Stünzi, Switzerland [k]

LONG DAY, *hinaga, lamba din*—Urdu (all). Though days begin to lengthen immediately after the **WINTER SOLSTICE** and the longest days come at **MIDSUMMER**, in spring we really notice the longer hours of daylight, making "the long day" a spring topic. See also: **LINGERING DAY,** the next topic.

Phir ik lamba din	Again a long day
jis ka katna lagta hai	this time it seems to me
ab ke namumkin	impassable

Mohsin Bhopali, Pakistan [k/s]

LINGERING DAY, *chijitsu* (all). As spring advances we respond to the added hours of daylight. We become more relaxed since there is more time to get things done before dark. Also: **slow day** (*osoki hi*).

the slow day . . .
in the empty motel corridor
a stack of dirty dishes

Anita Virgil, VA [k]

SPRING—THE HEAVENS

SPRING SKY, *haru no sora*, *Frühlingshimmel*—German (all). This suggests the sky of a mild spring day, the air less chill than in winter, possibly with thin white clouds.

Frülingshimmel blau.	Spring sky so blue.
Weiße Streifen aus Flugzeug:	White stripes from an airplane:
Welcher verblaßt zuerst?	Which will fade first?

Guido Keller, Germany [k]

SPRING SUN (all). In spring the sun rises higher in the heavens, stays with us longer, and begins to warm the earth toward the heat of summer. After the darkness of winter we greet it joyfully.

weightless—
the whole earth against my back
under spring sun.

Anna Vakar, BC [k]

SPRING MOON, *haru no tsuki* (all). The spring moon has special, almost enchanting qualities that set it apart from the moons of autumn or other times of the year. In haikai **MOON** by itself refers to an autumn moon. See also **HAZY MOON** (spring).

my shadow moves on the moving grass   spring moon

Michael McNierney, CO [k]

Mooing and mooing
Under the spring moon,
The cow cannot sleep.

Patrick Worth Gray, NE [k]

HUNGER MOON (early). North America is rich in moon lore, especially names for the months of the year. "Hunger Moon" refers to the moon itself, as well as to the lunar month roughly equivalent to February. It comes from the Algonquin and Ojibwa peoples of the St. Lawrence and Great Lakes region, and well describes the period between deep winter and early spring, when game is less plentiful and plants have not yet begun to produce much that is edible. Some other names for February's moon from Native American sources: **Moon of the Dark Red Calves** (Lakota), **Big Hoop and Stick Game Moon** (Cheyenne), **Frightened Coyotes Moon** (Pueblo). European colonists called it **Trapper's Moon,** and for several groups it was and is the **Snow Moon.** *The Moon Book* by Kim Long lists many names for each month's full moon (Johnson Books, 1988).

hunger moon
watching
as I turn forty

Jocelyne Villeneuve, ON [k]

SUGAR MOON (mid). One of several colonial American names for March and its full moon. Algonquins and other Native Americans call it **Sap Moon,** referring to the time when sugar-maple sap runs. Tapped, the sap is boiled down to maple syrup, and may be further reduced to maple sugar.

Sugar Moon—
stirring ghost stories
into maple fudge

Carol Purington, MA [k]

HAZY MOON, *oborozuki* (all). A classic evocation of spring in Japanese poetry, this phrase brings to mind a full moon partially obscured by a thin veil of clouds, mist, or haze, and is considered one of the most attractive images in the saijiki by haikai poets. Also: **misty moonlit night** (*oborozukiyo*), **moon hazy** (*tsuki oboro*). See "On Haze, Mist, Fog" at **AUTUMN MIST, FOG** for a discussion of these and related terms.

tsuki oboro	misty moon
buranko kasuka ni	playground swing moving
yurenikeri	ever so faintly

Jack Stamm, Japan [k]

SPRING HAZINESS, SPRING MISTINESS, *oboro* (all). Prominent in haikai mainly because of its contribution to **HAZY MOON,** this term focuses on the fact of obscurity in the nighttime atmosphere, more than on what is causing the diminished vision or hearing. Season words include: **hazy [spring] night** (*oboroyo*), **plants in [spring] haze** (*kusa oboro*), **bell in [spring] haze** (*kane oboro*), **looks hazy** (*oboro meku*). The word **misty** could be substituted for "hazy" in any of these. See the entry for **SPRING HAZE, SPRING MIST,** following terms relating to precipitation, below. See also "On Haze, Mist, Fog" at **AUTUMN MIST, FOG** for a discussion of these and related terms.

oboroyo no	a hazy night
haha ga byōfu mamoru	mother watches over sick father
komoriuta	singing lullabies

Yoshiko Yoshino, Japan [k]

SPRING DARKNESS, *haru no yami* (all). They say this traditional topic comes from *Kokinshū* #41: "The spring night's/ darkness is powerless;/ though the color/ of the plum blossoms is invisible/ can their scent be hidden?"

jitensha ni	I have been hit
tsuitotsu sareshi	from behind by a bicycle—
haru no yami	spring darkness

Sakuzō Takada, Japan [k]

SPRING WIND, *haru kaze* (all). Includes the early mild breezes and the later bold winds. The Japanese *haru kaze* may also be translated **spring breeze,** if appropriate. See also: **FIRST SPRING GUST,** and so on, below. Also: **soft spring wind, spring gales.***

hitotsu-zutsu	One by one
haru kaze watasu	He hands over the spring winds:
fūsen-uri	The balloon-man.

Kazuo Satō, Japan [h]

soft spring wind
even the maple in my bureau
stirs

James Handlin, NJ [k]

spring breeze
the dried flowers rustle
on the window sill

Robert Epstein, CA [k]

STRONG TRADEWINDS (mid). Strong tradewinds typically occur in March in tropical Puerto Rico, where the poem below was written, and they define the season there.

strong tradewinds—
palm fronds rattle
over the seething sea

Philip C. Specht, PR [k]

FIRST SPRING GUST, *haru ichiban* (mid). In Japan, as in many other places, the first winds from the equator can have a good deal of force, but are milder than the polar winds of winter.

haru ichiban	first spring gust
keiba shinbun	racing forms
sora o yuku	go through the sky

Haruo Mizuhara, Japan [k]

first spring gust
my flannel shirt
like a kite

Shōkan Kondō, Japan [k]

MARCH WINDS (mid). "March winds" are legendary in much of the northern hemisphere from long before Chaucer, noted for their gusty, blustery quality. They provide the force for flying a **TOY KITE** in March.

march winds—
hand held to his bald head
a man chases his hat

Martin Lucas, England [k/s]

SPRING RAIN, *harusame, lenteregen*—Dutch (all). Usually we think of a soft, mild rain as characteristic of spring, but rain can also come with gusty **SPRING WIND**, above. In the last poem below, "Blyth" refers to R. H. Blyth, author of the famous four-volume work *Haiku* which particularly influenced the Beat and San Francisco poets. He also wrote a comprehensive *History of Haiku* and three books on senryu, of which *Edo Satirical Verse Anthologies* is still available. His grave is in Kamakura, Japan, near that of D. T. Suzuki.

een duivenpaar	a pair of doves
in een mist van lenteregen	in a mist of spring rain
schouder aan schouder	shoulder to shoulder

Anton Gerits, The Netherlands [h]

Over Blyth's grave:
an offering of spring rain,
muddy knees, and brow.

James W. Hackett, CA [h]

MARCH SHOWER, *maartse buien*—Dutch (mid). March showers have a gustier aspect than the well-known, and usually gentler, **APRIL SHOWERS**. See also **MARCH WINDS.**

Maartse buien—	March showers—
twee heren in de regen	two men in the rain
handen aan de hoed.	hands on their hats.

Thea Witteveen, The Netherlands [k]

APRIL SHOWER, *natanezuyu* (late). The Japanese literally reads "herbs and seeds rainy season" or **seed rain,** characteristic of March and April and seen as a rain to make plants grow, as in "April showers bring May flowers." Note that singular "shower" is more likely than plural "showers" in haikai.

April shower
the gargoyles
start drooling again

Kaye Laird, MI [k]

LATE FROST, *wasurejimo* (late). The Japanese literally says "forgotten frost", meaning that it was left behind by winter, or that we had forgotten that frost was still possible. Placement of this topic in late spring shows that the tradition recognizes how late such a frost may be—despite the fact that Japan generally has a mild climate. In more polar latitudes or higher altitudes, the last frost may come a good deal later than April/October, but then the whole seasonal scheme shifts vis-a-vis the calendar in such places. Also called: **farewell frost** (*wakarejimo*).

hiza orite	knees bent
fuchi o fukikomu	I polish its edge—
wakarejimo	farewell frost

Nobuko Katsura, Japan [k]

SPRING THUNDER, *shunrai* (all). Thunder is considered most characteristic of summer, but occurs at all seasons.

hot bath water
cold on the breastless side
spring thunder

Yoko Ogino, Japan [k]

SPRING HAZE, SPRING MIST, *kasumi, brume*—French, *Frühlingsnebel*—German (all). While **SPRING HAZINESS** focuses on obscured vision at night, spring haze (or mist) refers to the haze or mist itself, usually during daylight hours. These related season words give an impression of its range of meaning: **thin [spring] haze** (*usugasumi*), **[spring] morning haze** (*asagasumi*), **haze in the offing** (*kasumi no oki*), **veil of haze** (*kasumigakure*). For any of these terms **mist** could be substituted for **haze**; in the following metaphorical expressions "mist" seems more appropriate: **sleeves of mist** (*kasumi no tamoto*), **nets of mist** (*kasumi no ami*). See **SPRING HAZINESS, SPRING MISTINESS,** above, following **HAZY MOON.** See also "On Haze, Mist, Fog" at **AUTUMN MIST, FOG** for a discussion of these and related terms.

Au loin	Far off
dans la brume du matin,	in the morning haze
l'appel du muezzin.	the call of a muezzin.

Rodolfo Giacalone, Morocco [h]

Vorüber der Frost—	The frost is over—
wie dampft der kahle Berghang	how the barren hillside steams
im Frühlingsnebel.	in spring mist.

Gerold Effert, Germany [k]

HEAT SHIMMER, *kagerō* (all). This refers to the distortion of visual images seen through the hot air over a heated surface. Though the phenomenon may be seen more often in summer and early autumn than in spring, it is a sure sign that things are warming up after the cold of winter. Also called **summer-colts** in parts of England, and **heat waves** by some. I suggest avoiding the latter, which is easily confused with the late-summer topic **HEAT WAVE** (*ensho*)—a period of some days or weeks of intense heat. (This topic sometimes includes the season word "gossamer" [*yūshi*], which was apparently at one time considered a similar phenomenon. In this saijiki **GOSSAMER** is a separate topic in autumn.) Also called: **shimmering heat.**

traffic jam—
dancing among the cars
shimmering heat

Ursula Sandlee, PA [k]

SPRING—THE EARTH

HILLS SMILE, *yama warau* (all). A traditional figure of speech for hills in springtime, from an old saying: "Spring hills faintly melting seem to smile; summer hills of pale green seem to trickle; autumn hills bright and clean seem all dressed up; winter hills faintly sad seem to sleep." Also translated: **mountains laugh.**

hiroshima no	never say
yama warau to wa	"Hiroshima's mountains
iu nakare	are laughing"

Yasuhiko Shigemoto, Japan [k]

SPRING FIELD, *haru no no* (all). A human mark on the landscape that clearly defines spring, a field between plowing and planting. Also: **plowed field** (*izorana livada*—Croatian).*

Na tek izoranoj	On the just-plowed
livadi već beru	meadow already picking
plodove—kokoši!	its fruits—the hens!

Milan Žegarac, Croatia [k/s]

BURNING FIELDS, *yakeno* (early). Fields burning from deliberate fires, set by farmers to kill off pests and clear fields for plowing. The farmers' work when they **BURN THE FIELDS** (*noyaki*) is also an early spring topic under Humanity.

burning fields,
the smoke reaches
a penthouse

Shōkan Kondō, Japan [k/s]

WATERS OF SPRING, *haru no mizu* (all). Water keeps moving, most noticeably during and after the spring thaw. This refers to everything from trickles down the side of a hill to the increase in streams and rivers. "Waters of spring" is also a good translation for Japanese *shunsui.*

shunsui ni	in the waters of spring
hitotsu no omoi	a certain thought
nagarekeri	flowed away

Sekishi Takagi, Japan [k]

REMAINING SNOW, *zansetsu* (mid). Snow on the ground, waiting for spring warmth to melt it off. There are many ways to express this image, including **left-over snow** (*nokoru yuki*), **snow left over** (*yuki nokoru*), **last patch of snow, patches of snow.** One of the most interesting invented by the Japanese is **shadow-snow** (*kageyuki*), which can mean snow left on the shady side of anything: a ditch, a hedge, a house, a tree, a mountain.

funeral too far to go . . .
snow left over
in this ground ivy

M. M. Nichols, NY [k]

a jogger's breath
hangs in the dusk
leftover snow

Michael Ketchek, NY [k]

last patch of snow:
a small black spider
lowers into it

Elizabeth St Jacques, ON [k]

patches of snow
the finger-warming breath
of a newborn lamb

Linzy Forbes, New Zealand [h]

SNOWMELT, *yukidoke* (mid). Runoff water from the melting snows of spring. Also called: **snow meltwater** (*yukige mizu*).

snowmelt . . .
she enters
the earth on her knees

Bill Pauly, IA [k]

snowmelt:
so many voices of stone
shape the current

Christopher Herold, CA [k]

hikaridō yori	from the Hall of Light
hito suji no	a single line
yukige mizu	of snow meltwater

Akito Arima, Japan [h]

yukidoke no	I skip over
hitosuji nagare	a single line of flowing
tobikoeru	snowmelt

Kimiko Horne, ON [k]

MELT OFF, *yukishiro* (mid). This refers to the melting of ice in streams and rivers, rather than to melting snow. Also: **stream melts.**

quiet rain—
the last stream melts
out of itself

Ross Figgins, CA [k]

THAW, *itedoke* (mid). When rising air temperatures and the warmth of the sun penetrate frozen ground, making the soil soft enough to work. Also: **thawing** (*odmrzava se*—Croatian), **thaws** (*topeţe*—Romanian).

Odmrzava se . . .	It is thawing . . .
Bude se	They awaken,
kamenovi u cesti.	the stones in the road.

Dubravko Ivančan, Croatia [h]

Zăpada se topeţe	The snow thaws
în jurul omului	all around the man
ce plânge.	who's crying.

Cristina Ionescu, Romania [k/s]

SPRING BREAKUP, *kōri toku* (mid). Literally "ice release" in Japanese; when the ice that has prevented navigation on rivers and streams lets go.

spring breakup
I hold my wife
a little closer

LeRoy Gorman, ON [k]

SPRING—HUMANITY

SPRING CLEANING (all). The Japanese *susuharai* has been translated "spring cleaning", but refers to an **END OF YEAR CLEANING** in preparation for the New Year; the cleaning used to occur at the tail end of the year and of winter, since the New Year began with spring. However, with the adoption of the Gregorian calendar, the Japanese have moved *susuharai* to the end of December, mid winter. Since "spring cleaning" per se is a European institution tied to the season, not the calendar, it seems appropriate to have it an all-spring seasonal topic. While **cleanup** (*schoonmaak*—Dutch) might not be a season word normally, in this context it seems clear.

Spring cleaning . . .
A Christmas card from someone
He doesn't know

Carlos Colón, LA [s]

Spring cleaning—
dust on the move
with legs and without

Eveline Rutgers, The Netherlands [s]

Zijn eerste brieven:	His first letters:
iedere schoonmaak opnieuw	at each cleanup again
overleven ze.	they survive.

Wanda Reumer, The Netherlands [k/s]

ROOF LEAK (mid). Roofs—especially thatched roofs, still not uncommon in Japan and parts of Europe—often suffer damage from winter freezes, causing leaks with the thaws of spring. Note the traditional mid-spring topic **REPLACING THE ROOF** (*yanegae*) and related season word **thatching the roof** (*yane fuku*). Also: **leaking roof.**

the roof is leaking
I play the rain drops as they
land on my music

Barry Edgar Pilcher, Ireland [k]

PLOW, *tagaeshi* (all). For many, the scent of ground newly broken with the plow in preparation for planting defines the arrival of spring. Also: **ploughing.**

Beneath rain showers
the clay ox ploughing
a field of rocks

Bill Wyatt, England [k]

TRACTOR (all). The tractor has replaced a farmer's draft animals in much of the world. Though it appears on the fields off and on throughout the growing season, the tractor comes to mind most often in connection with spring plowing.

From the sound
you know whose tractor—
neighbors

Ken H. Jones, Wales [k/s]

SEED PLANTING, *tanemaki* (late). Generally after farmers and gardeners think they've seen the last frost, planting goes forward in the fields.

the parsnip seeds:
I was about to plant them
when the wind blew

Anna Vakar, BC [k]

POTATO PLANTING, *jagaimo ue* (mid). Potatoes get planted more than once during the growing season, but the saijiki recognizes the first potato planting of the year, while the ground is still cold in mid spring, as a topic. Also: **planting early potatoes.**

Out in the cold sunshine
planting early potatoes
uncertain who I am

Ken H. Jones, Wales [k]

START IRRIGATION (late). In spring, after cleaning the ditches and plowing the fields, farmers **open the gates** to send water to the fields.

raising the stops: kids race irrigation water down the dry trenches

Richard Tice, UT [k]

FIRST MOWING, *premier fauchage*—French (late). Though **GRASS CUTTING** (*kusa kari*) and **MOWING HAY** (*hoshikusa*) are traditional summer activities, the first mowing usually takes place in spring. Exact timing will depend on general climate, weather, and what is being mowed. To suburbanites this topic suggests the **first lawn mowing,** while a farmer thinks of mowing (or buying) hay.

Premier fauchage.	First mowing.
La rouille de l'année	The rust of a year
disparait dans l'herbe.	disappears in the grass.

Jean Antonini, France [h]

BEACH-COMBING, *shiohigari* (late). A serious business in Japan, where sea products provide food and driftwood goes for firewood. "Beach morning glory" blooms late spring to mid autumn, unlike its cousins. Also: **gathering shells, search . . . conch** (*busco . . . concha*—Spanish).

search for shells—
the beach morning glory
out before us

Helen J. Sherry, CA [k]

La luna, en las olas.	The moon, in the waves.
Busco por la orilla	I search along the shore
una concha grana.	for a large conch.

Rafael Alberti, Spain [k]

TOY KITE, *tako* (all). A quintessential toy capitalizing on the winds of March and April. Also: **kite, kite festival.***

Kite festival:
when it ended sun and moon
in one sky

Gusta van Gulick, The Netherlands [h]

SOAP BUBBLES, *shabondama* (all). **Blowing soap bubbles** is one of the first activities of young children unfettered by snowsuits.

mata hitotsu	now another
aozora koware	blue sky is broken
shabondama	soap bubbles

Chizuko Sadoi, Japan [k]

rōkotsu no	not even a dream
tsuku yume mo nashi	of old bones breathing—
shabondama	soap bubbles

Hayao Sakai, ON [k]

SWING, *buranko* (all). We first take our children (or ourselves) for a swing in the spring. Also: **swings** (*schommels*—Dutch).

back and forth in the swing
a new child for the old tree

Elisabeth Marshall, CA [k]

Verlaten speeltuin—	Deserted playground—
roerloos hangen de schommels	the swings hang still
boven hun plassen.	over their puddles.

Nanneke Huizinga, Denmark [k]

SPRING—OBSERVANCES

FIRST COMMUNION (late). In the Roman Catholic Church, the ritual in which young people (generally age 7) and adult converts first participate in the Holy Eucharist, thus consciously acknowledging the presence of Jesus Christ in their lives. The time of year may vary, but April or May is most usual. Traditionally, First Communion has been observed during the Easter Vigil Mass on Easter Eve, especially for adult converts. First Communion is the second of three steps leading to full membership in the church. **BAPTISM** (all year) takes place shortly after birth or as the first step toward church membership by an adult, and signifies cleansing the individual of original sin. Traditionally observed in spring, it now may take place at any time of year. The final step, **CONFIRMATION** (all spring), at the age of about 12 or as an adult convert, signifies receiving the Holy Spirit and accepting the responsibilities of full adult membership in the church. Christians of Eastern Orthodox and many Protestant faiths observe similar rituals. See **EASTER.**

first communion:
light shining from the chalice
into the boy's face

Rich Youmans, NJ [h]

U.S. INCOME TAX (late). U.S. personal income tax returns are due 15 April. Some season words for this are obvious: **tax forms, deduction, tax-breaks**; should we also consider "accountant", "depreciation", "IRA" (for Individual Retirement Account), and the like? Also: **1040 forms.**

moonlight illuminates
1040 forms
spread out on my desk

Lesley Einer, AZ [k/s]

COCKFIGHT, *tori-awase* (late). Two game cocks, placed in the center of a ring, fight to entertain the betting crowd. Cockfighting was common in ancient Greece and Rome and is known in most of Europe. It was transmitted to the Japanese court from T'ang Dynasty China in the Nara Era (710–794) as a traditional spring event; samurai picked it up in the Kamakura Era (1252–1333), and it became an annual event for the third lunar month in the Muromachi Era (1338–1573). Also **fighting cocks** (*tōkei*).

tōkei no	the fighting cocks
bassa-bassa to	"hit'im hit'im" strikes
chū nareri	the very air

Setsuko Nozawa, Japan [k]

APRIL FOOL, *shigatsu baka* (mid). **April Fools' Day** or **All Fools' Day,** 1 April, is a traditional day for playing jokes and pranks on the innocent. It may have originated as the aftermath of moving New Year's Day from 25 March to 1 January. Various customs prevail in different countries. In France one sends a **poisson d'Avril**—an **April fish**—usually a fish made of chocolate. In many places the unsuspecting are sent on "fools' errands". In North America the credulous are told something untrue; when they begin to question their informant, they will hear the verdict "April fool!"—that is, a person caught believing such nonsense.

April fools in
this snow
daffodil and I

Minna Lerman, PA [k/s]

PILGRIMAGE, *henro* (all). Pilgrimage is a traditional spring activity in Japan, where many go on pilgrimages to specific religious sites or tour whole groups of sites spread over many miles. Special **pilgrim inns** (*henro yado*) accommodate them along the way, and they wear traditional clothes under a broad **pilgrim hat** (*henrogasa*) and may carry a **pilgrim staff** (*henrozue*) for the journey. Japanese pilgrims usually travel in groups, with peak activity taking place from March to May. The most famous circuit requires the pilgrim to walk the circumference of Shikoku Island, visiting each of eighty-eight temples, and is said to require forty days. Outside Japan, famous spring pilgrimages include the annual journey to the shrine of St. Thomas à Becket at Canterbury celebrated in Chaucer's *Canterbury Tales* (April), which draws pilgrims from all over Europe. Also: **blood of pilgrims** (krv hodočasnika—Croatian).

Krv hodočasnika	The blood of pilgrims
na kamenju, kamenje	on stones, the stones
im u koljenima.	in their knees.

Nediljko Boban, Croatia [k]

BUDDHA'S BIRTHDAY CELEBRATION, *busshō-e* (late). As with most ancient religious leaders, the actual date of birth of Siddhartha Gautama, the historical Buddha, is unknown, the year said to be 566 or 563 B.C.E. Japanese Buddhists celebrate the birth on 8 April. Religious observances include visiting the temple, where a small image representing the newborn Buddha will be standing in a bowl within a pavilion decorated with flowers. In the ceremony called **Baptising the Buddha** (*kanbutsu-e*) worshipers use a long-handled ladle to dip sweet tea from the bowl and pour it over the image. The name of the ceremony is also used as a synonym for the day itself. Priests chant special prayers honoring Buddha's birth. In some areas the day roughly corresponds to the beginning of **CHERRY BLOSSOM** season, and because of this—and the flower pavilions at temples—the holiday is also called the **Blossom**

Festival (*hanamatsuri*). In addition, Japanese Buddhists observe **BUDDHA'S ENLIGHTENMENT DAY** (*rōhachi-e*, literally "eighth day of the twelfth month" [lunar calendar]), now celebrated on 12 December (mid winter) and commemorating the day on which Siddhartha achieved perfect enlightenment and became a buddha. Buddhists in other parts of the world hold different observances; see, for example, **VESAK** (summer).

shironeko no	a white cat
matsu o orikuru	comes down a pine tree—
kanbutsu-e	Buddha's Birthday

Tsunehiko Hoshino, Japan [h]

VALENTINE'S DAY, *barentain no hi* (early). 14 February. Said to be the day on which St. Valentine, Catholic priest at Rome or the bishop of a nearby region (it seems uncertain whether there were one or two persons) was beheaded during the persecution of Christians under the reign of Emperor Claudius II (third century). St. Valentine is the patron saint of greetings, and the tradition of sending romantic greetings in the form of **Valentine cards** on this day may have originated with the earlier feast of the Roman goddess of love, Februata Juno, an orgiastic rite of purification held on 15 February. Another tradition says that on this date birds begin to pair in preparation for mating, though of course different species have different habits and timing in this regard. Also: **Valentine,** which can mean either the physical card or other greeting, or a person willing to receive one's affection, as in **be my Valentine**.

a candle
burning in the bathsteam
Valentine's Day

Allan Curry, BC [k]

after you leave—
your helium valentine
a presence

Yvonne Hardenbrook, PA [s]

SHROVETIDE, *shanikusai* (early). During these three days before **ASH WEDNESDAY** and the beginning of the Lenten fast, Christians traditionally confess their sins ("shrive") in preparation. Many people devote the day before Ash Wednesday, **Shrove Tuesday** or **Fat Tuesday,** to a pre-fast **Carnival** noted for rich foods, costume parades, buffoonery, and other worldly pleasures. The New Orleans **Mardi Gras** (French for "Fat Tuesday") is a world-famous example. Note: Distinguish between this capital-C "Carnival" and small-c **carnival** under the topic **SUMMER CARNIVAL.** Also: **Carnival parade** (*karnavalstoet*—Dutch).

De karnavalstoet.	The Carnival parade.
Op de schouders van vader	On father's shoulders
host de kleuter mee.	a child jigs in time.

Karel Hellemans, Belgium [k]

ASH WEDNESDAY, *hai no suiyōbi* (mid). The first day of **Lent** (from the Anglo-Saxon word for spring), the 40-day period of fasting which prepares Christians for **EASTER.** On Ash Wednesday itself, Roman Catholics attend a special service and receive a blessing, which is signified by the priest daubing **ashes on their foreheads.** Those observing the **Lenten fast** (*postul Paştelui*—Romanian) take no red meat (beef, pork, lamb, etc.) and abstain from various other luxuries, such as alcoholic beverages and gambling, throughout Lent. See also **SHROVETIDE,** the previous entry.

ash wednesday
a streetcleaner sweeps confetti
into the fire

Frank K. Robinson, TN [k]

Ash Wednesday—
on the playground children
compare smudges.

Ursula Sandlee, PA [k/s]

Urme-nlăcrimate	Traces of weeping
pe o masă de lemn	over a wooden table
în postul Paştelui.	in the Lenten fast.

Vasile Smărăndescu, Romania [k]

PASSOVER, *sugikoshimatsuri* (late). From the Hebrew *Pesach*. Celebrated on the eve of the 14th day and on the 15th day of the lunar month Nisan (usually between late March and late April, Gregorian). The beginning of spring in the Jewish tradition, Passover celebrates the sparing of the Israelites when God killed the firstborn of the Egyptians. The Israelites were directed to smear the blood of sacrificial lambs on their doorposts, so the plague would pass over them. This marked the beginning of their Exodus from Egypt and freedom from slavery. The main feature of the holiday is the **Passover seder**, a family gathering for a meal with **bitter herbs** (*maror*), **unleavened bread** (*matzoth*), and other foods symbolic of the Exodus, with a dialogue between children and elders and scripture readings that tell the story of the plagues, leaving Egypt, and arrival in the Promised Land. The ritual follows a special set of directions, the **Haggadah**.

Passover—
spring peepers also return
to my mother's house

Leatrice Lifshitz, NY [h]

EASTER, *fukkatsusai* (late). Feast of the resurrection of Jesus Christ, observed the first Sunday after the first full moon on or after the vernal equinox, or a week later should the full moon fall on a Sunday (thus, between 22 March and 25 April; slightly different in some eastern European churches). Principle observance of Christianity. Preparation begins on **ASH WEDNESDAY**, 40 days before. **Holy Week** leads up to Easter Sunday, with special observances: **Palm Sunday**, the week before, commemorates the entry of Jesus into Jerusalem; **Maundy Thursday** or **Holy Thursday** celebrates the **Last Supper**, when Jesus ate the Passover meal with his disciples; **Good Friday** commemorates the trial, crucifixion, and death of Jesus on the cross. Some Christians exchange the special greeting **"He is risen!"** on **Easter Day** (the response is "He is risen indeed!"), and Churches are decorated with **Easter lilies** (*Zephyranthes* *atamasco*). Many churches hold special **sunrise services** on Easter. Secular holdovers from pre-Christian spring and fertility festivals include decorated **Easter eggs** (hard-boiled hen's eggs), left for children in an **Easter basket** by the **Easter bunny** (so they are told), and an **Easter egg hunt**, in which children look for colored eggs that have been hidden about the grounds of a house or park. While French **Pâques** and the names of the holiday in most other European languages preserve its connection with the Jewish **PASSOVER**, the English "Easter" derives from the name of the Anglo-Saxon goddess of spring, **Eastre** or **Eostre**, whose feast was celebrated at the **SPRING EQUINOX**. In the poem following, **pine candles** is also a spring season word, under the topic **YOUNG GREEN**.

Easter sunrise
lighting the candles
in the longleaf pine

Kenneth C. Leibman, FL [h]

SPRING—ANIMALS

COLT, *wakagoma* (late). Unlike cows and many other domestic animals that commonly bear young at any time of year, horses typically give birth in the spring. Also: **small pony**.

the colt
wakes his groom
greening mist

Robert Reed, Japan [k]

the small black pony
forgetting how he got out
  waits at the gate

Elizabeth Nichols, CO [k]

LAMB (all). Lambs are typically born in early spring and soon become very active, though they have not made it into Japanese saijiki as yet. (Yes, sheep are raised in Japan.)

two lambs leap
and recoil, the space between them
invisible horns

Brent Partridge, CA [k]

CAT'S LOVE, *neko no koi* (early). Caterwauling and carrying on; the lovemaking of cats has been sung since haikai began. See the full "cat's love" entry from the *Japan Great Saijiki* in *The Haiku Seasons* (pages 97–98). In other contexts, **CAT** is an all-year topic. Also: **screaming cats** (*vrište mačke*—Croatian).

cats in love
old crow adding to
the din

Minna Lerman, PA [k/s]

pod prozorom	under the window
vrište mi mačke	a few cats are screaming
—sanjam velikog psa	—I dream a large dog

Robert Bebek, Croatia [s]

TADPOLES, *otamajakushi* (late). One of the great wonders of spring. The frogs have adapted to a wide range of difficult environments; their mysterious orphans, the tadpoles, start out looking like tiny long-tailed fish but grow so quickly into tailless adults that we can check their progress almost by the hour. I was fortunate enough to spend many such hours, as a child, and wonder if hours like those await future generations of humans. The interactions between humans and frogs go deeper than we know.

Tadpoles in a brook
make a circle
to the children's song

Shigemi Nagasawa, Japan [h]

FROG, ***kawazu, żaba***—Polish (all). Frogs bring word of spring with their vociferous singing. See the discussion of "frog" as a spring seasonal topic in *The Haiku Seasons*, pages 107-108. Also: **spring peepers.**

A frog jumps into a pond
the dog barks at the ripple.

Erna Taguchi, Japan [k]

3 a.m. . . . awakened
by a green frog swinging
on the prayer bell!

Cecily Stanton, Australia [k]

kap kap—puka deszcz	tap tap—rain knocks
do żabki, która mieszka	for the frog who lives
pod liściem szczawiu	under the sorrel leaf

Dariusz Piasek, Poland [h]

country road:
somewhere between
the stars and spring peepers

Muriel Ford, ON [h]

jinrui no	at the time
tasogare-doki o	of the twilight of humankind—
tōkawazu	distant frogs

Mutsuo Takahashi, Japan [k]

AMERICAN ROBIN (all). *Turdus migratorius*. The world abounds in robins and related birds. The Japanese robin, *komadori* (*Erithacus akahige*), is seen mainly in summer, when it has migrated from south China—and **JAPANESE ROBIN** is therefore a summer season word. The European **robin redbreast** (*E. rubecula*) has been thought of as a spring bird throughout British literature, since it comes back to the Isles in the spring. The American robin, even though overwintering throughout much of coastal and southern North America, retains the reputation. It tends to spend winter in the woods, living on berries, fruits, and nuts, and comes back to farms and towns in the spring to feed on grubs, worms, and insects, when its cheery song announces the beginning of the mating season that characterizes spring in so many species. Probably regions that have robins all year host a more northern-based group in the winter, which moves out as others come in from the south. Though paired in spring and summer for mating, robins gather in large flocks through the winter. I have seen trees full of robins on Christmas Day in the city of Santa Fe, New Mexico. Still, the word **robin** in English and American poetry will almost invariably be taken as indicating spring, without contrary information in the work.*

first robin
blinking, stamps
the snowbound lawn

Marshall Hryciuk, ON [k/s]

PHEASANT, *kiji* (all). Large nonmigratory birds, taken as game in Europe and North America, introduced in Australia and New Zealand. Noted for spring territory and courtship displays by male. The **ring-necked pheasant** or **Chinese pheasant** most commonly seen in the U.S. is a sub-species of the **common pheasant** or **green pheasant,** *Phasianus colchicus*, which is native to Japan.

out of tall grass
all the pheasants rise
at the same angle

Jim Kacian, VA [k]

startled in tall grass
the pheasant's wings beat
faster than my heart

Jackie Hardy, England [k]

pheasant drumming
in time with the blood
pounding in my ears

Janice M. Bostok, Australia [k]

BOBWHITE (late). While the **COMMON QUAIL** (*uzura*) is an autumn seasonal topic, the **northern bobwhite**'s whistling "bob-white" call announces territory and mating April through June.

Sirens . . .
then
bob-whites

Peggy Willis Lyles, SC [k]

SKYLARK, *hibari*, *alosa*—Catalan (all). *Alauda arvensis*. One of the most joyous of birds, skylarks have long been noted for their brimming songs in flight, to which poems about them typically refer. Native throughout Eurasia and in North Africa, they have been introduced in Australia and New Zealand. The North American **horned lark** (*Eremophila alpestris*), called **shore lark** in England, has similar habits. In their ranges, the word **lark** (*leeuwerik*—Dutch, *Lerche*—German) alone will usually be taken to refer to one of these birds.

kakete kuru	I catch
ko o uketomete	my kid come running—
hibari no no	skylark field

Sōshi Chihara, Japan [k]

Bij de ruïne	At the ruins
een-en-all oor voor de gids	tourists all ears for the guide
niet voor de leeuwerik.	none for the lark.

Adri van den Berg, The Netherlands [k/s]

Sie hängt am Himmel	It hangs in the sky
uber verschneiten Ackern—	over the snowy fields—
die erste Lerche . . .	the first lark . . .

Carl Heinz Kurz, Germany [h]

Els blats s'agiten:	The wheat stirs itself:
cogullades i aloses	crested larks and skylarks
els sobrefilen.	loop over it.

Miguel Desclot, Spain [h]

CHAFFINCH (all). *Fringilla coelebs*. The chaffinch summers throughout Europe, and is usually seen in flocks—except in breeding season when males mark out their individual territories with song.

At every station
The soliloquizing chaffinch.

Tito, England [k]

SWALLOW, *tsubame* (mid). *Hirundo rustica*. The **barn swallow** (North America and Japan, in Europe simply "swallow") is one of the most celebrated signs of spring, arriving in much of the north temperate zone in March and April, and as far north as Alaska by May. For more details of their range and migrations, see **SWALLOWS DEPART** in autumn. The **cliff swallow** (*Petrochelidon pyrrhonota*), celebrated in the popular song "When the Swallows Come Back to Capistrano" (music and lyrics by Leon Rene, 1940), is known only in the Americas and migrates in much the same way as the barn swallow. Legend says that cliff swallows come back to and leave their nests at the old Spanish mission of San Juan Capistrano, California, on the same dates every year, arriving on **ST. JOSEPH'S DAY** (*seiyosefusai*), 19 March, and leaving on the feast day of **ST. JOHN OF CAPISTRANO**, 23 October, which, like all saints' feast days, come under Observances in their respective seasons. The actual dates for first arrivals and departures seem to vary by as much as two weeks, depending on temperature and weather conditions.

swallows
skim the homing cars—
rush hour

T. M. Ramirez, CA [k]

CATBIRD (late). *Dumetella carolinensis.* The **gray catbird** of eastern North America summers from the Carolinas well into Canada. Its territorial song, which begins in mid to late April, closely resembles the meowing of a cat. Catbirds commonly nest in low shrubbery and thickets along roadsides and in gardens.

dawn
somewhere in the mist
a catbird wakens

John Wills, TN [k]

DEPARTING GEESE, *kigan* (mid). The Japanese literally says "returning geese" and refers to the large migratory geese of the northern hemisphere, mainly *Anser sp.* and *Branta sp.* In much of the U.S., western Europe, mainland Asia, and Japan, these geese overwinter, arriving in late autumn. After feeding on winter fields and marshes, they "return" to their extreme north temperate or arctic nesting grounds, away from populated areas, in large, V-shaped flight formations that take off in mid spring. The most familiar of these geese include the **Canada goose** (Japanese *shijūkaragan, B. canadensis*), **brant** or **brent** (*kokugan, B. bernicla*), **white-fronted goose** (*karigane, A. albifrons*), **greylag goose** (*haiirogan, A. anser*), and **bean goose** (*hishikui, A. fabalis*). Note that the names, or **GEESE** or **goose** by themselves, refer to the arriving birds of late autumn. Also: **geese go back** (*kari kaeru*), **geese leaving.**

NOTE ON "RETURN": In English the word "return" most often means *come back*. In Japanese, however, the Japanese word normally translated as "return" (*kaeru*) often means *go back*—home, or to some other place. In haikai, birds that only winter in Japan are said to "return" in spring, when they leave for their northerly continental breeding grounds. And those breeding in Japan during the summer but heading south in autumn "return"—to their winter feeding grounds in Southeast Asia. So we can usually assume that "returning birds" in Japanese means they are leaving after a sojourn, whereas the same idiom in English means they are reappearing after an absence. And when the Japanese simply use the name of the bird they mean that it has just arrived on the scene, or just begun some activity—like singing its mating song—that brings it to our attention. Since the Japanese have been noticing their birds this way for over a thousand years, we might make an effort to understand their usage, while retaining our own, or perhaps we should use "come back" instead of "return"—or otherwise give clear clues in the rest of the poem as to which end of the migration we mean. More important, translators should avoid using "return" for *kaeru* without thinking about the respective idiomatic understandings. See also **MIGRATING BIRDS** in autumn.

utsukushiki	beautiful sky
kigan no sora mo	of the departing geese
tsukanoma ni	just for a moment

Tatsuko Hoshino, Japan [k]

gomi omou	how much
koto ikabakari	I think of thee . . .
kari kaeru	the geese depart

Masajo Suzuki, Japan [k]

Night shift:

Arriving at work, the
geese
just leaving

Rod Tulloss, NJ [k]

TWITTERING, *saezuri* (all). This refers to the general twittering of songbirds in the spring; just the word **twitter** or **songbird** is enough to suggest this spring topic.

mayu sukoshi	eyebrow a little—
saezuru hō e	toward where they twitter—
age ni keri	raised

Kōko Katō, Japan [k]

sunny day
grass and songbird
so high

Lidia Rozmus, IL [h]

BIRDS MATE, *tori sakaru* (late). All manner of birds mate in the spring, migrating birds usually as far toward the pole as they are comfortable. Activity peaks in April, but note that specific species have their own schedules. Also: **ducks mating**.

getting on top
the quacking mallard
sunk the duck

Michael McClintock, CA [s]

SPARROWS' YOUNG, *suzume no ko* (late). This refers to young of the Eurasian tree sparrow (*Passer montanus*) in Japan, where its habits are much like those of the more widely distributed house sparrow (*Passer domesticus*, formerly called the English sparrow in North America). Toward the end of spring **baby sparrows** (*kosuzume*) come out of the nest to try their wings; they set up such a chatter it is hard to ignore them. Adult **SPARROWS** of both kinds are seen all year. Note, however, that there are many other sparrows, especially native to the Americas, several of which are migratory.

genbaku dōmu	Atom bomb dome
kosuzume kuguri	baby sparrows duck among
nuke ni keri	the rusted girders

Tokihiko Kusama, Japan [k]

BIRD'S NEST, *tori no su* (all). Large numbers of songbirds nesting in spring makes this a spring topic. The following poem illustrates an indirect or unstated reference to a seasonal topic. Also: **nest building, plovers are nesting, line the nest.**

an old woolen sweater
taken yarn by yarn
from the snowbank

Michael Dylan Welch, CA [k]

This time of year
wear a hat in the paddocks:
plovers are nesting.

Norman Talbot, Australia [k/s]

brushing my old dog—
a house wren waits
to line her nest

Hank Dunlap, AZ [k]

SPARROWS' NEST, *suzume no su* (all). This refers specifically to the nests of the house sparrow and—in Japan—the closely related Eurasian tree sparrow. Both of these old world sparrows have been introduced into North America, where the house sparrow in particular nests throughout the continent except in the far north, and is especially fond of human cities and farms. Like many birds, house sparrows hatch from two to several broods a year, and consequently nest-building and repairing goes on more or less continously from February through July and again in late autumn and early winter, with the spring phase being most prominent. Sparrow nests are usually concealed within foliage such as ivy or evergreens, or in a birdhouse or hole previously occupied by another bird. They consist of straw or dried grasses and other plant materials, often with human trash mixed in. Young may be present any time from March through August. See also **SPARROWS' YOUNG**, above, and **SPARROW** (all year).

Vrabia în zbor	Sparrow on the wing
cu alt pai din pieptarul	with one more straw from the vest
sperietoarei	of the old scarecrow

Stefan Theodoru, NY [k]

FLEDGLING *sudachidori* (late). While the young of different birds in the feathering-to-flying stage are seen at many different times of year depending on species and locale, in haikai "fledgling" refers to the young of the passerines—the "perching" songbirds that we most often see in or near our own environment—toward the end of spring. In fact, a fledgling, at the spring of its own life, is one of the most archetypal symbols of the season.

Heartbeat
of the fallen fledgling
filling my hand

Steve Shapiro, South Africa [k]

SMOLT (late). These are young salmon (*Oncorhynchus sp.*, Pacific) at the stage of swimming downriver to the sea, usually a year or two after they hatch in freshwater streams and often older for Atlantic salmon, *Salmo sp.*

stars at dusk:
churning in the waves,
sea-bound smolt

Richard Tice, UT [h]

SMELT RUN (mid). In North America various smelt run upstream to spawn shortly after frozen rivers and streams break up in spring. The most widely fished species, **rainbow smelt** (*Osmerus mordax*), ranges up to 13" (33 cm) long, and is taken by hook and line through winter ice, by net during spring spawning runs. (Note that smelt is a February seasonal topic in Japan.)

Here a lantern, there a face
waiting
for the smelt to run.

Arizona Zipper, Maine [k]

SEASHELLS (all). Japanese saijiki include many named shells or shell-bearing animals, but no generic term such as "seashells" for the shells of any and all marine whelks, clams, snails, oysters, and so on.

wrapped in seashells
the voices of their mothers
of their fathers

vincent tripi, CA [k]

WHELK, *sazae* (all). Family Buccinidae and related large-shell mollusks. As a shell, the whelk is one of the fancier finds on the beach; as a living animal, one variety or another inhabits the bottom in waters from just below low-tide to 200' (60 m) deep in virtually all ocean waters. Also: **neptune, conch.**

futa o shite	lid tightly shut
sazae no yume wa	a whelk dreams
mizu no yume	water dreams

Jack Stamm, Japan [k/s]

SCARAB BEETLES EMERGE (mid). The scarab beetles—family Scarabaeidae with 1,300 species in North America alone—include several sub-families, each with different habits. Unless otherwise indicated, the word "scarab" in haikai refers to the "sacred scarab beetle" or "dung beetle" of Egypt (*Scarabaeus sacer*), which emerges in mid spring. But note that other members of the same subfamily, such as the **TUMBLEBUG** (*Canthon sp.*), are active in autumn. The 300,000 or so different species of beetles (order Coleoptera) emerge as adults at different times of the year ranging from mid spring through mid autumn. Many of the most obvious beetles are active in summer, accounting for the traditional placement of the general topic **BEETLE**. Note also **GROUND BEETLES EMERGE** (*jimushi ana o izu*), a mid-spring topic referring to members of the Carabidae family that become active at this time. Also: **scarabs everywhere.**

Ancient tombs
in the desert—
scarabs everywhere.

Bakos Ferenc, Hungary [h]

ANTS EMERGE, *ari ana o izu*, *mravi izviru*—Croatian (mid). The Japanese literally says "ants come out of their holes"—and relates to the first appearance of ant activity in mid spring.

Izviru	Emerging
iz zemlje. Teku.	from the ground. Flowing.
Mravi.	Ants.

Nada Zidar-Bogadi, Austria [k]

BUTTERFLY, *chō*, *farfalla*—Italian, *mariposa*—Spanish (all). Who has not been charmed by the beauty of butterflies and by their life cycle? In Japan one cannot think of butterflies without recalling Chuang-tzu's parable of the man who dreamed he was one. The Japanese also take special note of the **first butterfly** of spring.

In haikai any given type of butterfly is associated with the season in which adults first emerge and fly. Most of the **small white** butterflies become active in spring. The **cabbage white** (*Artogeia rapae* formerly classified as *Pieris rapae*, *monshirochō* in Japanese) flies from last frost to first frost throughout Eurasia and North America and has been introduced to Australia and South America. Sometimes just specifying the color is enough to capture the essence of a moment, as in **white butterfly** (*shiro chōcho*, *bijeli leptir*—Croatian), which is a spring season word associated with the small whites.

As with many insects and plants, common names can confuse the image. For example, since childhood I have known these small white butterflies as "cabbage moths", but they are in fact butterflies. And there is a true "cabbage moth" (*Mamestra brassicae*), emerging May to October, dark brown with shining white kidney-shaped spots on wings, night-flying, found in Eurasia and North Africa.

SUMMER BUTTERFLY includes most varieties of **sulphur** or **yellow** (same family as the whites, Pieridae), but there are exceptions such as Britain's **brimstone** (Gonepteryx rhamni), which appears February-October, and the North American **common sulphur** or **clouded sulphur** (*Colias philodice*), March-December; both types are spring season words.

Similarly, the majority of swallowtails (family Papilionidae) are summer butterflies, but the North American **pipevine swallowtail** (*Battus philenor*) and **zebra swallowtail** (*Eurytides sp.*) begin flying and are often most numerous in spring.

Representatives of the family Nymphalidae that first fly in spring include the **small tortoiseshell** (*Aglais urticae*), **large tortoiseshell** (*Nymphalis polychloros*), and **peacock butterfly** (*Inachis io*) in England, and most of the *Polygonia* species in Eurasia and North America—the **comma, question mark,** and the **anglewing** butterflies.

Only a few members of the mothlike **skipper** family (Hesperiidae) appear in spring, most notably varieties of **sootywing** (*Staphylus sp.*) and **duskywing** (*Erynnis sp.*) in North America.

In addition, **migrating monarch** belongs to spring (see **SUMMER BUTTERFLY**). See also the essay "Butterflies Through the Year" following the poems below, and the entries for **SUMMER, AUTUMN**, and **WINTER BUTTERFLY**, and for **MOURNING CLOAK** (all year).*

shiro chōcho	the white butterfly
tobisari nanika	flew away—something
ushinai shi	has been lost

Ayako Hosomi, Japan [k]

on the patio
the afternoon drifts along
with the butterfly

Patricia Machmiller, CA [k]

Ala con ala	Wing to wing
due farfalla a baciarsi	two butterflies kissing
sulli arso muro.	on the burnt wall.

Fabrizio Virgili, Italy [k]

Iz beskonačne	From the distant
daljine doliječe	void there arrives
bijeli leptir.	a white butterfly.

Vladimir Devidé, Croatia [k]

Tired by the long flight
the wandering butterfly
slept at the world's margin.

Liliana Gradinaru, Romania [k]

¿Por qué tantas	Why all these
mariposas rondando	butterflies wheeling around
al caballo muerto?	the dead horse?

Humberto Senegal, Colombia [k]

BUTTERFLIES THROUGH THE YEAR

What we usually call a "butterfly" is only the final stage in the life cycle of an individual organism of the order Lepidoptera, which includes both butterflies and moths. But it is the most visible and aesthetically pleasing stage. Generally, butterflies fly by day and moths by night. Butterflies make up only about one tenth of the 170,000 or so Lepidopteran species; since we are also diurnal, we are more conscious of them than we are of moths.

We most notice butterflies of a particular kind shortly after the adults come out of their cocoons, dry their wings, and fly. For many butterfly species this occurs only once a year; others may produce a new "flight" of fresh individuals two, three, or more times a year, if weather and climate remain in the normal range. Some species may have more or fewer flights per year in one area than another; members of a widespread species may follow quite different schedules in different areas.

Each species of butterfly depends mainly on a particular plant group or species for its food, and its stages—egg, larva, pupa, and adult—are timed to accord with the seasons of the host plants as well as the more general climate. Thus individuals of a particular species tend to go through the same stages at about the same time in a given region.

In haikai each season has its butterflies. The word "butterfly" by itself will always be taken to mean a butterfly of spring, and many species appear for the first time in that season. Note that even though a species may have flights in more than one season, naming the species in a haikai verse puts the poem into the season in which that species' first flight typically occurs—unless another season word carries the poem into a different season. A butterfly that normally appears only in spring and another that has flights on and off from spring through autumn will usually both be considered spring butterflies in the saijiki.

Often we call butterflies by names that represent a group of related species or even whole families. Butterfly species may vary considerably from region to region, but members of the same family often have similar habits in widely different areas. The following four butterfly families are among those most common in the mid-temperate regions of the British Isles, the United States and Canada, and Japan. Note that there are some fifteen families of butterflies, and that those prominent in one or another region may have no representatives in others. Observations similar to the following could no doubt be made for the butterflies of any region.

Family Pieridae: whites, orange tips, and sulphurs (or sulfurs)—Japanese *shirochōka*. While there are exceptions, most of the "cabbage butterflies" become active in spring. In the same family, almost all of the mainly yellow-colored "sulphurs" begin flying in summer. A few Pieridae appear only in autumn, and most of the tropical "giant sulphurs" (sometimes found in extreme southern states of the U.S.) have several flights which may appear at any time of year.

Family Papilionidae: swallowtails—Japanese *agehachōka*. The only circumpolar swallowtail, *Papilio machaon*, is widely distributed in Eurasia and North America and flies in summer and autumn. In England it is the only representative of its family, and is called simply "swallowtail"; in the U.S., "old world swallowtail". In North America the black, giant, and tiger swallowtails mainly begin their flights in summer, but the pipevine and zebra swallowtails first appear in spring. In Japan about half the several swallowtail species get started in late spring, but all are most commonly seen in the summer landscape.

Family Lycaenidae: hairstreaks, coppers, and blues—Japanese *shijimichōka*. The majority of these species first show up in summer, but both hairstreaks and blues include several varieties that fly in the spring and a few that appear only in autumn.

Family Nymphalidae: fritillaries, admirals, and vanessids—Japanese *tatehachōka*. This varied family includes Britain's "tortoise shells" and the commas, question marks, and anglewings, all of which get started in spring. The many fritillaries take to the air in summer, along with Japan's "blue admiral" and "emperor" butterflies. Other admiral and "painted lady" species may become active in either spring or summer, depending on species and locale. One common species of tortoise shell butterfly, known as the "mourning cloak" in North America, may be seen in any month throughout most of its range there, but appears in England under its British name "Camberwell beauty" only in autumn.

This last example illustrates one of the problems involved in trying to create an international saijiki. Many kinds of butterflies have very different seasonal cycles in different regions. The same species may be active year-round in the tropics, but characterize a specific season in the temperate zone. This is only the most obvious difficulty. Others, like the Camberwell beauty/mourning cloak, may routinely appear at very different times in different places with similar habitats and climates.

Perhaps in recognition of this fact, or simply because of the incredible variety of butterflies, Japanese haikai poets have tended to use generic terms for the butterflies of different seasons. But in the minds of many poets these generic terms will themselves suggest specific types of butterfly: The simple "butterfly" of spring usually calls to mind a small white; one prominent poet and creator of saijiki says that he specifically imagines a "summer butterfly" to be a swallowtail; and so on. Thus the Japanese terms are not as vague to their readers as literal translations may seem to us.

To see how all this might work into the saijiki system, look over the various entries relating to "butterfly" in *Haiku World*, which are: **BUTTERFLY** (spring, above); **SUMMER BUTTERFLY, AUTUMN BUTTERFLY, WINTER BUTTERFLY**, and **MOURNING CLOAK** (all year).

The butterflies mentioned in this essay and the entries only represent a very small portion of all the world's butterflies. To determine the seasonal placement of any specific butterfly or group in your area it is best to consult a guide or field book—or butterfly expert—for your own region, remembering that butterflies are usually placed in the saijiki during the season in which they typically first appear. At the same time, do not forget that the seasons of haikai differ from those commonly associated with spring, summer, and so on in field guides. For example, "late spring" in a field guide usually corresponds to early summer in haikai.

Finally, a poet may "move" a butterfly species appearing in a season different from that of its typical first flight by including another appropriate season word to govern the seasonal aspect of the poem. This may be necessary when a butterfly that normally flies throughout spring and summer is involved in a summer poem, or sometimes when unusual weather or the like may cause a butterfly to appear quite outside of its normal timespan. (The resulting poem would appear in a saijiki under the governing seasonal topic rather than that for the type of butterfly.)

There are other general seasonal topics like **BUTTERFLY**, for example **INSECT** and **MUSHROOM**, both in autumn. Neither means nor implies that all insects or all mushrooms are to be found only in autumn. Rather, because many insects sing so prominently in autumn, the general term applies to that season (which is August through October). Similarly, several different kinds of mushrooms are available in autumn, and the general term relates to the fact that many Japanese go mushroom-gathering then. In haikai the words "butterfly", "insect", and "mushroom" each typify their respective seasons. But when one names a particular type or species, that specific animal or plant has its own appropriate position in the seasonal cycle.

BEE, *hachi* (all). Japanese *hachi* includes **honeybee** and **bumblebee; wasp** (*yāchal*—Gujarati), **yellow jacket**, and **hornet**, among others. Unspecified, "bee" in English will usually be taken to mean the honeybee, known for pollinating flowers as it flies from one to another collecting nectar. Honeybees exist both wild and farmed in a **beehive** (*košnica*—Croatian) by a **beekeeper**. Bumblebees are a bit more frightening than honeybees because of their size and loud noise, but are similar to honeybees in their behavior. Some wasps and hornets build a **wasps' nest** of mud or a papery material which they make, often in or near buildings, and may become aggressive when disturbed. The entire group is capable of administering a painful **sting**. Stings can be serious or fatal to humans and other animals if they are stung repeatedly; some allergic persons must avoid all stings. In the last poem below, "champa flower" refers to the pungent yellow blossoms of *Michelia champaca*—

"champac" or "champaka" in English—a tree of the magnolia family from the tropics of eastern India.

bewildered bee
on her wedding bouquet
walks down the aisle

Robert Henry Poulin, FL [k/s]

Košnica u potkrovlju.	A beehive in the loft.
Zlatni odsjaj	The golden gleam
ispunjava tamu.	fills up the gloom.

Nediljko Boban, Croatia [h]

yāchal ēmī	Wasps after her . . .
bhamara nē anbōḍē	she sticks in her coiffure
gūnthē ē chanpō	a champa flower.

Jhinabhai "Sneharashmi" Desai, India [k]

SPRING—PLANTS

PLUM BLOSSOMS, *ume* (early). *Prunus mume.* In early classical Japanese poetry the word *hana* referred to plum blossoms, rather than to cherry blossoms, as it does now. As the first blossoms, and because of the scent, plum blossoms are still highly prized in Japan, and in haikai. The phrase will normally be taken to refer specifically to **white plum blossoms** (*hakubai*), since the image is important enough to grant a separate topic to **pink** or **RED PLUM BLOSSOMS** (*kōbai*), which appear just a little later, but are still an early spring topic. **LOOKING FOR PLUM BLOSSOMS** is a late winter topic, as they may appear in January shortly after the holiday period. Note that while generations of translators have called this tree by the name "plum", to English and American gardeners it is the "Japanese apricot", sometimes grudgingly referred to as "flowering plum". Also: **plum tree blooming.**

Plum tree still blooming
against an old wooden house
when the builders come

David Burleigh, Japan [k/s]

KOWHAI (early). *Sophora sp.* The kowhai tree (pronounced KO-why) bears one of the most beautiful and earliest flowers of New Zealand forests, where it usually grows in open spaces or at the edges. The pendulous yellow flowers blossom before the new leaves, and attract honeyeaters (nectar-eating birds of the family Meliphagidae). The kowhai is considered the semi-official national flower of New Zealand, though it is also found in Chile and on some intervening islands. The closely related Japanese **PAGODA TREE BLOSSOMS** (*enju no hana*) appear in early summer. Also: **first kowhai.**

another bitter morning
and then—
the first kowhai

Cyril Childs, New Zealand [h]

QUENUAL SHEDDING, *quenual muda su piel*—Spanish (early). *Polylepis sp.* The *quenual* (*quiñual* in Equador) grows in the Andes at altitudes of 8,000' (2,700 m) and above; some species have loose bark which sheds in early spring—August in Peru, where the poem below was written.

Brisa tranquila	Soft breeze
un quenual de oro	a golden quenual
muda su piel	sheds its skin

Alfonso Cisneros Cox, Peru [h]

CAMELLIA, *tsubaki* (all). Japanese **tsubaki** is usually understood as deep red in color, American "camellia" as white; therefore it makes good sense to specify the color.

Falling with the rain
a white camellia blossom
The moss darkens

Peter J. Kendall, OR [k]

CHERRY BLOSSOMS, *sakura* (late). One of the two most important images in all traditional Japanese poetry (the other being the moon). However, while there are many poems specifically on cherry blossoms, its most common evocation comes with the simple word **BLOSSOMS** (*hana*), which is itself a seasonal topic (see next entry). Also: **cherries blossom, cherry in bloom, eyes in the cherry tree** (*ochi în vişinul*—Romanian).

Cherries blossom—
a light breeze is blowing
in my heart

Edna Kovacs, OR [k]

one more spring
part of the cherry tree
in bloom

Michael Ketchek, NY [k]

Azi dimineaţă,	Under my window
o mie de ochi	this morning, a thousand eyes
în vişinul de sub geam.	in the cherry tree.

Nicolae Stefanescu, Romania [h]

BLOSSOMS, *hana* (late). Unless some other blossom is specified, in Japan the word blossom or blossoms (*hana*) will be taken to mean the blossoms of the ornamental cherry. Because of a more varied environment in North America, some renku poets there have suggested that "blossoms" in English-language renku be understood as the blossoms of any spring-blossoming tree. While the Japanese word *hana* translates both as "blossom" and as "flower", in English we usually—but not always—employ "blossom" for the flowers of trees, and "flower" for the blossoms of other plants, such as garden flowers and wildflowers.

Some North American renku poets have suggested accepting this distinction between "blossoms" and "flowers" as a rule. Also note that named blossoms, such as **PEACH BLOSSOMS** and the like, each have their own status as seasonal topics. This includes **CHERRY BLOSSOMS.** Also: **blossoming sky** (*hana no sora*), **abundant blossoms** (*Blütenübersät*—German).

hana ikite	arranging blossoms
nokoriga shimiru	my fingers are cold with
yubi hiyuru	the lingering fragrance

Kayoko Hashimoto, Japan [k]

tetsubō ni	once around
ikkaiten no	on the horizontal bar
hana no sora	blossoming sky

Tsubaki Hoshino, Japan [k]

Blütenübersät—	Abundant blossoms—
wird das Auto den Frühling	will the car carry spring
durch die Stadt tragen?	into the city?

Barbara Lindner, Germany [k]

FLOWERING DOGWOOD, *hanamizuki* (late). *Cornus florida*. This is the common dogwood of eastern North America, which has been cultivated world-wide for its 3-4" (7.5-10 cm) wide "blossom"—actually composed of four creamy white or pink bracts surrounding a cluster of small greenish flowers. The tree grows up to 30' (9 m) high. Though most American guides say flowering dogwood blooms in May, in the southern United States it blooms as early as February; Japanese guides show it in April and May. The bracts of the flowering dogwood are notched at the outer ends, rather than pointed like the **MOUNTAIN DOGWOOD** of Japan or the **Pacific dogwood** of North America, which are discussed in summer. The inner and outer ends of flowering dogwood bracts quickly shade to a reddish brown, which has combined with other characteristics to suggest a Christian symbol for the passion and purity of Jesus' crucifixion, the flower-cluster representing the crown of thorns, the brown color the blood, the white purity, and the overall shape the cross. In autumn the clustered, oblong fruits turn red. Note that in English the word **dogwood** alone will usually be taken as referring to the flowering of this tree, though other dogwoods may come to mind for readers in their regions. (It may also be useful to know that in parts of the mountains and plains area of the western U.S. "dog-wood" refers to sagebrush wet with rain, said to smell like a wet dog.)

last light—
at a crossroads
the flowering dogwood

James Chessing, CA [h]

BLUEBELLS (late). Full name **Virginia bluebells** (*Mertensia virginica*). These light blue trumpet-shaped flowers (about 1"/2.5 cm) bloom March Through June on erect stems 8-24" (20-60 cm) tall, in the eastern half of North America. This and related species range from Ontario to the Carolinas and west to Minnesota and Kansas. Also called: **Virginia cowslip**. Bluebells is a common name of some other wild and garden plants. Those found in spring include: **English bluebells** or **Scottish bluebells** (*Endymion* or *Hyacinthoides non-scripta*)—a bulb of western Europe; **Spanish bluebells** (*H. hispanicus*); and some varieties of **grape hyacinths** (*Muscari sp.*). One kind of **HAREBELL** (*Campanula sp.*) is also called bluebell and blooms late summer and autumn (*C. rotundifolia*).

Bluebells
Up through dead leaves
Sound of the surf

Miriam Sagan, NM [h]

SWEET DAPHNE, *jinchōge* (mid). A Eurasian laurel (*Daphne odora*) growing 3-6' (1-2 m) high, noted for clusters of sweet-smelling, pinkish-white blossoms March through April.

sweet
daphne
snow
capped

Michael Fessler, Japan [k]

neko iede shite	the cat goes out
jinchō no	sweet daphne's
yami nokoru	darkness remains

Kin'ichi Sawaki, Japan [k]

CALLA LILY (all). *Zantedescia aethiopica*. Also known as **white arum**, or **Lily of the Nile**, the calla lily is native to South Africa, where it produces large flowers with pure white spathe and yellow spadix in spring; it is a common houseplant in north temperate regions. Not a true **LILY**, which see in summer.

Dusk
the arum holds its light a little
longer

Steve Shapiro, South Africa [h]

FORSYTHIA, *rengyō* (mid). *Forsythia sp.* One of the cheeriest signs of spring, commonly in single clumps or wild-looking hedges of brilliant yellow, often seeming to outshine the sun.

forsythia!
  the minimum speed
    forty miles per . . .

Joan Bulger Murphy, NY [k/s]

the door closing—
forsythia petals left behind
on the elevator floor

joan iversen goswell, PA [k]

rengyō no	the forsythia's
hana ga akashi no	blossoms . . . lamp for
neko no tsuka	a cat's grave-mound

Kazuo Satō, Japan [k]

LILAC, *rairakku* (late). Of central Asian origin, *Syringa vulgaris* is now found world-wide. In some areas, blossoms peak in early summer.

all my life
smelling that childhood
lilac tree

Virginia Brady Young, CT [k]

lilac morning
the rooster opens his wings
to each hen

Marian Olson, VA [k]

JACARANDA, *jacarandá*—Spanish (mid). (*Jacaranda sp.*, about 50 species.) Tropical American trees of the family *Bignoniaceae*, blooming in March and April (the dry season, often called *verano*—"summer" in Spanish-speaking Central America, and most equivalent to that season in temperate zones). Blossoms in the pink-lavender-blue range. Also called: **False rosewood.**

the night shift over . . .
covering my old car
jacaranda blossoms

Richard Burri, CA [k]

Dedos del viento	A bit of wind
bajo el jacarandá	under the jacaranda
grama celeste.	sky-blue grass.

Beatriz Piedras, Argentina [k]

AZALEA, *tsutsuji* (late). A large group of evergreen shrubs in the rhododendron family. Their hardiness and bright colored, fully flowering bushes make them popular in gardens.

azalea display!
but look how their shadows are
all the same color

Dorothy A. McLaughlin, NJ [k]

MAGNOLIA, *mokuren*, *magnolia*—Spanish (mid). Of the dozen or more *Magnolia* species and hybrids, most bloom in April. This seems to be true in Japan as well as outside of Japan, but many Japanese gardens will have an early blooming species, such as *M. stellata* or *M. heptapeta*, with showy white blossoms, which accounts for the mid-spring assignment in the saijiki. Also, **magnolia buds** become prominent long before they bloom, perhaps adding to the sense of their early blooming.

Lunar magnolia,	Lunar magnolia,
el fuego diurno	the diurnal fire
tocó su carne.	has touched your flesh.

Javier Sologuren, Peru [k]

ALMOND BLOSSOMS, *flori de migdal*—Romanian (all). Blossoms of *Prunus amygdalus, P. dulcis*, etc. This almond tree is widely cultivated for its early pink to white blossoms in mid spring, and orchard-grown for its nut. However, the word "almond" is the common name of many related nut-bearing trees with a variety of spring bloom times, including one grown in Japan that blooms in late spring (*hatankyō*) and others blooming as early as February. So this might best be considered an all-spring topic.

flori de migdal	almond blossoms
se deschid în lumina	are opening in the light
ochilor de copli	of a child's eyes

Olga Duţu, Romania [h]

PEAR BLOSSOMS, *nashi no hana* (late). *Pyrus sp.* Like many orchard trees, pears provide clusters of white blossoms in late spring, before the trees leaf out. Also: **flowering pear tree.**

a neighbor's
white-flowering pear tree
storm clouds overhead

Mary E. Durham, TX [k]

APRICOT BLOSSOMS, *anzu no hana, cvijetu marelice*—Croatian (late). *Prunus armeniaca*. One of the more lovely and delicate blossoming fruit trees, originated in China and now spread throughout the southern part of the north temperate zone. In the southwestern U.S. these small trees are frequently snuggled close to houses in patios and gardens, and bring a special light to their surroundings. In some areas, the blooming may be interrupted by a late frost. Also: **apricots bloom** (*anzu saki*).

apricot blossoms
mostly beyond the reach
of my nose

John F. Turner, Australia [k/s]

Raskošno trepti
u cvijetu marelice
jedna nit sunca.

Luxuriously twinkling
in the apricot blossom
one thread of sun.

Katarina Pšak, Croatia [h]

anzu saki
jiai kiwamaru
waga mensu

apricots bloom
self-love in extremis
my menstruation

Shinko Tokizane, Japan [k/s]

APPLE BLOSSOMS, *ringo no hana* (late). *Malus sylvestris* or *M. pumila* varieties. The apple is the most widely cultivated fruit in the temperate zones, thanks in part to the efforts of Jonathan Chapman (1774–1845)—better known as "Johnny Appleseed"—who carried seed of this Eurasian native from Pennsylvania to Illinois. Today, many regions have orchards of apple trees covered with pinkish-white blossoms in March, April, and May. (Large commercial orchards tend to be in cooler regions, with heavy bloom beginning in April.) Between natural and human development, more than 3,000 varieties are known, though the number is shrinking as market pressures favor those producing fruit of consistent size and color. **CRABAPPLE BLOSSOMS**, of which there are many species native to North America, produce smaller, irregular fruit. They are widely cultivated for their white, pink, or reddish blossoms of early summer; in warmer regions some varieties may bloom from early spring on. See also **APPLE** in autumn. Also: **apple petals** (*latice jabuke*—Croatian).

Stablo jabuke—
krava ispod krošanja
pase latice.

Apple tree—
a cow under the branches
grazes on petals.

Zvonko Petrović, Croatia [h]

TREE BUDS, *ko no me* (mid). Buds actually form on most trees in autumn and winter, but spring warmth and moisture bring swelling and visibility, especially as buds crack to reveal hints of color. Also: **budding**.

. . . still gusty
surveyor tapes fluttering
on the budding slope

R. J. Trayhern, VA [k]

PINE CANDLES, *waka midori* (late). The Japanese literally says "young green". The new growth of pine trees looks very like candles at the tips of branches. One Japanese name for them translates as "pine wicks" (*matsu no shin*). They have been documented for a variety of months in different places, like many seasonal phenomena. Aldo Leopold devotes a long, lyrical passage of *A Sand County Almanac* to pine candles, which he notes in Wisconsin in May. See also their appearance at **EASTER** in Florida in this saijiki.

after sunset
the pine candles still hold
the light

Samantha Gates, TN [k]

WILLOW, *yanagi* (late). *Salix sp.* In haikai this always refers to one of the many varieties of **weeping willow** (*shidare-yanagi* or *itoyanagi*), known for their luxuriant green foliage in spring. Other willows such as the **PUSSY WILLOW** (*nekoyanagi*, early spring), and other aspects of the weeping willow including **WILLOW FLUFF** (*ryūjo*, mid spring), have their own status as topics. Also: **willows** (*sălcii*—Romanian).

Pe lac, lopata	On the lake the oar
adunînd, risipind	gathers, disperses
soare şi sălcii.	sun and willows.

Radu Dumitru, Romania [h]

ALDER CATKINS, *hannoki no hana*, *Erlenkätzchen*—German (mid). *Alnus sp.* The catkins—flowers—of most alder trees bloom in mid spring, before the leaves are fully formed.

quiet croaking of a crow
on the leafless alder
old cones—new catkins

Martin Lucas, England [k]

Der Erlenbaum hängt	The alder tree hangs
die Blütenkätzchen über	its blooming catkins over
die Friedhofsmauer.	the cemetery wall.

Gisela Schermer, Germany [k]

PUSSY WILLOW, *nekoyanagi* (early). *Salix discolor* (North America) and *S. gracilistyla* (Japan). A most welcomed early sign of spring.

kite mireba	came looking for them—
hoho kechirashite	the heads all are scattered
nekoyanagi	pussy willows

Ayako Hosomi, Japan [k]

WILLOW FLUFF, *ryūjo* (mid). *Salix sp.* The majority of these water-loving trees develop their **willow catkins** (*yanagi no hana*) in mid spring.

Also called **flying willow fluff** (*ryūjo tobu*, *wilgepluisje*—Dutch), **willow cotton**. The "ninety" in the poem below refers to kilometers per hour; over 55 mph.

Ik rijd negentig.	I'm doing ninety.
In mijn auto zweeft rustig	In my car gently floats
een wilgepluisje.	a willow fluff.

Bart Mesotten, Belgium [k]

DAFFODIL, *rappa suisen*, *narcisa*—Croatian (mid). *Narcissus sp*. While the twenty-plus species of narcissus, jonquils, and daffodils are all in the same genus, and there are flowers called "narcissus" that closely resemble what we commonly think of as "daffodils" and vice-versa, most people will image the **common daffodil** (*N. pseudonarcissus*) as bearing a yellow flower with a longish yellow corona or "trumpet" at center—in mid spring. Also in mid spring, according to Japanese saijiki: **yellow narcissus** (*kizuisen*), various species with all-yellow flowers. And late spring includes what translates as **red-mouth narcissus** (*kuchi beni suisen*), which resembles **poet's narcissus** (*N. poeticus*) in American and British gardens. In haikai **narcissus** (*suisen*) by itself always means late winter (such varieties of *N. tazetta* as the **paper-white narcissus**). When reading it seems best to accept the Japanese tradition of **narcissus** as late winter and **daffodil** as mid spring. When writing haiku or hokku it is better to write naturally of what one observes than to worry too much about seasonal associations, but for stanzas in the body of a renku the traditional associations should be observed.

Starica u crnini	An old woman in mourning
narcisa joj viri	yet a daffodil peeps
iz torbe	from her bag.

Smiljka Bilankov, Croatia [k]

SIBERIAN WALLFLOWER (all). *Cheiranthus allionii*. Also called **early wallflower** (*muurbloempje*—Dutch), with hardy yellow-orange flowers. Not to be confused with the highly fragrant yellow, red, or copper-colored **WALLFLOWER** (*C. cheiri*) of summer.

Zo'n muurbloempje!	This early wallflower!
rechtop uit brokken baksteen	standing up from broken brick
en een verweerde voeg.	and a weathered joint.

Ton Koelman, The Netherlands [k]

DAISY, *hinagiku* (all). The common name "daisy" refers to a few related wildflowers with composite flower heads, white ray florets forming one or more flat disks surrounding a bright yellow central button. The two that most commonly come to mind are the English daisy (*Bellis perennis*) and the oxeye daisy. The former blooms from March through October (earlier and later in warmer climates), and is native to Europe and western Asia, but can be found in North America—and Japan. Its flower heads rise up to 8 in. (20 cm) on individual stalks from a rosette of leaves at the base; this is the flower of the **daisy chain**. The somewhat larger-flowered (head 2"/5 cm across) and taller (to 3'/1 m) **OXEYE DAISY** (*Chrysanthemum leucanthemum*) was also introduced from Europe into North America, and has become common. It blooms June through August, making it appropriate to all summer, along with its garden hybrids, varieties of **Shasta daisy** developed by Luther Burbank and others.

subway woman asleep
picked daisies
in her hand

Raffael de Gruttola, MA [k]

SNOWDROP, *sunōdoroppu*, *Schneeglocken*—German (early). *Galanthus sp.* Snowdrops are members of the daffodil family, and their drooping white blossoms are among the earliest wildflowers seen in their native Europe. There are a number of cultivated varieties, now distributed worldwide.

Das Gesicht des Sees	The face of the swells
ändert minütlich: blau, grün;	changes by the minute: blue, green;
Schneeglocken zittern.	snowdrops tremble.

Lili Keller-Strittmatter, Switzerland [k]

CROCUS, *kurokkasu* (early). One of the first garden flowers to bloom, while the breath of winter seems still with us.

Crocus in bloom
one thin shadow
leaning

Pat Shelley, CA [k]

BABY'S BREATH, *kasumisō* (late). The Japanese literally reads "mist plant". The small white flowers of *Gypsophila sp.* bloom in dainty sprays from late spring to early summer; plants grow up to 3' (1 m) tall.

ubaguruma	as a baby buggy
tōreba soyogu	passes by . . . the swaying
kasumisō	baby's breath

Yatsuka Ishihara, Japan [h]

GREENING BARLEY, *aomugi* (all). A staple crop in Japan; barley fields take on a rich yellow-green color in spring. Also: **green of barley** (*mugi no aosa*).

shinzō ni	into the heart
mugi no aosa ga	the green of barley
jojo ni jojo ni	slowly, slowly

Tohta Kaneko, Japan [h]

VIOLETS, *sumire*, *viooltjies*—Afrikaans (all). One of the most traditional signs of spring, the **common blue violet** or **meadow violet** (*Viola papilionacea*) of North America blooms March to June. In Europe the best-known is the similar **sweet violet** (*V. odorata*); in Japan *sumire* (*V. mandshurica*) has a more lavender flower in April and May. There are white and yellow varieties also (some summer-blooming), but the word "violet" will always be taken to mean one of the many blue or "violet-colored" violets unless something else is specified.*

long ago
I would have picked
these violets

Sylvia Forges-Ryan, CT [k]

TRILLIUM (mid). *Trillium sp.* Native to North America, the trilliums are also known as **wake robin**, perhaps in connection with their appearance in the woods about the same time as the **AMERICAN ROBIN** moves from its winter range to fields and towns more in human view. Most varieties have white blossoms growing from a few inches to a foot (30 cm) or more off the ground, but some have deep red flowers.

woods walking
in a time of trilliums
my hand in her hand

anne mckay, BC [k]

trilliums rippling . . .
under her scarf
her pulse

Rod Willmot, PQ [k]

CLOVER, *umagoyashi* (late). A common lawn plant, clover also grows among wild grasses; typical leaves come in threes, but a **four-leaf clover** is said to bring good luck.

at the hazardous
waste site
an eight-leaf clover

Carlos Colón, LA [k/s]

DANDELION, *tanpopo* (all). One of the most ubiquitous plants, worldwide. Dandelions bloom spring through autumn, but are most noticeable in spring. Detested by some, who prefer smooth lawns, they are loved by others as a source of greens and dandelion wine. Also: **dandelion seeds** (*păpădia*—Romanian).

tanpopo no	the dandelions
hanazakari nari	have come to full bloom—
rusu no niwa	garden of my absence

Chie Kamegaya, BC [k]

păscînd iarba	grazing grass
calul împrăştie	a horse spreads
păpădia	dandelion seeds

Ion Codrescu, Romania [h]

PRIMROSE, *sakurasō, jaglac*—Croatian (late). *Primula sp.* A family of low-growing plants with five-petalled flowers. *Sakurasō*, literally "cherry-blossom grass" (*P. sieboldi*), is also called *purimura* in Japanese and has pink flowers in late spring. The common primrose (*Primula vulgaris*) of England has sulphur-yellow flowers March through May. They are popular with florists, who can supply them from early spring on.

outside the deli
primroses and daffodils—
I open my coat

Perdita Finn, NY [k]

Između stabala	Among trees
jaglaci su procvali	primroses begin to bloom
žutim mirisom.	with a yellow smell.

Katarina Pšak, Croatia [h]

HEPATICA, *suhamasō, blåsippa*—Swedish (early). *Hepatica sp.* Also called **liverleaf** or **liverwort,** hepaticas grow 4-6" (10-15 cm) tall and sometimes offer their white-sepalled blossoms in snow. They are common to rocky woodlands of Europe, eastern and central North America, and Japan. The various species all seem to bloom consistently in March and April, with some lingering into May, according to wildflower guides from Massachusetts to Florida and west to Illinois (and from Japan)—though one indicates some bloom in February. The placement in "early spring" may have as much to do with habitat and tradition as with time, since in many areas hepatica is the first woodland plant to flower. Note the variation indicated in the poem from Sweden—where May would very likely be early or mid spring in any reasonable haikai calendar.

can i learn from the hepatica root-tangled in jagged rocks

Marlene Mountain, TN [k/s]

Kom redan i mars	Come already in March
maj månad förra året	in the month of May last year
kära blåsippa.	dear hepatica.

Gun Wahrenby, Sweden [k]

ANEMONE, *ichirinsō* (late). The European, American, and Japanese **wood anemones** (*Anemone nemorosa, quinquefolia,* and *nikonensis,* respectively, *vitsippor* in Swedish) are also known as **windflowers.** These wild members of the buttercup family grow 4-12" (10-30 cm) high and present bright white-sepalled flowers from mid to late spring well into summer. Several cultivated anemones bloom at about the same time, some with bright colors; in Japan these are known collectively as *anemoni*, also a late spring topic. Note that the so-called **JAPANESE ANEMONE** (Japanese *kibunegiku*, *A. hupehensis*) native to Asia has red or white flowers in mid autumn. The **OXEYE DAISY** mentioned in one of the following poems is an all-summer topic.

From the wind
Along with the scented cat
Spring the anemones.

Gerald Robert Vizenor, CA [k]

Många mil mellan	Many the miles between
vitsippor och prästkragar	wood anemone and ox-eye daisy
mellan vår och sommar.	between spring and summer.

Gun Wahrenby, Sweden [k]

FIDDLEHEAD FERNS, *warabi* (mid). Also translated **fernbrake,** *warabi* refers to a number of large ferns that sprout up in the shape of the end of a violin before the leaves fully open.

kōsofu no	great-great grandfather's
bonji warabi no	Sanskrit letters—tomb
naka no haka	among the fiddleheads

Kyoko Tsuruta, Japan [k]

MINT (all). A large family of low-growing perennials that have aromatic oils in the leaves. "Mint" will normally mean **peppermint** (*Menthe piperita*) or **wild mint** (*M. arvensis*). Also: **new mint.**

Raking last winter's leaves
all at once
a breath of new mint

Rebecca M. Osborn, PA [h]

THISTLE, *azami* (late). Plants of the botanical tribe Cynareae. In haikai "thistle" by itself indicates the earliest-blooming pink-to-purple thistles, such as the Japanese **wild thistle** (*no-azami, Cirsium japonicum*) and North American **cluster thistle** (*C. brevistylum*). The stout **yellow thistle** (*C. horridulum*) of the eastern U.S. blooms as early as March in the south. But most varieties of thistle bloom in summer and on into autumn, accounting for the topics **SUMMER THISTLE** (*natsu-azami*) and **AUTUMN THISTLE** (*aki-azami*). Summer finds a number of kinds of **white thistle** blooming in the Pacific states, along with varieties of yellow **sow thistle** (*Sonchus sp.*) originally native to Europe and now found also in the eastern U.S. The **nodding** or **musk thistle** (*Carduus nutans*) of Europe and North America and the similar-looking **devil thistle** (*oni-azami, Cirsium borealinipponense*) of Japan are purple summer-bloomers that linger well into autumn. Thistles that just begin blooming in late summer or autumn include the Japanese **beach thistle** (*ama-azami, Cirsium maritimum*) and **Fuji thistle** (*fuji-azami, C. purpuratum*), and the **Santa Fe thistle** (*C. ochracentrum*) of the U.S. high plains. In the following poem "oryoki" (Japanese *ōryōki*) refers to Buddhist eating and begging bowls, and the formal manner of eating from them.

Mad at Oryoki in the shrine-room—Thistles blossomed late afternoon.

Allen Ginsberg, NY [k/s]

SUMMER

The following entries appear under Summer, in the categories indicated.

---- The Season ----
Summer
May
The Coming of Summer
Midsummer
July
Summer Day
Blaze of Midday
Summer Afternoon
Summer Evening
Summer Night
Short Night
Dog Days
Hot
Hot Day
Sultry
Burning Hot
Summer's End
---- The Heavens ----
Summer Light
Billowing Clouds
Midnight Sun
Summer Moon
Pleiades at Dawn
Summer Dusk
Summer Wind
Evening Calm
Dust Devil
Summer Rain
Rainy Season
Monsoon
Hail
Summer Mist, Summer Fog
Sea Fog
Summer Haze, Summer Mist
Thunder
Summer Afterglow
Drought
---- The Earth ----
Summer Field
Flood
Fountainhead
Waterfall

---- Humanity ----
Splash Pattern
Summer Pajamas
Sunglasses
Parasol
Ice Cream
Beer
Hammock
Air Conditioner
Electric Fan
Airing Clothes
Shower Bath
Sidewalk Sale
Flea Market
Water the Garden
Grass Cutting
Midsummer Plowing
Swimming
Swimming Pool
Sand Castle
Fireworks
Morris Dance
Baseball
Night Game
Bouquet
Hide-and-Seek
Naked
Barefoot
Washing Hair
Sweat
Summer Lethargy
Sun-Bathing
Sunburn
Midday Nap
End of School
Class Reunion
---- Observances ----
Vesak
Mother's Day
A-Bomb Day
Dominion Day
Independence Day
Memorial Day
Festival
Holidays
Takako's Day

---- Animals ----
Bats
Grazing Cows
Hedgehog
Turtle
Toad
Giant Salamander
Lizard
Snake
Cuckoo
Hummingbird
Brown Hawk-Owl
Waterbird's Nest
Loon
Heron
Egret
Willow Warbler
Chickadee
Sweetfish, Trout
Goldfish
Killifish
Flying Fish
Pike
Crab
Jellyfish
Summer Butterfly
Moth
Hairy Caterpillar, Woolly Bear
Caterpillar
Firefly
Beetle
Soldier Bug
Chafer
Ladybug
Leaf Beetle
Cicada
First Cricket
Damselfly
Fly
Fruit Flies
Mosquito
Gnats
Mayflies
Cockroach
Fleas
Ant
Spider
Millipede
Snail
Earthworm
---- Plants ----
Leafing Cherry (Trees)
Cherries
Rose
Hydrangea
Geranium
Jasmine
Orange Blossoms
Maple Keys
Grape Blossoms
Raspberry
Cloudberry
Salmonberries
Shade of a Tree
Mountain Dogwood
Poinciana Blossoms
Poplar Seeds
Iris
Datura
Sweet Alyssum
Water Lily
Lily
Century Plant
Zinnias
Berries
Moonflower
Queen Anne's Lace
Melon
Grain
Corn Tassels
Bindweed
Mullein
Moss Blossoms
Duckweed
Morel
Mold, Mildew

Note: An asterisk at the end of an entry's text indicates that additional poems and season words on the topic may be found in Chapter 6 of *The Haiku Seasons.*

SUMMER—THE SEASON

SUMMER, *natsu*, *leto*—Serbian (all). Technically, in haikai "summer" means the period from about 6 May through about 7 August and centering on the summer solstice, or commonly May through July (November to January in the southern hemisphere). Poems on the season per se may be included here. Generally, the word "summer" adds a sense of heat and lushness to a poem. Additional season words associated with this topic include **all summer** (*sanka*, literally "three summer [months]"), **90 days of summer** (*kyūka*), **fiery summer** (*enka*), and **god of fire** (*entei*). See the discussion of the names of seasons in the introduction to the saijiki, pages 32–33.

entei no	in the fire god's
ikari ni waga no	anger my hair gets
kami midare	all tangled up

Yasushi Ueno, Japan [k]

Pusta obala	Deserted beach
Letos nema turista	No tourists this summer
Caure i skoljke	Seashells and gunshells

Vid Vukasovic, Yugoslavia [k]

MAY, *gogatsu*, *Mai*—German (early). The **merry month of May** exactly expresses the feeling associated with this month for the northern hemisphere. By now the last vestiges of winter are gone in most populated areas, and people are out enjoying the mild weather. The heaviest of the farm work is done until harvest, and flowers bloom in profusion. It is a time for relaxation and socializing.

Das Wiedersehen:	The reunion:
ein alter Freund wird müde.	an old friend grows weary.
Mai-kuhle zur Nacht.	A May night's coolness.

Günther Klinge, Germany [k]

COMING OF SUMMER, *rikka* (early). This expresses the idea of "summer is just now coming"; in haikai such phrases as "the coming of summer" must be justified in the rest of the verse with an image that completes the feeling. Also called: **became summer, summer has come** (*natsu no kishi*).

A big old cockroach
walks across the kitchen floor.
Spring became summer.

Edith Marcombe Shiffert, Japan [k]

umi ga mata	the sea again
wagako yūwaku su	seduces my son—
natsu no kishi	summer is come

Kyōko Hori, Japan [k]

MIDSUMMER, *chūka* (mid). The period around the **SUMMER SOLSTICE**; see the discussion of "midsummer" and "midwinter" in *The Haiku Seasons*, page 106. Also: **midsummer morning**.

midsummer morning—
the dead tree's shadow
stretches upstream

Adele Kenny, NJ [k]

JULY, *shichigatsu*, *Āshāḍha*—Gujarati (late). Seventh month in the Gregorian calendar, it is associated with many festivals and holidays, and with high heat, in the northern hemisphere. It may be more universal to refer to **LATE SUMMER** (*banka*), which corresponds to January in the southern hemisphere.

the gnat in amber
gleaming in July sun
on her throat

Paul O. Williams, CA [k/s]

Vitē Āshāḍh
khētara khālī . . . jhankhun hun
dādura rava.

End of July
empty fields . . . I look
for frogs' croakings.

Jhinabhai "Sneharashmi" Desai, India [k]

SUMMER DAY, *natsu no hi, ljetni dan*—Croatian (all). The Japanese words also mean **summer sun,** but since the primary meaning is "summer day" the topic is included here rather than under The Heavens.

One still summer day
As I watched the butterflies
I heard their wings flap

David Stelfox, BC [k]

Čitavu noć
zvjezdanim nebom put
za ljetni dan.

The whole night
a starlit skyway
to a summer day.

Dragan Vučetić, Croatia [h]

BLAZE OF MIDDAY, *enchū* (late). By late summer the glare and heat of noon have become almost unbearable. Also **burning sun, blazing sun, midday heat, sun beats down** (*ghrian áit éigin*—Irish).

shōkasen
enchū no jiken o
mokugeki su

a fire hydrant
the sole witness of an event
under the burning sun

Sōichi Furuta, NY [k]

midday heat
soldiers on both sides
roll up their sleeves

Lenard D. Moore, NC [k]

scalann an ghrian	somewhere the sun
áit éigin ar a colpaí	beats down on her calves
a murnáin	her ankles

Gabriel Rosenstock, Ireland [k]

lottery tickets
on the parking lot pavement
in the blazing sun

Jerry Ball, CA [k]

SUMMER AFTERNOON (all). Relates to the general slowing of activity during the **BLAZE OF MIDDAY** and taking a **MIDDAY NAP**, also summer topics.

Summer afternoon:
through bars of light your shoulder
rising and falling.

D. C. Trent, England [k]

SUMMER EVENING, *natsu no yū* (all). Summer evening, dusk, twilight; after the sun has set and it begins to cool. Also: **summer dusk** (*ljetni sumrak*—Croatian).

Ljetni sumrak.	Summer dusk.
Dvije gitare traže se	Two guitars seek each other
čistim tonovima.	in clear tones.

Tomislav Maretić, Croatia [k]

SUMMER NIGHT, *natsu no yo, notte d'estate*—Italian (all). The quality of air and sound changes from season to season, especially at night.

summer night
the *cha!-ch-ch, cha!-ch-ch . . .*
of switch engines

Pat Gallagher, CA [k]

Notte d'estate	Summer night
nel silenzio	in the silence
respiro de grilli	the breathing of crickets

Tamara Colombaroni, Italy [k]

SHORT NIGHT, *mijika-yo* (all). As the days grow longer the nights become shorter, and we have an **early dawn**. Also: **early light**.

early dawn
the roadrunner's coos echo
down the chimney

Sheila Wood, NM [k]

early dawn:
at last the new baby sleeps
in his mother's arms

Dorothy A. McLaughlin, NJ [k]

Early light—
the gravedigger sweats
over his spade

Matthew Louvière, LA [k]

DOG DAYS, *doyō* (late). Traditionally in Japan the dog days of summer fall in the last week of July and the first week of August, the period known as the **GREAT HEAT** (*taisho*) in the old Chinese solar calendar. See also Winter, **COLD TIME**.

dog days
even the sand lizard
takes his time

Nina A. Wicker, NC [k]

HOT, *atsushi*, *chaud*—French (all). Classic definition of summer. If one says **summer heat**, there best be some other heat around as well.

Les arbres, l'herbe	The trees, the grass
ne bougent—le silence	don't budge—the hot
chaud du midi	silence of midday

Carolanne Reynolds, BC [k]

HOT DAY, *atsuki hi* (all). Hot days may linger into autumn—indeed **LINGERING HEAT** (*zansho*) is an autumn topic. But the words "hot day" surely bring summer to mind. Also: **hot afternoon** (tarde calurosa—Spanish).

Tarde calurosa.	Hot afternoon.
Los hombres callados	The quiet men
dicen lo mismo	say it again

Alfonso Cisneros Cox, Peru [k/s]

SULTRY, *jokusho* (late). Stiflingly damp and hot; in colloquial Japanese, *mushiatsui* (*mushiatsushi* in haikai). Also: **sweltering** (*schwüler*—German), **humid stillness.***

humid stillness . . .
men load bricks
by candlelight

Kim Dorman, India [k]

Schwüler Sommertag:	Sweltering summer day:
in den Tanz der Mücken stüzt	into the dance of gnats dive
blau der Schwalbenschrei.	the blue cries of swallows.

Gerold Effert, Germany [k]

BURNING HOT, *yakuru* (late). This is the **increasing heat** of July, summer fully realized. In the following poem **locusts** refers to **CICADA,** also a late summer topic. Also: **increasing heat.**

increasing heat
locusts and the neighbors
raise their voices

Karen Sohne, NY [k/s]

SUMMER'S END, *natsu no hate* (late). Just past the peak of **HIGH SUMMER** (*natsu fukashi*, late) while the days are as hot as ever the nights begin to cool, especially in the countryside, and we are aware that something has shifted. Thoughts turn to the beginning of harvest and other autumn activities. Also: **summer is gone** (*vara s-a sfârşit—Romanian*).

summer's end
the quickening of hammers
towards dusk

Dee Evetts, NY [k]

Un fir de nisip	A thread of sand
în puşculiţa goală—	in the empty piggy-bank—
vara s-a sfârşit.	summer is gone.

Clelia Ifrim, Romania [k]

Summer gone . . .
older now
than my father

Dave Sutter, CA [k]

SUMMER—THE HEAVENS

SUMMER LIGHT (all). Each season has its characteristic light. **SPRING LIGHT** (*shunkō*) has a misty quality; summer light can be bright and glaring.

the cat asleep
in the room's darkest corner—
summer light

Delilah Nagoset, AZ [k]

BILLOWING CLOUDS, *kumo no mine* (all). The Japanese literally reads **cloud peaks.** Refers to **cumulus clouds** (*chiluan yün—Chinese*) or **cumulonimbus,** sometimes called **thunderheads.** Also: **tall clouds.**

Billowing clouds—
poplars by the river bank
bend in a breeze

Lorraine E. Harr, OR [h]

tall clouds—
at the bottom of the sky
stands a sheep

Hina, Australia [h]

chiluan yün	cumulus clouds
tien-k'uang ping-yüen	hospital for the insane
tsêng-chu tsung	getting an addition

Lingiy Huang, Taiwan [k]

MIDNIGHT SUN (mid). The sun seen above the horizon at midnight, which occurs near **MIDSUMMER** in the arctic or antarctic. At latitudes closer to the pole than the arctic or antarctic circle, the sun remains above the horizon for a number of days and nights varying inversely with the distance from the pole. The following poem was composed in northern Sweden.

friends from the south—
a great bowl of strawberries
in the midnight dusk

Dee Evetts, NY [h]

SUMMER MOON, *natsu no tsuki* (all). The summer moon brings with it a suggestion of cooling after the heat of the day.

The sea breeze
ripples the hair on my chest—
summer moon

Ty Hadman, Peru [k]

yokisha chō	night train lights—
kokkyō wa senri	the border a thousand miles
natsu no tsuki	summer moon

Kimiko Horne, ON [k]

PLEIADES AT DAWN (mid). Since the earliest civilizations the Pleiades, a star cluster in the constellation Taurus, has provided a calendar for the growing year, the elements of which certainly qualify as seasonal topics. In the northern hemisphere: When the **PLEIADES FOLLOW THE SUN DOWN** in April or late spring it is the beginning of the growing season. After this they remain unseen until: The **Pleiades rise just before the sun** around the time of the solstice—midsummer, and the height of the growing season. In November the **PLEIADES RISE JUST AFTER SUNSET**, indicating the beginning of winter. The cluster is so prominent in the eastern sky early in the night then that November is sometimes called **PLEIAD MONTH**. The name "Pleiades" comes from Greek mythology, in which they represent the "Seven Sisters", the daughters of Atlas and Pleione. It is said that Zeus turned the daughters into stars in the sky to save them from **ORION** (a winter topic), who was pressing unwanted affections upon them. Today only six stars can be seen with the naked eye, though telescopes reveal many more in the cluster; some astronomers believe that the ancient Greeks could see a seventh star, which has since dimmed. The Japanese name for the Pleiades is ***subaru***, which has not previously been included in saijiki.

In the half-light of dawn a few birds warble under the Pleiades.

Allen Ginsberg, NY [k]

SUMMER DUSK (all). In summer, dusk brings with it relief from the heat of the day.

Summer dusk
Pebbles in the vineyard
still warm

Pierre Constantin, French Polynesia [k]

SUMMER WIND, *natsu no kaze* (all). While **SPRING WIND** provides pleasant warmth after the cold of winter, summer wind tends to bring heat, even though it may seem cooler than still hot air. Special winds of summer which rate topics of their own include the warm **SOUTH-WIND** (*minami*, appropriate to the northern hemisphere) and **BALMY BREEZE** (*kunpū*) of all summer and the **DOG DAYS WIND** (*doyō kochi*) and **COOL BREEZE** (*suzukaze*) of late summer.

hair tightly coiled
in the summer wind
shaking it free

Jean Jorgensen, Alberta [k]

EVENING CALM, *yūnagi* (late). In clear summer weather at the seashore, after sunset when the air temperatures over land and sea become relatively uniform, there is usually a period of a few hours with little or no wind. A similar phenomenon at morning yields the topic **MORNING CALM** (*asanagi*). In Japan this generally occurs after the **RAINY SEASON** (see entry below), making these both late-summer topics.

Evening calm . . .
I echo the train whistle
For the baby's smile

Miriam Sagan, NM [k]

DUST DEVIL (all). Common all summer over desert and dry scrub-land, a dust devil looks like a tornado but, unlike the similar-looking waterspout, is differently caused and less dangerous. Dust devils seem to arise from intense ground heating combined with turbulent air conditions, and frequently appear under clear skies. Some dust devils last for several hours, are tens of yards (or meters) wide, and carry sand up to 2000' (600 m) high, but the term is also applied to much smaller **dust whirls**, extending for only a yard or two and dissipating in a moment. Also called **dancing dervish, desert devil, sand auger,** and other names.

a blue pickup
rattles over the cattle guard:
dust devils

Elizabeth Searle Lamb, NM [k]

SUMMER RAIN, *natsu no ame* (all). There are many kinds of rain specific to summer, such as the **RAINY SEASON** and **MID-SUMMER RAIN** of mid summer and all summer's **DOWNPOUR** (*yūdachi*) and **MONSOON,** all of which are independent topics. "Summer rain" simply means any rain of summer which does not exhibit the specific characteristics of one of these others.

after love
her heartbeat
summer rain

nick avis, NF [k]

RAINY SEASON, *tsuyu* (mid). The Japanese literally says "plum rain". This is the **seasonal rain** of Japan, which normally comes for three to four weeks beginning about the middle of June. During this period skies remain overcast most of the time and it rains for at least a part of virtually every day. Since these rains have been essential to the growing of rice, the staple food of Japan, they are most welcome to farmers. Also called: **MID-SUMMER RAIN** (*samidare* or *satsuḳi ame*), literally "fifth-month rain", which relates to the lunar calendar. An **EMPTY RAINY SEASON** (*ḳara-tsuyu*) brings no rain, and presages food shortages and drought.

rainy season—the ground glass of the swimming pool

James Kirkup, Andorra [k]

MONSOON (all). Different tropical climates have monsoons at different times. The area in which the following poem was written, the southwestern coast of Sri Lanka, experiences the **southwest monsoon** from late May through October, as does the southwest coast of India. The **monsoon season** features heavy rains and southwest winds that sometimes cause severe flooding, mudslides, and the like, especially in coastal areas. Necessary for agriculture, and a welcome relief from the

HOT DRY SEASON of February through early May when temperatures rise into the mid-90s F. (mid-30s C.) with high humidity, the storms can still create a grim, grey time.

Note: In some tropical areas, for example Central America, the **WET SEASON** is called "winter" (Spanish *invierno*), but it is also a very fertile time. Other tropical areas will differ as to the timing of wet and dry seasons. I recommend that any renku written in the tropics, or involving natives of the tropics, include seasonal topics appropriate to the "monsoon" or wet season and the hot or **DRY SEASON** once each in place of summer or winter in the mid-section of the renku—and in the hokku, if the poem is written there. Future attempts at international saijiki may contain a substantial number of wet- and dry-season phenomena, warranting the creation of these as new seasons in the saijiki.

Monsoon sky
Monsoon sea—a boat
And no horizon.

Anne Ranasinghe, Sri Lanka [k]

HAIL, *hyō* (all). Hail is a frequent accompaniment to a summer **THUNDERSTORM**; hailstones normally range from grain- or pea-sized pellets to the size of hens' eggs, though some as large as grapefruit are reported every few years. In North America the heaviest **hailstorms** (*hyō no ōfuri*) take place in June and July on the great plains east of the Rocky Mountains, and can inflict serious damage on crops and livestock, property and persons. (Note that *arare*, sometimes translated as "hail", actually refers to **SNOW PELLETS**, which see in winter.)

Sun back out
and the fields all
glittering hail.

Mary Raoul, MS [k]

SUMMER MIST, SUMMER FOG, *natsu no kiri* (all). Refers to summer fogs and rising mists, generally a bit more palpable and obviously damp than those of **SUMMER HAZE, SUMMER MIST**, which see below. **SEA FOG**, also below, is generally thicker. See also "On Haze, Mist,

Fog" at **AUTUMN MIST, FOG** for a discussion of these and related terms.

> Summer fog—
> moonlight blowing
> from tree to tree
>
> Dave Sutter, CA [k]

SEA FOG, *jiri* (late). When a large body of water cools the air above it to the dew point, fog forms. Dense white fogs roll in from the sea and obscure the moon during June and July along Japan's Pacific coast, especially from central Honshu north. Similar heavy fogs dominate the summers of San Francisco Bay and a good deal of the U.S. Pacific coast, increasing from May to August and subsiding through autumn. From a mountain top one can look down on this **SEA OF CLOUDS** (*unkai*), another summer topic. See **SUMMER MIST, SUMMER FOG**, above, and **SUMMER HAZE, SUMMER MIST**, below. See also "On Haze, Mist, Fog" at **AUTUMN MIST, FOG** for a discussion of these and related terms.

> Breakers gone,
> but out there in the fog
> the buoy's bell.
>
> James Carnisol, CA [k]

SUMMER HAZE, SUMMER MIST, *natsugasumi* (all). Typically, this is the uniform haze or mist of summer that makes each more distant ridge appear a paler blue. Substantial amounts of dust in the air, especially in the later afternoon, may shift its color with a yellow or reddish tinge. Sometimes called heat haze, though this may also be a synonym for **HEAT SHIMMER**, a quite different phenomenon classified as a spring topic. See **SUMMER MIST, SUMMER FOG** and **SEA FOG**, both above. See also "On Haze, Mist, Fog" at **AUTUMN MIST, FOG** for a discussion of these and related terms. Also called: **violet mist** (*ceaţa violetă—Romanian*).

natsugasumi ichimai iwa no kanki kana	summer haze the joy of this one rock

Banya Natsuishi, Japan [h]

Dunga munţilor— *o şosea violetă* *traversând ceaţa.*	Crest of mountains— a violet lure highway traveling the mist.

Clelia Ifrim, Romania [h]

THUNDER, *kaminari* (all). This topic includes such terms as **thunderstorm** (*raiu*), **violent thunder** (*gekirai*), **distant thunder** (*enrai*), **thunder and lightning** (*raiden*), **Thunderer** or **Thor** (*raijin*), **thunderbolt** (*rakurai*), and **lightning-strike fire** (*raika*—literally "thunder-strike fire"). But note that while these season words all traditionally relate to summer, **LIGHTNING** is a traditional autumn topic. Perhaps the division comes because farmers tend to stay indoors during summer thunderstorms—where they mainly hear them—but are out in the fields harvesting rice in autumn where they are very conscious of seeing the lightning. See **LIGHTNING** in autumn.

distant thunder—
the beach vendor uproots
his pinwheel display

Patricia Neubauer, PA [k/s]

a rumble of thunder
on the kitchen roof—I chase
off the squirrels

Chris Torrance, Wales, UK [k/s]

SUMMER AFTERGLOW, *natsu no zankō* (all). The traditional haikai word for **AFTERGLOW,** *yūyake*, literally says "burning evening", and is restricted to bright red skies of late summer. In the following poem the poet has selected another Japanese word that translates more literally as "afterglow", but is not usually a season word. By adding "summer" he creates a new seasonal topic, one with broader application than the always red *yūyake*, and which is free of the latter's previous literary associations. The *shite* (pronounced "she-tay", but more clipped than English) is the princial actor in a noh drama.

shizukasa ni	in stillness:
natsu no zankō	the summer afterglow
shite no men	the mask of the *shite*

Ryokufyū Ishizaki, Japan [h]

DROUGHT, *hideri, suša*—Croatian (late). In Japan, drought may come after the summer rains end (usually by mid July), and extend into autumn. In other places it may be hot and dry throughout summer. In some of the tropics "summer" means the dry season; see "Tropical Seasons" in the introduction to the saijiki (pages 21–23). The phrase **only the wind** (*doar vântul*—Romanian) in the second poem below seems to argue for its placement here, though technically the absence of peonies is the only seasonal concept overtly expressed in the poem. In the third poem, **lows for rain** (*chüjt mördöön*—Mongolian) seems more directly apropos.

Ljetna suša.	Summer drought.
Blistavilo zvijezda	The dazzling stars
sve je blijeđe.	all become pale.

Marijan Čekolj, Croatia [k]

Amurg sângeriu	Blood-red sunset
nici un bujor în grădină—	not a peony in the garden—
vântul, doar vântul . . .	wind, only the wind . . .

Mioara Gheorghe, Romania [k]

amaa ödördzin angajdź	mouth gaping
atan temee nücgen bijendee	all day long the gelding camel
chüjt mördöön dzogsono	lows for rain

Jawuuchulan Begdzijn, Mongolia [k]

SUMMER—THE EARTH

SUMMER FIELD, *natsuno* (all). Often translated **summer meadow** or **summer moor,** natsuno suggests a profusion of wildflowers.

tateyoko ni	high and wide
fuji nobite iru	Fuji stretches out—
natsuno kana	this summer meadow

Nobuko Katsura, Japan [h]

FLOOD, *demizu* (mid). All seasons have their characteristic floods, but those of summer are quintessential. Also: **river rising, floodwaters.**

tennis shoe
drying on a branch
over floodwaters

Charles Bernard Rodning, AL [k]

The Mississippi
a mile wide at Winona
and still rising

L. A. Davidson, NY [k]

FOUNTAINHEAD, *izumi* (all). As with waterfalls, we are most conscious of **springs** in summer, when their waters mean refreshment as well as sustenance. In English **spring** meaning fountainhead must be used carefully, so as not to be confused with "spring"—the season.

highway construction
a spring trickles from a pipe
in the concrete wall

Torrey Hansen, RI [k]

WATERFALL, *taki* (all). In Japan waterfalls are at their best in summer, during or after the **PLUM RAINS** (*tsuyu*). Also: **torrent** (*torrent*—French).

Hysteric
laughter breaks and tumbles
at the waterfall

Tino Icatlo, Japan [k]

Une seul pierre déplacée	One single stone displaced
suffit à changer	suffices to change
le rire du torrent	the torrent's laughter

Bruno Hulin, France [k]

SUMMER—HUMANITY

SPLASH PATTERN, *shirogasuri* (late). A lightweight white cloth with a free, "splashed" pattern dyed in and used in summer-weight kimono. Also called: **white-ground cloth** (*shiroji*), as in having a pattern on a white background.

shiroji kite	in white-ground cloth . . .
sanko no uo ni	oh to be a fish
narabaya to	of the mountain lake

Setsuko Nozawa, Japan [k]

SUMMER PAJAMAS (all). The lightweight sleepwear of summer. Also: **gauzy night things.**

sea breeze—
gauzy night things stir
in an open drawer

Mitzi Hughes Trout, GA [k]

SUNGLASSES, *sangurasu* (all). Though they may be worn year-round, the percentage of people wearing sunglasses jumps dramatically in summer. The colloquial **shades** has its own power, as the senryu below demonstrates.

As the sun sets
In his glasses the blind man
Feels the night coming.

Jacques A. Navarro, Japan [k]

standing on a stump
the land developer
in green shades

Peter Yovu, VT [s]

PARASOL, *higasa* (all). This handy portable shade protects one from both sun and unwanted glances.

higasa toji	closing her parasol
genbaku dōmu	she looked up at
aogikeri	the a-bomb dome

Yasuhiko Shigemoto, Japan [k]

ICE CREAM, *hyōka* (all). This popular dessert has special appeal in the summer, when **ice-cream carts** patrol beaches and **ice-cream trucks** come to city and suburban neighborhoods, ringing their bells, inviting people to come and buy their wares. Related confections which also may be taken as treats during hot afternoons or evenings include a fruit-flavored **ice** (*kōrigashi*) or **sherbet** (*shābetto*). Ice cream itself is often served in an **ice-cream cone**, or with sweet toppings in a **sundae** or **banana split.** Also: **ice-cream parlor, ice-cream vendor.**

stormy afternoon—
between peals of thunder
the ice-cream man's bell

Brian Tasker, England [k]

BEER, *biiru, Bier*—German (all). Some foods that are consumed year-round still have a strong association with one or another season. Who would deny the special appeal of a cold beer in summer? The Japanese include a number of related terms under this topic: **dark beer** (*kurobiiru*),

draught beer (*namabiiru*), **beer hall** (*biyahōru*), **beer garden** (*biyagāden*), **canned beer** (*kanbiiru*), to which I would add the related drinks **ale, bitters,** and **stout.***

fishing
through the ice
for a beer

Jim Kacian, VA [s]

HAMMOCK, *hanmokku* (all). This is a good place to take a **MIDDAY NAP** or **siesta** (*hirune*), also a summer topic.

Overhead leaves rustling
Soft sounds of swinging fabric
The empty hammock.

Edythe Polster, NM [k]

AIR CONDITIONER, *reibō* (all). Artificial relief from summer heat, **air conditioning** can be a contributing cause of many summer illnesses, though a boon to those with pollen allergies. Note that the English-derived Japanese word *eakondishonā* means interior atmospheric control, and includes both heating and cooling.

Crashing
against the air conditioner—
ice pellets

Richard Marx Weinraub, NY [k/s]

ELECTRIC FAN, *senpūki* (all). Electric fans include the **standing fan, table fan,** and **box** or **window fan.** In haikai the word **fan** by itself means the **FOLDING FAN** (*ōgi*), but phrases associated with electrical appliances such as "switch off" or "turn on" indicate the electic fan. The folding fan and **ROUND FAN** (*uchiwa*), which immediately precede electric fan in a Japanese saijiki, can easily be carried on the person, but a **portable fan** is probably electric.

switching on the fan
white waves rise and fall
far out at sea

Richard von Sturmer, New Zealand [k]

AIRING CLOTHES, *mushi boshi* (late). The Japanese literally says "drying out bugs". Anyplace where the climate is as damp as Japan, especially during the moist heat of summer, people must air out clothing, bedding, and paper products to avoid infestations of various insects and **MOLD, MILDEW** (a mid-summer topic associated with the **RAINY SEASON**). Also: **airing books** (*bakusho*).

clothes line:
his winter woollies
out for an airing

Mildred Williams Boggs, KY [k]

shaded from bright sunlight
an open book airs beside
the sickroom window

Wally Swist, MA [k]

SHOWER BATH, *shawā* (all). While something many of us do all year, a **shower** has special appeal in summer when we may use an **outdoor shower** at the beach.

shawā ima	now in the shower
otome no koi o	the maiden's first love
nagashikeri	is washed away

Shigeru Ekuni, Japan [k]

SIDEWALK SALE (all). As the weather warms, and after **INVENTORY** (a New Year topic), shopkeepers put past-season and older merchandise on tables outside their stores, hoping to attract buyers with cheap prices. Beginning in spring and continuing into autumn, sidewalk sales peak in summer, sometimes taking on a carnival atmosphere as several stores in a city block or shopping mall participate and advertise together. A **FLEA MARKET** (see below) has a similar atmosphere, except that usually the outdoor tables (often under tents) are the vendors' shops, and most goods are either secondhand or made expressly for sale at the flea market; there are no stores with "regular" merchandise.

sidewalk sale—
wind twists a lifetime
guarantee tag

Tom Clausen, NY [k]

FLEA MARKET (all). An outdoor market featuring mainly hardgoods and clothing, often used. Sometimes flea markets are set up at an established location, sometimes in a field or parking lot. Although some flea markets operate from spring to autumn, the peak of activity is summertime, when vendors travel from region to region on regular circuits. (See also **SIDEWALK SALE**, above.)

All the old boots
lined up by a sawhorse—
flea market morning.

Alice Dartley, NJ [k]

WATER THE GARDEN (all). This is the main gardening task through the summer, along with **PULLING WEEDS** (*kusatori*).

Watering the garden
I listen to the soil
whispering in the dark.

Miriana Bozin, Yugoslavia [k]

GRASS CUTTING, *kusakari* (all). Whether cutting by hand with a sickle, as *kusakari* means literally, or **mowing the lawn** with a **lawnmower**, this activity stays at its peak all summer long. The **SORREL** (*Oxalis corniculata*) in the following poem commonly grows in California lawns all year. Also: **mowing, grass cuttings.**

mowing the sorrel
with its yellow flowers—
I dull the yard

Paul O. Williams, CA [k/s]

raking grass cuttings—
the beautiful girl asks if
I'm ever depressed

Colin Blundell, England [k/s]

MID-SUMMER PLOWING (mid). While we usually think of the **PLOW** in connection with spring, farm fields in much of the temperate zone produce two or more harvests per year, rotating among grains and vegetable crops. Hence poems including images from both harvest and preparation for the next sowing may refer to this topic; many second crops are planted in June. However, note that several specific crops are planted at other times of the year, such as **SOWING WINTER WHEAT**, a late-autumn topic. Also: **stubble . . . furrows** (*éteule . . . sillons*—French).

L'éteule fraîche *et déjà quelques sillons* *tracés au matin.*	Fresh stubble and already a few furrows traced on the morning.

Yves-Marie Moullec, France [h]

SWIMMING, *oyogi* (all). A major summer receation, carried on at seashore and lakeside beaches, or at a **SWIMMING POOL** or **swimming hole**. While there are those who swim year-round, taking advantage of an **INDOOR POOL** in winter, many more people go **swimming** in the summer. Also: **wading, waist-deep in water** (*do pojasa u vodi*—Croatian).

Biti do pojasa *u vodi: ni čovjek* *niti—riba.*	To be waist-deep in water: neither man nor—fish.

Mile Stamenković, Croatia [k]

SWIMMING POOL, *pūru* (late). Some people prefer the relative calm of a swimming pool to **OCEAN BATHING** (*kaisuiyoku*), also a summer topic. Those without access to an artificial pool or beaches may prefer a **swimming hole,** a relatively calm section of a river or a natural pond taken over for the purpose. While "swimming pool" implies a city or suburban setting, either at an institution such as a **community pool** or club or a **backyard pool** in a private yard, "swimming hole" suggests a rural environment.

in the swimming pool
pregnant women aqua-dance
to slim instructions

Colin Blundell, England [s]

SAND CASTLE (all). From the simple tower molded in a **beach pail,** to fanciful creations for summer contests and rivaling late winter **SNOW SCULPTURE** (*setsu-zō*), the vulnerability of sand castles to wind and tide makes them ephemeral and adds to their appeal. The best sand for building on the beach occurs at or just below the high-tide line. This topic includes other objects fashioned of beach sand, such as **sand tarts** (*zand taartjes*—Dutch).

captured sand crabs
will make fine moat monsters
for our castle

Gary Warner, AL [k]

in het natte zand	in the wet sand
bakken de kleuters taartjes	the toddlers bake little tarts
tot de zee ze eet	till the sea eats them

Silva Ley, The Netherlands [k]

FIREWORKS, *hanabi* (late). The Japanese literally means "blossom fire". Fireworks were imported from China into Japan, where they were once part of the **BON FESTIVAL** of early autumn and have been a common summer amusement for a long time. In the United States they coincidentally have been part of the **INDEPENDENCE DAY** celebration since its first anniversary, 4 July 1777. They also feature in Canada's **DOMINION DAY** celebrations, 1 July. But since fireworks are associated with **GUY FAWKES DAY**—5 November —in England, I think we must acknowledge that the season for fireworks varies from region to region and even from country to country. The poems below all refer to experience in Japan or the U.S.

okujō ni	to the roofgarden
zen hakobasete	I carry a room-service order—
tō hanabi	distant fireworks

Kazuo Takagi, Japan [k]

hanabi oe	fireworks finish
kitai no yami no	the darkness of anticipation
nao tsuzuku	continues

Dhugal Lindsay, Australia [k]

sunrise . . .
a fireworks wrapper
tumbles down the street

Ebba Story, CA [k]

MORRIS DANCE (all). Thought to have come to England from Spain in the fourteenth century (the name derives from "Moorish Dance"), morris dancing soon became associated with the legend of Robin Hood. The dancers dress to represent various characters, including Robin Hood, Maid Marian, Friar Tuck, a hobby-horse, clowns, and so on. Wearing bells they dance about in fantastic mummery beginning with the **May games** of **MAY DAY** (late spring) and continuing on into the summer.

Morris dancers stamp
the sound of bells and laughter
into the earth

Susan Rowley, England [k]

BASEBALL, *yakyū* (all). One Japanese saijiki says "baseball season is summer", and though baseball now begins in spring and carries through into mid autumn, it still suggests summer. Also: **home plate.**

Squeeze play
umpire whisk brooming
home plate.

Arthur Goodrich, IL [k/s]

NIGHT GAME, *naitā* (all). The Japanese word derives from the American English "nighter", a baseball game played **under the lights. GNATS** is also an all-summer topic.

Night game
softball soars
through swarms of gnats

David Elliott, PA [k]

BOUQUET (all). Also called a **nosegay** (*pušlec*—Croatian) or **posy**, a bouquet of flowers cut from a garden or in the wild—or purchased from a florist—provides a visual and olfactory treat long associated with summer and with courtship. A **wedding bouquet** will be the bride's major accessory during the **WEDDING CEREMONY** at any time of year.

the blindman
flower by flower
smells the posy

Brian Tasker, England [k]

Putuje sam	Traveling alone
zaboravljen pušlec	a forgotton nosegay
u autobusu.	in the bus.

Milan Žegarac, Croatia [k]

HIDE-AND-SEEK (all). A game, usually played by children outdoors in summer. One player who is "it" covers eyes and counts out loud up to a certain number (usually 10, often higher), to allow the other players (usually two to five) to disperse and hide, then calls **Ready or not, here I come.** "It" then seeks to find and call out the name of one of the others before any of them gets back to base, the place the game started from. The caught player is "it" for the next game. If a player gets back to base without being seen by "it", he or she cries **allee-allee-in-free** or the like, alerting the others that "it" has lost and must try again in the next game. Hide-and-seek may be played at dusk, becoming more difficult as darkness falls. There are many local variations. Also: **hide-and-go-seek.** Related to **PEEK-A-BOO**, a game between an adult or older child and an infant, and to **TAG**, both commonly played all year.

The little boys play
hide-and-seek among the rocks,
so seriously.

Ivor Garb, South Africa [s]

NAKED, *hadaka* (late). For obvious reasons, people are more likely to remain **stark naked** (*mappadaka*), **nude** (*maru hadaka*), or at least **STRIPPED TO THE WAIST** (*hadanugi*) or **BAREFOOT** (*hadashi*)—also summer topics—during the summer than at other times of the year, even in a nudist camp.

wife of the only
man without a shirt
looks slightly guilty

Fred Schofield, England [s]

from the sequence "Senryu from a Nudist Camp"

Secretly,
  imagining her dressed
    the chairman's daughter.

Eric Amann, ON [s]

Sun pouring down
on the nudist beach
hats essential

Jeanette Stace, New Zealand [s]

BAREFOOT, *hadashi* (all). What better symbol of summer than feet's freedom from shoes and socks?

kyobashi nite	on the great bridge
neru matenrō e	sleeping, bare feet
hadashi muke	toward the skyscrapers

Takashi Kodairi, Japan [k]

WASHING HAIR, *kami arau* (all). Of course people wash their hair at all times of year, but during summer the sweat and dust accumulate more quickly, and we tend to wash our hair more often. It gives a cool, fresh feeling on a hot summer day. Also: **shampoo.**

Tonight
while shampooing my hair
for the first time
I felt my skull.

Pat Donegan, Japan [k]

SWEAT, *ase* (all). The body's main means of cooling off when the environment is hot, sweating includes such terms as **beads of sweat** (*tama no ase*), **in a sweat** (*ase-midoro*), **sweaty** (*asebamu*), and the **smell of sweat** (*ase no ka*).

tearing down the wall:
sweat blends with fine adobe flakes
  that cling to their backs

Federico C. Peralta, Philippines [k]

MIDDAY NAP, *hirune* (all). Especially in the central and southern regions of the temperate zone, people frequently avoid activity during the heat of midday and take a nap, often under the shade of a tree or porch. The Spanish word **siesta** has been adopted in English, and is an excellent translation for the Japanese *hirune*, though siesta also suggests the image of people asleep sitting up and wearing a broad-brimmed *sombrero* as shelter from the sun. Also called: **nap** (*ne*).

Nubes de alas	Clouds of wings
y sombras de pájaros	and shadows of birds
cruzan mi siesta.	cross my siesta.

Palle Seiersen Frost, Mexico [k]

shinbunshi	a newspaper
shiki sekkō no	spread out the stone-mason's
sanshakune	three-foot nap

Kazuo Takagi, Japan [k]

SUMMER LETHARGY (all). A lassitude more physical than the mental state of **SPRING FEVER**, which is a laziness associated with the desire to enjoy the newly mild weather, summer lethargy suggests a kind of unthinking sluggishness brought on by the heat.

Every now and then
kookaburra interrupts
summer lethargy.

Faye Davis, Australia [k/s]

SUN-BATHING (all). While **BASKING IN THE SUN** applies to winter, sunbathing is a summer pastime often associated with ocean beaches, lakeshores, and swimming. It leads to **SUNBURN** for the careless, though light-skinned people may achieve a pleasing **suntan** if they control exposure. **A WINTER VACATION** may include a **WINTER TAN**. Also: **bronze skin** (*gebronsde huid*—Dutch).

Vroeg op het strand—	Early on the beach—
dromen van een gebronsde huid	dreaming of a bronzed skin
in wit kippevel.	in white goose-flesh.

Ton Koelman, The Netherlands [s]

SUNBURN, hiyake (all). A kind of overindulgence, increasingly dangerous to health as the ozone layer diminishes. Often produces **peeling sunburn** for those of light skin-color.

Hole in the ozone
my bald spot . . .
sunburned

Garry Gay, CA [k/s]

END OF SCHOOL (mid). In North America the end of the school year usually comes in May or June. The seasonal aspect of **school's out** may vary substantially from one region to another, like that of **CLASS REUNION**, below. In Japan one school year ends in March and the next begins the first week in April, making **ENTERING SCHOOL** (*nyūgaku*) a mid-spring topic, whereas **SCHOOL OPENS** is an early autumn topic in the United States, where the new school year typically begins around **LABOR DAY**, the first Monday in September. Note also that Labor Day is celebrated on other dates in different countries.

school's out—
a boy follows his dog
into the woods

Randy Brooks, IL [k]

CLASS REUNION (mid). College class reunions generally occur in May or June in North America, just after the end of the spring semester.

class reunion—
with my old girlfriend
her girlfriend

Lee Gurga, IL [s]

SUMMER—OBSERVANCES

VESAK (early). In Sri Lanka, the day of the full moon in May. On this day the Lord Buddha is said to have been born, achieved enlightenment, and died. It is the main Buddhist festival of the year, featuring much decoration and festivity. While I am placing this entry in "early summer" in order for it to fall in May, the seasons of tropical Sri Lanka bear little relation to those of the temperate zone. See **MONSOON**.

A Vesak poem
about a Buddha statue:
the cockroach survives.

Anne Ranasinghe, Sri Lanka [k]

MOTHER'S DAY, *haha no hi* (early). The second Sunday in May is a day of recognition for the service mothers give in bearing and raising their children. The holiday is celebrated mainly at home—my mother typically received breakfast in bed; some families take mother out to dinner. Christian churches often recognize the day with special music and a sermon on the topic of motherhood. Similarly, **FATHER'S DAY** comes in mid summer on the third Sunday of June. These holidays are observed in the U.S., Canada, Japan, and elsewhere.

Mother's Day
gift-wrapped box of chocolates
one piece missing

Francine Porad, CA [s]

A-BOMB DAY, *genbaku no hi* (late). Commemorates the dropping of the first atomic bombs used in warfare, on Hiroshima and Nagasaki, Japan, 6 and 9 August 1945, toward the end of World War II. As a memorial to the thousands of people who died from the blast, fire, and radiation, Hiroshima celebrates a **Peace Festival** (*heiwasai*) on 6 August. The city and its festival have become a center for the worldwide movement to ban nuclear weapons and seek peaceful means of resolving disputes between nations. Also: **A-bomb Anniversary** (*genbakuki*), **A-bomb epicenter** (*genbaku-chi*).

genbaku-chi	A-bomb epicenter
ko ga kagerō ni	a child in the heat-shimmer
kieyukeri	disappeared

Yatsuka Ishihara, Japan [k]

DOMINION DAY (mid). 1 July, Canada. This anniversary celebrates the confederation of the Canadian provinces in 1867. Among other things, it provides an opportunity for a display of **FIREWORKS**, also a summer topic. (See **INDEPENDENCE DAY**.)

Dominion Day:
after all the fireworks, the stars
still there

George Swede, ON [k/s]

INDEPENDENCE DAY, *dokuritsusai* (mid). Also called the **Fourth of July**, the holiday celebrates the signing of the **Declaration of Independence** by representatives of some American colonies, on 4 July 1776, in Philadelphia. Thus officially began the American Revolution against England, which ended with recognition of the United States in the Treaty of Paris, 3 September 1783, though the fighting stopped after the Battle of Yorktown, in October 1781. Like Canada's **DOMINION DAY**, this celebration almost always includes **FIREWORKS** (*hanabi*), which happens to be a late-summer topic in the Japanese saijiki.

Fourth-of-July party
family and friends
last year's argument

Richard Wiman, UT [s]

MEMORIAL DAY (early). Also **Decoration Day**, celebrated 30 May in U.S., or on 26 April, 10 May, or 3 June in some Southern states. Instituted in 1868 to honor veterans of the American Civil War, the holiday now features decorating the graves of all veterans and the most important **parade** of the year in most cities. Unofficially marks the beginning of summer. See also **ARMISTICE DAY**, winter.

Memorial Day—
two Buddy Poppies
in a young girl's hair

Norma S. Hass, IL [k]

scraping his shoe
on the curb . . .
the passing parade

Alan Pizzarelli, NJ [s]

FESTIVAL, *matsuri* (all). Summer is festival time in Japan. Almost every city and town has one, usually sponsored by a Shinto shrine. Activities include a parade or public display, perhaps associated with games or performances, and purification rituals. Also: **festival flutes** (*matsuribue*).

matsuribue	festival flutes
taiga nagarete	as the great river flowed
kure ni keri	dusk settled in

Nōichi Imoto, Japan [h]

HOLIDAYS (mid). "The Holidays" in countries dominated by the Judeo-Christian heritage and the Gregorian calendar means the period between Hannukah or Christmas and New Year's Day. In the U.S. the phrase may be extended to include Thanksgiving. In the northern hemisphere, this corresponds to mid winter, and will be associated with snow and cold. However, the poem below is from New Zealand, where the holiday period is in mid summer, and often includes visits to the beach.

after
the holiday   sand
in my pocket

Cyril Childs, New Zealand [k/s]

TAKAKO'S DAY, *takakoki* (early). Died 29 May; Takako Hashimoto (1899-1963) was a leading poet of her time, having studied haiku with

Hisajo Sugita and Seishi Yamaguchi. She edited haiku magazines and was associated with Sanki Saitō. In the following poem, **WASHING HAIR** is also a summer topic. Also: **Takako's anniversary**.

Takako's anniversary . . .
trickling even now
my fresh-washed hair

Lesley Einer, AZ [k]

SUMMER—ANIMALS

BATS, *kōmori* (all). Order Chiroptera. Cave-dwelling night-flyers of many kinds. Typically bats leave daytime roosts in large numbers at dusk. They may roost in farm outbuildings, attics, or abandoned houses, though most live in caves. "Bleu roi" is dark blue, referring to the color of the sky. A **flying fox** is a kind of **fruit bat** (*Pteropus sp.*).

canyon dawn
a bat folding dark
into a crevice

Ruth Yarrow, NY [k]

bleu roi
a thousand flying foxes
quarter moon

Alan J. Summers, Australia [k]

GRAZING COWS, *grazende koeien*—Dutch (all). While cows are certainly a year-round feature of rural landscapes, a field dotted with grazing cows seems to express the essence of a calm summer day.

Over het weiland
traag-bewegende tongen
grazende koeien.

Across the meadow
the slow-moving tongues
of grazing cows.

Piet Zandboer, The Netherlands [k]

HEDGEHOG, *igel*—German (all). *Erinaceus sp.* This Eurasian, mainly insectivorous mammal is nocturnal, and curls into a spine-covered ball for defense. Hedgehogs range up to 12" (30 cm) or more long, with light-colored fur on underparts, the spines colored in bands of chocolate brown, yellow, or white giving an overall mottled appearance, with some quite light or albino. Hedgehogs generally hibernate until late spring, but occasionally come out for brief periods before becoming fully active. They are not related to the **PORCUPINE** (family Hystricidae), a good deal larger animal with more-dangerous quills that does not hibernate—making it an all-year topic.

nachts kommen igel	at night a hedgehog
über die maulwurfshügel:	comes across a molehill:
ich weiß nichts von dir!	i know nothing of you!

Gerald Albin Rödler, Austria [k/s]

TURTLE (all). Refers to freshwater turtles, not normally found in Japanese saijiki, which do include **SEA TURTLES** (*umi kame*), also in Summer.

Dusk over the lake;
a turtle's head emerges
then silently sinks

Virgil Hutton, IL [k]

TOAD, *hikigaeru, pad*—Dutch (all). *Bufo* sp. and related. Known more for their lumpy appearance and preference for dry land than for song, toads come into view mainly in summer. Their life cycles closely resemble those of frogs, except that the adults of most species spend much of their time on or in the ground rather than in water. In temperate climates they hibernate for some months, usually in underground burrows. See also **FROG,** spring.

Een paddenpaar ligt	A pair of toads lies
op weg naar de voortplanting	on the way to propagating
tot een prent geplet.	flattened to a print.

Wiel Claus, The Netherlands [k/s]

Puffing up dust
as it follows a toad
the dog's nose.

Colin Oliver, England [k]

GIANT SALAMANDER, *sanshōuo* (all). *Andrias japonicus* grows fat, and up to a yard (1 m) long, living in Japan's clear mountain waters.

ikisugite	living to the fullest
wasureraruruna	and not to be forgotten!
sanshōuo	giant salamander

Shugyō Takaha, Japan [h]

LIZARD, *tokage, sopîrlă*—Romanian (all). Covers many kinds of land-dwelling reptiles, including **monitor, chameleon, horned lizard** or "**horny toad**".

the cat's eyes glitter
as the lizard plays dead
in its mouth

Penny Harter, NM [k]

Foşnet de frunze	Rustling leaves
Doi ochi de sopîrlă	The lizard's eyes
Mă privesc curiosi	Watch me curiously

Laura Văceanu, Romania [k]

no seabreeze
even the lizard just ambles
out of sight

Alex McQueen, Australia [k]

SNAKE, *hebi, şarpe*—Romanian, serpe—Italian (all). Includes many kinds of snakes. The *aodaishō* is a **green constrictor** (a kind of rat snake, same family as the American blacksnake).

aodaishō
kono hi otoko to
onna kana

a green constrictor . . .
this day we are man
and woman

Nana Naruto, Japan [k]

Pietre . . .
Printre ele
respiraţia şarpelui

Stones . . .
Among them
the snake's breath

Valentin Busuioc, Romania [k]

Giro de luna,
gioca nuova la serpe
all'avventura.

Turn of the moon,
the snake ventures again
on its luck.

Argo Suglia, Italy [k]

CUCKOO, *kankodori* (all). *Cuculus canorus*, the **common cuckoo** also called *kakkō* in Japanese and by similar onomatopoetic names in many languages. This is the most common representative of a global family; almost all cuckoos are highly migratory, spending summers in temperate breeding areas and winters in the tropics. The cuckoos of Eurasia are legendary for depositing their eggs in the nests of other birds. Most cuckoos are noted for their distinctive calls, which vary considerably from one species to another. In Japanese haikai, the most famous is the **LITTLE CUCKOO** (*C. poliocephalis*), sometimes called in English by its Japanese name, **hototogisu**, that mimics its five-note call often heard in the summer woods, though the bird is rarely seen.

umi to iu
ōkina mimi ni
kankodori

into the large
ear called a lake—
cuckoo song

Shugyō Takaha, Japan [k]

HUMMINGBIRD, *colibrí*—Spanish (all). Hummingbirds are found throughout the year in Central America, but migrating species spend summers in the temperate zones of both North and South America.

Atardece:	Late afternoon:
el verde colibrí	the green hummingbird
libando la roja flor.	sucks a red flower.

Gloria Inés Rodríguez Lodoño, Colombia [k]

BROWN HAWK-OWL, *aobazuku* (all). *Ninox scutulata.* While many owls are considered mainly winter phenomena, this bird migrates to Japan in summer.

matchi sureba	strike a match
mori no yururu yo	and you shake the woods—
aobazuku	a brown hawk-owl

Katsuo Sekimori, Japan [k]

WATERBIRD'S NEST, *mizudori no su* (all). Many waterbirds nest on the water, usually attaching their nests to a plant with roots in the bottom. Also: **moorhen's nest** (*waterhoentje nest*—Dutch).

Het waterhoentje	The moorhen
op zijn nest in de rietkraag—	on her nest in the reed's edge—
het oog slechts beweegt.	only her eye moves.

P. A. Dietze, The Netherlands [k]

LOON (all). *Gavia sp.* Loons go north for the summer, when their striking breeding plumage and calls and displays make them a seasonal topic around lakes in the northern reaches of the north temperate zone. (Japan and most of coastal U.S. see loons in winter, when their plumage is dull and their habits less noticeable.)

all night in dreams
howling dogs   loon
    dialogue

Phyllis Walsh, WI [k]

HERON, *aosagi, garza*—Spanish (all). The Japanese refers specifically to the grey heron (*Fischreiher*—German) of Eurasia and Africa (*Ardea cineria*), similar to the **great blue heron** of the Americas (*A. herodias*) and the darker **white-necked heron** of Australia (*A. pacifica*); all about 36" (1 m) long. Breeds in tall trees throughout summer.

Borda la garza *El sueno de la playa* *Andar descalza!*	The heron weaves What the beach dreams To walk barefoot!

Ana Rosa Núñez, FL [k]

Kein Wind überm Teich— *reglos starrt der Fischreiher* *auf sein Spiegelbild.*	Calm over the pond— motionless, a grey heron stares at its image.

Gerold Effert, Germany [k]

after sunset
  the black-crowned mountain
    the night heron

Marlina Rinzen, CA [k]

EGRET, *shirasagi* (all). *Egretta sp*. Group of large, mostly white birds of the heron family, distributed worldwide and breeding in summer at mid-temperate latitudes.

at her "shush"
the egret lifts
a yellow foot

Hal Roth, MD [k]

WILLOW WARBLER (all). *Psylloscopus trochilus*. A particularly migrant member of its family, the willow warbler winters in Africa, arriving in Europe and Siberia during mid and late spring, departing in late autumn. Authorities cite it as one of the most abundant visitors to northern Europe. It nests on the ground in areas of low, bushy vegetation. The small insect-eater (4.25"/11 cm) is olive brown above with a pale yellow breast shading to dusky white underparts, and is noted for its melodious, melancholy song. Also called: **Peggy-whitethroat, willow wren** (but note that it is not a **wren** or **NORTHERN WREN**, which see in winter).

A forbidding place
But high among the dark pines
The willow wren's small voice

Cicely Hill, England [k]

CHICKADEE, *shijūkara* (all). *Parus sp.* Genus of several small black and white birds noted for acrobatic antics in bushes, and "chick-a-dee-dee" call. Breeds in summer; seen more often in winter in some areas.

lazy afternoon—
a chickadee answers the calls
on my bird tape

Wally Swist, MA [k]

SWEETFISH, TROUT, *ayu* (all). The sweetfish (*Plecoglossus altirelis*) of Japan lives only in fast-moving streams and rivers, and is a table delicacy. Various **trout** (*trucha*—Spanish, *Salmo sp.*) occupy a similar place in Europe, North America, and elsewhere; "trout" has been used to translate Japanese *ayu*.

hikari au	meeting the light
ikesu no yo no	of a restaurant fishtank's night
otori ayu	the alluring *ayu*

Momoko Kuroda, Japan [k]

My cat
tries to catch Schubert's trout
on the piano keys

Pierre Constantin, French Polynesia [k/s]

happy to catch it,
the boy now cries when he sees
the cleaning of the trout

Frank Higgins, MO [k/s]

La trucha—cantando al sol—disuelto.

The trout—singing of the sun—dissolved.

Palle Seiersen Frost, Mexico [k]

GOLDFISH, *kingyo* (all). In Japan these and many kinds of **TROPICAL FISH** (*nettaigyo*) are sold at temple festivals and outdoor fairs, which gives them the summer connection. I have placed this topic here in deference to the tradition, but in the U.S. tropical fish sell more in winter, as people's activities shift indoors near the gold-fish bowl or aquarium. Since we may see an aquarium in a home, a doctor's waiting room, or a restaurant at any time of year, it may make sense to consider these as all-year topics outside of Japan.

A small jar
has bent
the goldfish.

Hamish Turnbull, Scotland [k]

KILLIFISH, *medaka* (all). The small killifish (family Cyprinodontidae) and **minnows** (technically members of the family Cyprinidae, but commonly meaning any small fishes) are often taken by net and used for bait in sports fishing.

the child swings
his pail of minnows
around a new world

Mary Thomas Eulberg, IA [k]

FLYING FISH, *tobi-uo* (all). *Cypselurus sp.* Flying fish generally grow to 12" (30 cm) long, and have greatly enlarged pectoral fins compared to other fish. They often swim close to the ocean surface building up speed with their powerful tails, then seem to leap from the water and glide on outstretched pectoral fins a few feet above the water for some distance. Some flights have been recorded as long as 1,000' (300 m), but the average seems to be 100-300' (30-90 m).

tobi-uo no	flying fish
tsubasa hirogeshi	its wings spread
mama shi seri	even in death

Dhugal Lindsay, Australia [k]

PIKE, *kawakamasu* (all). Pike and other large freshwater fish such as the **muskellunge**, or **muskie** are generally considered prime game in summer.

somewhere out in his lake
that muskie
he never caught

Joyce Walker Currier, IL [k]

CRAB, *kani* (all). From the **mole crab** and **fiddler crab** to **blue crab,** there are numerous genera of these crustacea, many edible. Most of them molt much like insects such as grasshoppers. In the second poem below, "Morib" is an area south of Kuala Lumpur on the Strait of Malacca.

soft rain
a crab backs out
of its shell

Lenard D. Moore, NC [k]

I remember
You remembering crabs scurrying
Across the Morib stillness.

Edwin Thumboo, Singapore [k]

JELLYFISH, *kurage* (all). Free-swimming marine coelenterates with a jellylike body in the medusa stage. In the following poem the East River is the eastern boundary of Manhattan, New York City.

condom
floats with the jellyfish
down the East River

Raffael de Gruttola, MA [k]

(jellyfish)
(in a
coolness)
(without
edges)

Rod Willmot, PQ [k]

SUMMER BUTTERFLY, *natsu no chō* (all). This topic includes the generic **swallowtail** (*ageha*) since the majority of swallowtails emerge for their first flights during the summer months. Some saijiki even advise that "swallowtail" is the proper image to have in mind on finding "summer butterfly" in a poem. Among those most commonly seen in summer in North America are the **giant swallowtail** (*Heraclides sp.*), **tiger swallowtail** (*Pterourus sp.*), and varieties of **parnassian** (*Parnassius sp.*)—which do not have the characteristic tails but are still members of the family Papilionidae. Known as the **old world swallowtail** in North America, *Papilio machaon* is also the only representative found in England, where it is simply "the swallowtail"; it flies in summer in both regions. In Japan "swallowtail" (ageha) alone may be taken to refer to the **Chinese yellow swallowtail** (*Papilio xuthus*), but several other Papilionidae are prominent in summer, including the **blue-green swallowtail** (*karasu ageha, Papilio bianor*), **Gifu swallowtail** (*gifuchō, Luehdorfia japonica*), and the tailless **common blue bottle** or **blue triangle** (*aosuji ageha, Graphium sarpedon*). (Note that some specific swallowtails do appear in spring—see **BUTTERFLY.**)

In North America the many species of **blue** and **hairstreak** butterflies (family Lycaenidae) divide almost evenly between those that first fly in spring and others appearing in summer, but those of Britain and Japan are seen mainly in summer, making them summer season words unless a poem refers to a specific spring-flying species, or one of the few that appears under **AUTUMN BUTTERFLY**. Universally summer is the **common blue** (*uranamishijimi, Polyommatus sp.*) of Eurasia and North America. In the same family the many varieties of **copper** fly in summer. The widespread **small copper** (*benishijimi, Lycaena phlaeas*) is also counted in the summer saijiki, though it may be seen April to October in Britain and Japan, and in North America, where it is known as the **American copper** or **flame copper**.

Among the Pieridae most of the **sulphurs** or **yellows** (*kichō, Eurema hecabe* in Japan, *Colias sp.* in Europe and North America) first appear in summer, but note that some other species appear last frost to first frost, placing them under the spring topic **BUTTERFLY**.

Japan's striking summer butterflies include the **blue admiral** (*ruritateha, Vanessa canace*), the **purple emperor** (*komurasaki, Aptura ilia*)—closely related to the more widespread Eurasian **purple emperor** (*A. iris*)—and **Japanese emperor** (*ōmurasaki, Sasakia charonda*), and the **map-wing butterfly** (*ishigakechō, Cryestis thyodames*). England and North America feature many types of **fritillary** and **admiral** in summer, along with the **painted lady** (*Vanessa cardui*), all in the family Nymphalidae.

Most members of the mothlike **skipper** family (Hesperiidae) first appear in summer, with many lingering well into autumn. (A few are first seen in spring or autumn.)

In North America one cannot leave this topic without mentioning the **monarch** (*Danaus plexippus*), the orange and black butterfly that performs annual migrations worthy of waterfowl. From April to June monarchs move north from winter quarters in central Mexico's Sierra Madre mountains to reach most of the rest of the continent. The movement comes in waves, as successive generations fly north, breed, lay eggs, and die, the eggs soon hatching into caterpillars which quickly eat, form pupae, and emerge as adults to continue moving north. This cycle continues until a brood of adults reaches the summer range. Following the haikai tradition, I will designate **migrating monarchs** a spring season word under the topic **BUTTERFLY** and **monarchs leaving** under **AUTUMN BUTTERFLY**. The single monarch, like Japan's related **yellow tiger** (*asagimadara, Danaus tytian*), is a summer season word.

Finally, in addition to the generic "summer butterfly" the Japanese have the term **plum-rain butterfly** (*tsuyu no chō*), which refers to any butterfly that comes out during a sunny break in the **RAINY SEASON** (*tsuyu*). For further information see the brief essay "Butterflies

Through the Year", following the entry for **BUTTERFLY** in spring. See also **AUTUMN BUTTERFLY, WINTER BUTTERFLY,** and **MOURNING CLOAK** (all year).

the empty highway:
a tiger swallowtail
follows the divider

Nicholas A. Virgilio, NJ [k]

MOTH, *ga, moljac*—Croatian (all). Predominantly night-flying, male moths navigate and find mates by smell, which involves their large, feathery antennae. Many species are also attracted to lights, becoming noticeable to humans as we move our activities outdoors on mild summer nights.

suddenly moths
into the headlights . . .
skunkscent

Ron Simbeck, TN [k]

the cat yawns in
a moth—
her attack stance

sally l. nichols, MA [k]

tiho zatvorih	quietly, I shut
ormar da ne ometem	the wardrobe to not disturb
moljce pri jelu	the moths as they eat

Visnja McMaster, Croatia [k]

HAIRY CATERPILLAR, WOOLLYBEAR, *kemushi* (all). Hairy larvae of various moths, including **tiger moth larvae, gypsy moth larvae,** and **tent caterpillars.** (The first of the following poems need not be read as referring to the latter.) While the Japanese *kemushi* refers to any hairy caterpillar, the English word "woollybear" refers specifically to the furry larvae of certain members of the tiger moth family (Arctiide), which are frequently seen—especially in autumn—walking on the ground, across roads or sidewalks, looking for an appropriate place to pupate. One of these may be called an **AUTUMN WOOLLYBEAR**.

no breeze—
the sound of caterpillars
inside the tent

Kenneth C. Leibman, FL [k]

nature trail gossip—
a mullein caterpillar
on water figwort

Norman Barraclough, England [s]

CATERPILLAR, *shakutori* (all). The Japanese literally refers to the **looper, inchworm, measuring worm, spanworm,** or **stick caterpillar** (*dobinwari*), larvae of any of the moths of the family Geometridae (Japanese *shakuga*), which move by drawing the rear up to the front—causing the body to arch out in a loop—then releasing the forelegs and stretching out full length to a new front grip, and so on. Bodies are relatively smooth and characteristically green, reddish brown, or brown. Some species hang from trees (apple, birch, maple, oak, etc.) on silken threads. In Japanese the generic equivalent to the common English word "caterpillar" is *yōchū*, which has the broad meaning of "larva" and is not a seasonal topic. While there are many kinds of caterpillars, and many of them come out at different times of year, I believe that most North Americans will imagine a looper unless something in a poem names a different kind, such as a **HAIRY CATERPILLAR**, and so on. So I recommend that in English-language haiku "caterpillar" be taken to mean "looper", "inchworm", or the like, unless the poem suggests otherwise. Note that many species of caterpillars and adult Lepidoptera normally eat, lay eggs on, and suck nectar from specific plants with which they are associated.

inchworm
just ahead of
evening shadows

Suezan Aikins, NS [k]

FIREFLY, *hotaru, cocuyo*—Spanish (mid). The common summer insect, family Lampyridae, also called **lightning bug** in English. **Glowworm** (*luciérnaga*—Spanish) usually refers to a wingless female or larva, but is also sometimes used for the flying male.

Un cocuyo *tratando de iluminar* *el oscuro guadual.*	One firefly is trying to illumine the dark field.

Gloria Inés Rodríguez Lodoño, Colombia [h]

Las primeras luciérnagas *un niño corre a buscarglas* *para su amigo enfermo.*	The first glowworms a boy runs to catch some for his sick friend.

J. Teillier, Chile [k]

In the summer dusk,
the flickering starlight of
pale topaz glowworms

James Kirkup, Andorra [h]

BEETLE, *kabuto mushi* (all). Order Coleoptera. A large group of insects, some 300,000 species, all featuring forewings developed into hard wing-casings that cover the membranous flying wings. Patterned wing-casings give many species distinctive appearances. The life cycle features eggs, grubs, pupae, and adult beetles, which emerge and mate in spring or summer. Some are carnivorous, eating other insects, while many eat plants. Many specific beetles are also summer topics, for example **CHAFER**. Also: **darkling beetle, ground beetle** (*jimushi*).

A darkling beetle
crosses in front of the cat's
black nose.

Samuel Hastings, OH [k]

rain beats on the roof—
upside down a beetle struggles
to regain its feet

Dick Holmes, SC [k]

a ground beetle
 stands on his head
  with each clap of thunder

Hank Dunlap, AZ [k/s]

SOLDIER BUG (all). Family Pentatomidae. Soldier bugs and **stink bugs** are shield-shaped, with glands that secrete a foul-smelling fluid when they are disturbed. Size 1/4 to 3/4" (6 mm to 2 cm); many colors. Most notable in North America are the **green soldier bug** (*Acrosternum hilare*); **two-spotted stink bug** (*Cosmopepla conspicillaris*), with two black spots on an orange yoke across its otherwise black wing case; and the orange and black **harlequin cabbage bug** or **calico bug** (*Murgantia histrionica*). Members of the group are often taken as beetles, hence another common name, **shield beetle.**

contra dance—
a shield beetle works its way
across the plaza

Tom Clausen, NY [k]

CHAFER, *koganemushi* (all). Members of the beetle subfamily Melolonthinae. This includes the **Japanese beetle** (*Popillia japonica*), and several other garden pests along with the **May beetle** or **June beetle** (also called **June bug**, an erroneous but common name), called **cockchafer** in England (*Melolontha, Phyllophaga*, and related genera). (In English the names "May beetle" and "June bug" will normally be taken to refer to early and mid summer, respectively.)

across the room
a junebug struggles
to right itself

Carl Patrick, NY [k]

LADYBUG, *tentōmushi* (all). Family Coccinellidae. A great garden protector, and a subject of poems the world over. Also called **ladybird beetle,** named after "Our Lady Mary"—the mother of Jesus.

tentōmushi	ladybug
tanagokoro yori	from cupped hand
tanagokoro e	to cupped hand

Naomi Y. Brown, TX [k]

LEAF BEETLE (all). Family Chrysomelidae. This includes the **tortoise beetle** (subfamily Cassidinae), **leaf-mining leaf beetle** (subfamily Hispinae), and several other beetles mostly about 1/4" (6 mm) long or smaller that feed on many garden plants and crops, particularly grains and potatoes. Also: **potato bug.**

out of the ground
potato bugs
feeling their way

Francine Porad, WA [k]

CICADA, *semi, cigarras*—Spanish (late). Also called **harvestfly,** and occasionally in English by its Italian name, *cicala*. Frequently called **locust** in parts of North America, though technically "locust" refers to various large and destructive members of the grasshopper family. One important variety of cicada, in particular, is often called the **seventeen-year locust,** since its adults appear en masse seventeen years after the previous appearance. There is also a **thirteen-year locust;** these and others with long periods between appearances being *Magicicada sp*. Other cicadas commonly encountered in North America include the **dogday harvestfly** (eastern, *Tibicen canicularis*) and **grand western cicada** (*T. dorsata*). Since most North American species are known for their harsh, piercing cries, it may be difficult for Americans to understand the charm Japanese find in their cicadas. But Japan's cicadas are generally sweeter-voiced, and there are several types, most notably the **oil cicada** (*aburazemi, Graptosaltria calorata*) of late summer, and the **CLEAR-TONED CICADA** or **DAY DARKENER** (*higurashi, Tanna japonensis*) and **MONK CICADA** (*tsukutsukubōshi*), both seasonal topics of early autumn. Cicada cries of one kind or another generally begin in mid-to-late summer, and continue well into autumn, varying by species and location.

from the shadows
ceaseless as song of cicadas
sex-show sex-show

Angelee Deodhar, India [k/s]

Verano tórrido.	Torrid summer.
En el molino quieto	In the quiet mill
solo cigarras.	only cicadas.

Neri L. Mendiara, Argentina [k]

Locust wings
I carry them home
in my blouse.

Florence Miller, NJ [k]

FIRST CRICKET (mid). Crickets begin singing in June or July, become increasingly noticeable in August, and continue until frost. See also **CRICKET** (autumn).

first crickets—
the pulse
in my wrist

Adele Kenny, NJ [k]

DAMSELFLY, *itotonbo* (all). Family Coenafrionidae. Unless otherwise qualified, "damselfly" may be taken to refer to the **narrow-winged damselfly,** the most prominent family of these varied insects. Several species are active around ponds and swamps throughout summer and into autumn. Some of the more commonly seen include various types of **bluet** (*Enallagma sp.*), which usually have blue or red bodies, and **dancer** (*Argia sp.*), the most striking of which is the **violet dancer** (*A. violacea*). The closely related **spread-winged damselfly** of the family Lestidae is the only damselfly to hold its wings parted at rest. The various kinds of **BROAD-WINGED DAMSELFLY** (*kawatonbo*), family Calopterygidae, have broader wings and are associated with rivers and streams; they form a separate all-summer topic. All damselflies have very narrow, jewel-like bodies.

for one bright moment
the damselfly
impossibly blue

anne mckay, BC [k]

FLY, *hae, gîză*—Romanian, muva—Serbian (all). Includes the many varieties of household flies plus those of field and barn.

Carelessly,
brushing away a fly
into a cobweb

Peggy Heinrich, CT [k]

Busy with words
he drinks the fly
in his cup

John Brandi, NM [k/s]

Flyswatter broken
the fly and I
wring our hands

Kaye Laird, MI [s]

Buze şi gîză	Lips and fly
pe marginea paharului.	on the rim of the glass.
Setea, aceeaşi.	The same thirst.

Radu Dumitru, Romania [k]

Tišina sobe.	Quiet room.
Odnekud	From somewhere
uzlete muva.	a fly rises.

Nebojša Milenković, Yugoslavia [k]

FRUIT FLIES, *shōjōbae* (all). Any of various small flies whose larvae feed on fruit or decaying vegetables. Includes those technically known as "fruit flies", members of the family Tephritidae, which are also called **peacock flies** for their habit of flexing their colorful irridescent wings as they walk, and members of the family Drosophilidae, those most commonly found indoors and more correctly called **pomace flies** or **vinegar flies,** though they are the "fruit flies" of the city-dweller. The Drosophilidae are half the size of the Tephritidae or smaller, with bodies 1/16-1/8" (2-4 mm) long, and have been used in genetics experiments because of their brief life-cycle of one-to-two weeks.

as the day heats up
the fruit flies settle
on the kitchen sponge

Richard von Sturmer, New Zealand [k]

MOSQUITO, *ka* (all). Perhaps the most universal summer pest.

hand raised
I stop to admire
the mosquito's leg

Carl Patrick, NY [k]

A dandelion seed floats above the marsh grass with the mosquitos.

Allen Ginsberg, NY [k]

GNATS, *buto* (all). Includes **midges** and **sandflies,** the families Ceratopogonidae, Chironomidae, Phlebotominae, and others. Small biting insects, gnats mostly appear in swarms.

open boxcar doors
the evening sun slips
into a swarm of gnats

James Chessing, CA [k]

MAYFLIES (all). There are many families of "ephemera" (order Ephemeroptera), estimated to include over 2000 species, more than 500 in North America. Habitat is in and over fresh-water ponds and lakes, streams and rivers. The order name comes from the Greek *ephēmeron*, meaning "dayfly"—for these delicate flies typically live only one day as full adults. Adult mayflies mate in midair, where they are called **spinners**, after which the male drops to the water and dies while the female lays her eggs within the hour on the surface of the water and then also dies. In a few hours to a few weeks, depending on species, the eggs, attached to aquatic plants by thin filaments or lying on the bottom, hatch into wingless naiads or **nymphs**, which live mainly underwater. After a feeding period of from a few weeks to two or more years, nymphs rise to the surface and molt into subimagos—also known as **duns** for their usual color. (This emergence is called a "hatch" by those who fish for trout.) Duns float on the water with their wings upright until they can fly to stream-side vegetation to spend a few hours or at most two days becoming the adults which again molt, leaving their dun shells behind as they become spinners. Only the nymphs eat, but fish, especially trout and shad, eat mayflies in any stage of life or death. Many of the "flies" used in fly fishing mimic mayflies.

While the English common name suggests that all adults emerge in May—the peak period in the British Isles—different species appear as adults somewhere in North America anytime from late March through early October. The majority of North American species appear from May to July, so I have assigned mayflies and **shadflies** (named after one of the fish that feeds on mayflies) to all summer, but most readers will associate "mayfly" with May, and "shadfly" with the timing of the **SHAD RUN** that coincides with mayfly appearances in their areas, as late as June inland from southern Canadian coasts. The southern hemisphere may have its own timing. Note also the somewhat similar-looking non-ephemerids **GREEN LACEWING** (Japanese *kusakagerō*, late summer) and **ANTLION** (Japanese *usubakagerō* refers to adult, late summer). In Japan, August is most important for **EPHEMERA** (Japanese *kagerō*, see autumn).

billboard girl
only shadflies
have come to your lite

LeRoy Gorman, ON [k]

COCKROACH, *aburamushi* (all). Family Blattidae. The Japanese name literally means "oil bug". The most obvious members of this family are those which live in houses and commercial buildings, coming out at night to feed on kitchen waste and producing an unpleasant odor. Efforts to exterminate cockroaches have made some species extremely pesticide-resistant. Tropical insects related to grasshoppers and crickets, they are found mainly in the warmer parts of the temperate zone. All have flattened bodies, making it easy for them to hide in cracks; most are a medium brown with long antennae and have an oily appearance. Common names for particular species include the **German cockroach** or **Croton bug** (*Blatella germanica*), and **American cockroach** or **waterbug** (*Periplaneta americana*)—the latter common name perhaps deriving from their association with plumbing which frequently provides holes in the walls through which they travel. The black **oriental cockroach** or **shad roach** (*Blatta orientalis*) appears in large numbers about the time shad swim into freshwater to breed.

crossing the table
beside a book on zen
the cockroach pauses

L. A. Davidson, NY [k/s]

FLEAS, *nomi* (all). Japanese sometimes feel affection for these insects, as seen in the works of Issa. In some parts of the world they may be carriers of bubonic plague.

Suffocating smoke—
our friends burn their sleeping bags
along with the fleas

Peggy Willis Lyles, SC [k]

ANT, *ari* (all). Family Formicidae. All of the many kinds of ants, plus **anthill**, are included in this topic. Note that **ANTS EMERGE** is a mid-spring topic, which see.

necklace of bone . . .
ants have finished
with the snake

Margaret Manson, Australia [k]

ant exploring
finger to finger
shadow of my hand

John Hazelton, NM [k]

SPIDER, *kumo* (all). When grass is high and insects are out in full force, spiders emerge. Also: **spider web** (*kumo no su*), **cobwebs** (*kumo no ito*). See also **GOSSAMER** (*yūshi*) in autumn.

spider
silvered
morning

Chris Mulhern, England [h]

Circle of gnats
held still into twilight—
orb weaver's web

Carol Purington, MA [k]

Evening on the porch
"Is he coming
before the spider finishes his web?"

Keiko Kakami, Japan [k/s]

Spiderweb thread—
I walk through it unthinking
two days running

Katherine Gallagher, England [k/s]

MILLIPEDE, *gejigeji* (all). Also **millepede, milliped.** A wormlike, many-legged, segmented arthropod. The millipede is a plant-eater, unlike its flatter cousin, the **CENTIPEDE** (*mukade*), which is larger and eats insects, also of summer. Millipedes have two pairs of legs per segment, centipedes one pair per segment.

Millepede
lost in my hand
the feel of starlight

vincent tripi, CA [k]

SNAIL, *katatsumuri, slak*—Afrikaans, *caracol*—Spanish, *puž*—Serbian (all). Refers to land snails normally seen in summer gardens and fields, comprising the order Stylommatophora. The order also includes the **SLUG** (*namekuji*), a separate all-summer topic. Snails are legendary for carrying their cumbersome shells with them and for moving slowly.

the snail who doesn't move
—next time you look for him
he's somewhere else

Fred Schofield, England [k/s]

Skielik alleen	Suddenly alone
die gaste het vertrek—	the guests having departed—
Slak teen die ruit	Snail at the window

Hélène Kesting, South Africa [k]

El caracol lleva	The snail carries
su casa.	its house.
La nuestra se quedó.	Ours stayed behind.

Berta G. Montalvo, FL [s]

Na vlati trave	On a grass blade
Odsjaji puževog traga	Reflected in a snail's trail
Sunce zalazi	The setting sun

Svetlana Mladenović, Yugoslavia [k]

the snails
oh my God
they get erections of light
with those eyes of theirs

Alvaro Cardona-Hine, NM [k/s]

EARTHWORM, *mimizu* (all). Segmented worms or *Annelidae* are legless and live in the soil; they are valuable to agriculture for conditioning and enriching the soil. A soaking summer rain brings **worms** to the surface of lawns and fields at night, where they are often found the next morning.

After rain a little girl straightening worms.

Florence Miller, NJ [k/s]

you kiss my neck
a bird plucks a worm
from warm earth

Patricia Heim, NJ [k]

SUMMER—PLANTS

LEAFING CHERRY (TREES), *hazakura* (early). After cherry blossoms have fallen, the young leaves come out.

buchimaketa	let's have
hanashi o shiyō	a really frank talk—
hazakura da	it's leafing cherry time

Seitenjō Seto, Japan [k]

CHERRIES, *sakura no mi, trešnja*—Croatian (early). Refers to the fruit, which ripens in early summer (throughout summer for some commercial types). Note that late spring's showy **CHERRY BLOSSOMS** are mainly decorative varieties resulting in fruit of interest only to wildlife.

Crvene trešnje	Red cherries
Zriju u boji djedove	Ripen in the color of grandpa's
Kovačke vatre.	Forge fire.

Franjo Krizmanić, Croatia [h]

ROSE, *bara* (early). In Japanese saijiki this refers to cultivated roses, which would also be understood in English if the word "rose" were used by itself. A number of well-known varieties could be named; I imagine that most Americans will picture a red rose unless the poem indicates otherwise. But in both Europe and North America there are several kinds of summer-blooming native **wild roses**. These include the **multiflora rose** (*Rosa multiflora*) with clusters of small white flowers, common from southern New England south; **Virginia rose** (*R. virginiana*) with pink flowers, Newfoundland south to North Carolina and west to Missouri; and **wrinkled rose**, also called **beach rose** (*R. rugosa*) with rose-lavender or white flowers, especially noted along roadsides, in seashore thickets, and on sand dunes, and cultivated both for show and to prevent erosion, ranging from eastern Canada south to New Jersey, west to Wisconsin. Despite its name, the white **Cherokee rose** (*R. laevigata*) was introduced from China, but has gone wild, especially in much of the south-central U.S. England has the pink-flowering **sweet briar** (*R. rubiginosa* or *eglanteria*)—also known as **eglantine**—and **dog rose** (*R. canina*). The wild rose of Japan is the yellow-flowered **MOUNTAIN ROSE** (*yamabuki*) of late spring. Also: **white roses**.

reading a mystery—
a cool breeze comes through
the beach roses

Cor van den Heuvel, NY [k]

along the trail
everywhere a fragrance
of Cherokee roses

Carol Dagenhardt, MD [h]

For a moment
there is a silence in the garden
like that in the rose.

Miriana Bozin, Yugoslavia [h]

headlights
flashing the roses
back to red

Jeanette Stace, New Zealand [k]

barefoot
under the moon
stealing white roses

Linzy Forbes, New Zealand [k]

HYDRANGEA, *ajisai* (mid). Blooms June in Tokyo area; common American varieties bloom June or July. Most tend to hold their blossoms for a month or two, during which they may change color to green, blue, lavender, or pink, depending on variety and soil conditions.

On Mt. Rokko
Spent hydrangeas stand like giant
Minnesota blackberries.

Scott Wright, MN [k]

GERANIUM, *zeranyūmu* (all). Usually refers to the annual garden plants *Pelargonium sp*., perennial in their original tropical habitat; often potted or used in window boxes, with red, pink, salmon, white, or lavender flowers, red being most common. Blooms May to October, most noticeably in June, so listed here as "all summer" though considered "early summer" in Japanese saijiki. The scientific name *Geranium* refers to another genus of summer-blooming perennials with common names "geranium", **cranesbill,** or **hardy geranium.** Also: **red geranium.**

red geraniums
rips in the awning
leak sunlight

Ellen Compton, DC [k]

JASMINE, *matsurika, jazmín*—Spanish (late). *Jasminum sp*. In haikai refers to **common jasmine** or **jessamine** (*J. officinale*), which originated in Persia (the English name derives from Persian *yasmin*) and the Himalayas and has been spread both east and west.

Jazmín	Jasmine
blanca,	white,
sencillamente blanca,	simply white,
abierto al blanco espacio.	open to white space.

Javier Sologuren, Peru [k]

clouds and moon
on dark earth
scattered jasmine

Stephen Hobson, Australia [k]

ORANGE BLOSSOMS, *daidai no hana, flor del taronger*—Catalan (early). The Japanese refers to the common or **sweet orange** (*C. sinensis*). The **MANDARIN ORANGE** and **tangerine** (*mikan*, both varieties of *C. reticulata*) also bloom at this time, but the **Seville** or **BITTER ORANGE** (*Citrus aurantium*) blooms in mid summer. Also: **blossoming orange tree** (*florecer del naranjo*—Spanish).

No veo el florecer	I don't look at the blossoming
del naranjo, oigo	orange tree, I listen
subir su canto.	to its rising song.

Javier Sologuren, Peru [k]

La flor del taronger	The orange blossom
ja no la colliré,	still haven't picked it,
que ve l'hivern.	that it might ban winter.

Rosa Leveroni, Spain [k]

MAPLE KEYS (early). Maple trees (family *Aceraceae*, genus *Acer*) provide many topics already in traditional saijiki, but the distinguishing feature of all maples, the maple keys or **maple wings**, has not previously been included. These are the paired seeds with thin membranous wings that hang in great clusters in the trees. While the seeds do not mature for most maples until autumn, in early summer they are delicate and easily dislodged from the trees in a wind, to float down in a spiral. Soft, light green—with a tinge of red or yellow in some species, these young dual seed pods can be split, and each half partially split again, revealing its still-green seed. Thus split into a "Y", the seed casing can be placed on the end of one's nose, holding on by means of the sticky fluid inside, to create a **pucker-nose** that sticks up like a green banner, to the great amusement of children. The box elder common in much of the eastern and midwestern U.S. is also a maple, with keys. **Brown** or **DRIED MAPLE KEYS** would be an early-autumn topic.

after rain
spilled maple keys
a red barbecue slowly smoking

Marshall Hryciuk, ON [k]

recess over
the children all wearing
pucker-noses

William J. Higginson, NM [k]

GRAPE BLOSSOMS, *budō no hana* (early). *Vitis sp.* Clusters of small, greenish flowers on long racemes. Also: **budding grapes.**

machine gun cackle:
the roadrunner beneath the
budding grape vines

Mary E. Barton, TX [k]

RASPBERRY, *ki-ichigo* (all). *Rubus sp.* **Wild raspberries** and **thimbleberries** mature in mid-to-late summer, but commercial raspberries come in earlier.

just as it's touched
the over-ripe raspberry
drops off

Gayle MacDonald, OR [k/s]

morning meditation—
a raspberry seed
between my teeth

James Ferris, WA [k/s]

CLOUDBERRY (late). *Rubus chamaemorus*. "Cloudberry" or **baked-apple berry** grows on erect plants with single, white blossoms in isolated sites in the northeastern U.S.

cloudberries:
tasting
the word

Jerry Kilbride, CA [k]

SALMONBERRIES (all). *Rubus spectabilis*. Blooms mid spring through summer, with ripe fruit from summer into autumn.

salmonberries
the second one picked
plunks into the pail

Mark Arvid White, AK [k]

SHADE OF A TREE, *ko no shita yami* (all). In winter we hope to **BASK** in sunshine; in summer we seek the shade of a tree. Also: **shade** (*ombra*—Italian), **hemlock shade**.

Raro s'incontra l'amico	Rarely does one meet a friend
ancor pigro nell'ombra	still idling in the shade
e di narrare sazio.	and sated with storytelling.

Galilea Loperfido, Italy [s]

Here the river hooks
through cliffs and hemlock shade;
the smell of a still

Robert Spiess, WI [k]

MOUNTAIN DOGWOOD, *yamabōshi no hana* (early). The Japanese phrase here translated "mountain dogwood" literally reads "mountain priest". In English it is usually called **Japanese dogwood** (*Cornus kousa*). Wild in Japan and cultivated widely, the tree grows 10-26' (3-8 m) high and blooms for about a month beginning in May or June. Its 2-4" (5-10 cm) wide "blossoms" consist of a greenish flower cluster surrounded by four creamy-white petal-like bracts which end in sharp points. The **Pacific dogwood** (*C. nuttallii*) of North America, also called "mountain dogwood", grows up to 50' (15 m) or more high and is frequently found in the understory of coniferous forests. Its "blossoms" are similar to but larger than those of its Japanese cousin: 4-6" (10-15 cm) across with four to seven bracts, usually six. It begins blooming in April in some areas, but peaks in early summer, often blooming again in autumn. Both Japanese and Pacific types have red leaves in autumn. There is also an **evergreen dogwood** (*C. capitata*) introduced in Europe and growing to 33' (10 m) high which has similar blossoms. The somewhat earlier-blooming **FLOWERING DOGWOOD** of eastern North America is a spring seasonal topic. Note that in English the word "dogwood" alone will usually be taken as referring to the more wide-spread and hardier flowering dogwood, though Pacific, Japanese, or evergreen dogwoods may come to mind for readers in their locales.

Tips rising
as the sun burns through—
mountain dogwood.

William J. Higginson, NM [k]

POINCIANA BLOSSOMS, *fenghuang hua*—Chinese (all). *Delonix regia*. The **royal poinciana**, also called **flamboyant tree, flame-tree,** and **peacock flower**, originated in Madagascar, and is now widely cultivated in the tropics, including southern portions of Florida and California, Puerto Rico and the West Indies, and from Mexico to Brazil as well as the orient. This deciduous tree can reach a height of 50' (15 m) with a broad crown spreading half-again as wide. From May to July or August it produces abundant racemes of brilliant scarlet blossoms, often tinged with yellow, initially from an otherwise barren tree—perhaps accounting for the Chinese name *fenghuang*, or "phoenix". Leaves appear during the blooming period. Its fruits, dark brown to black, are flat woody pods up to 2' (60 cm) long, resembling machetes; they mature in autumn and persist to spring.

fênghuang hua	poinciana blossoms
chin-chao i-pieh	parting this morning
ko hsi tung	to east and west

Ts'aiwên Yang, Taiwan [h]

POPLAR SEEDS (all). Catkins of the white poplar mature in May or June and their seeds go airborn on cottony tufts. Though now widespread in eastern North America, the white poplar (*Populus alba*) is native to central and southern Europe and the eastern Mediterranean. Its modern common and genus names derive from the name of this tree in Roman times, *arbor populi*—"the people's tree". Also: **poplar fluff** (*Pappelflocke*—German), **white-poplar seeds** (*sjemenke topole*—Croatian).

Granični prijelaz	Frontier crossing:
nehajno prelijeću	leisurely flying over,
sjemenke topole.	white-poplar seeds.

Maja Rijavec, Croatia [k]

Hand greift ins Leere.	The hand grasps at the void.
Entwischte Pappelflocke	The slipped-away poplar fluff
streichelt mein Gesicht.	caresses my face.

Guido Keller, Germany [k/s]

IRIS, *airisu* (early). *Iris sp.* The irises make up a large group of plants including species that bloom at many different times in spring and summer, but this topic refers to varieties of tall, bearded **western iris** originating in western Europe and commonly blooming in mid summer.

Note that several irises are native to Japan, and constitute popular midsummer topics on their own, such as **WALL IRIS** (*ichihatsu*), and **BLUE FLAG** (*kakitsubata*).

Last night lightning
this morning
the white iris.

Pat Donegan, Japan [h]

DATURA, *dachura* (late). *Datura stramonium*. A deadly member of the nightshade family common on dry, waste ground. Has showy, trumpet-shaped white or violet flowers up to 4" (10 cm) wide, blooming from July to October on plants 1-6' (2 m) tall. Native to central America, introduced north by Native Americans. The common name **jimsonweed** is a corruption of "Jamestown", where the plant was apparently first encountered by Europeans. Related species include **angel trumpet** (*D. wrightii*) and **entire-leaved thorn-apple** (*D. metel*) in the southern U.S.; the **entire-leaved thorn-apple** or **Indian apple** (*D. meteloides*) in the Southwest and Pacific states begins blooming in April. Probably introduced for its medicinal properties—or possibly by accident when shipped with other field crops—it is now found wild in Japan and England. A poison if taken internally, it can also cause a skin rash.

in kiva ruins
a sacred datura bud
unfolds shadows

Ruth Yarrow, NY [h]

SWEET ALYSSUM (all). *Alyssum maritimum*. A hardy annual, with fragrant pale blue or white flowers blooming May to October.

new moon
sweet alyssum hanging
over the cracked wall

Gene Doty, MO [k]

WATER LILY, *suiren* (late). *Nymphaea sp*. Many wild and cultivated varieties grow in ponds, lakes, and river eddies. They come in many colors, but most notably in white and yellow. In the following poem, **LOON** is also a summer topic, which see.

White water lilies
in the moonlight
the loon's voice

June Moreau, MA [h]

LILY, *yuri* (late). Common name of many wild and cultivated members of the genus *Lilium* with funnel- or bell-shaped flowers. Most varieties peak in late summer, including **Turk's-cap lily** (*L. superbum*, North America; also *L. martagon*, northern Europe) and **tiger lily** (*L. tigrinum, oniyuri*, East Asia, cultivated and escaped worldwide; also *L. columbianum*, North America). Not to be confused with a number of plants in other families which also include "lily" in their names, such as **CALLA LILY** and **Easter lily**, which see under **EASTER**. Also: **orange lilies, white lilies** (crin—Romanian).

Shinnyodo's far bell
while the wind blows back and forth
the orange lilies.

Edith Marcombe Shiffert, Japan [h]

flori albe de crin	white lily flowers
in grădina bunicii	in my grandma's garden
—muzică de Grieg	—the music of Grieg

Ana-Olimpia Sima, Romania [h]

CENTURY PLANT (all). *Agave sp.* Also called: **Agave, maguey.** One of the best-known century plants, A. *deserti*, has spikes of orange-yellow blossoms in the California desert May to July. Others bloom for one or two months from April to August. Individual plants grow 12–15 years before sending up a single flower stalk, up to 25' (8 m) tall, then die after they set seed.

orange agave buds
against the white mission wall
shadows of gravestones

Donna Gallagher, CA [k]

ZINNIAS, *hyakunichisō* (late). The Japanese literally reads "hundred-day plant". Bright, in varied colors, zinnias practically defined summer during my childhood in New York City and New Jersey.

Taking a snapshot
of these bright zinnias
and my own shadow

Don L. Holroyd, PA [s]

BERRIES (early). Various wild berries ripen in early summer, some later. Includes **blackberries** (*more dai rovi*—Italian).

Gogliendo more	Picking blackberries
dai rovi del sentiero	from the brambles by the path
salgo alla vetta.	I climb to the summit.

Margherita Guidacci, Japan [k]

MOONFLOWER, *yūgao* (late). *Lagenaria sp.* The Japanese literally means "evening face"; also called: **evening-glory**, **bottle-gourd flower**, **calabash flower**. The vines are native to the tropics; their flowers bloom on summer evenings and fade before morning. "Evening-glory" may be a translator's invention, since the white blossoms resemble those of the autumnal **MORNING-GLORY**, called *asagao* ("morning face") in Japanese. A plant of lowly status, the moonflower is not found in Japanese poetry before *The Tale of Genji* (11th century C.E.), where *Yūgao* is the name of an important character. Thus it has become part of the literary trio including morning-glory and **BINDWEED** (*hirugao*, "noon face"). The moonflower's fruit, **CALABASH** or **bottle gourd**, frequently hollowed out for containers, is an early-autumn seasonal topic. Note that the **OXEYE DAISY** of midsummer is also called "moonflower" in England, and the name is applied to some other plants as well.

yūgao ni	for the moonflower
kaerihagureshi	he strays from the way home—
kumanbachi	the giant hornet

Saichi Hoshino, Japan [k]

QUEEN ANNE'S LACE, *ninjin no hana* (all). *Daucus carota*. **Wild carrot** is believed to be the foundation plant for the domestic carrot (known for thousands of years). Blooms May to October, most prominent June to August, when flower heads may be seen at all stages of development; has wide flat umbels of small white blossoms with one dark maroon floret at center. Also called: **lace flower** (not to be confused with the cultivated **blue lace flower** [*Didiscus caeruleus* = *Trachymene caerulea*] that blooms about the same season in Western Australia); **bird's-nest**, for the incurving cluster as it matures; **devil's weed**, for the difficulty of rooting it out of farm fields. In the following poem, "Tornado season" varies considerably according to region; see **TORNADO** (all year).

brown lace flower
teetering
into tornado season

Shawn Lindsay, IN [k]

MELON, *uri, pepeni*—Romanian (late). *Cucumis melo var.* Usually refers to **muskmelons** (*makuwa-uri*), varieties of the reticulatus melon group, which may also be erroneously called **cantaloupe** in U.S. (Technically, cantaloupe is a particular variety of *C. melo* not grown in the U.S.) **MELON BLOSSOM** (*uri no hana*) and **MUSKMELON BLOSSOM** are early-summer topics. See also **WATERMELON** and **WINTER MELON** in Autumn.

produce stand
the pregnant girl thumps
a melon

Kenneth C. Hurm, KY [k/s]

Pe câmpul verde	The green field
scarabei uriaşi—	scarab beetles, huge—
pepeni galbeni.	yellow melons.

Dumitru D. Ifrim, Romania [h]

GRAIN, *mugi* (early). Most grains, including barley, oats, and wheat, are sown in winter to produce early summer crops. "Ears" of grain are the heads containing the ripening or ripened grains in their husks. Also: **wheat ear** (*klas pšenice*—Croatian), **oats** (*civada*—Catalan).

Klas pšenice—	A wheat ear—
ljuljuška se vrabac	a sparrow rocks itself
sa svojom gozbom.	with its feast.

Zvonko Petrović, Croatia [k]

Tractors sorollen	Tractors shake
unes feixes vetustes.	some ancient plots.
Civada i ordi.	Oats and barley.

Miguel Desclot, Spain [h]

CORN TASSELS, *tōmorokoshi no hana* (late). *Zea mays.* The major grain of the Americas, cultivated for over 5,000 years, and now used for human food and animal fodder worldwide. Modern varieties all derive from Indian maize. Corn tassels (blossoms) appear a given number of days from planting, depending on variety. Late summer provides a good average for many of the temperate zone's preferred varieties. Also: **tasseling corn.**

In the tasseling
corn
fireflies
swap light

Eve Triem, WA [h]

GREEN PAMPAS GRASS, *aosusuki* (all). *Miscanthus sinensis.* Lush green pampas grass is characteristic of summer in many places, where it adds to the general impression of abundance. Just the name **PAMPAS GRASS** (*susuki*) by itself, however, yields the image of the silvery fronds of the mature plant, and is an autumn topic.

yamabiko wa	the mountain echo
otoko narikeri	has become a man—
aosusuki	green pampas grass

Mizue Yamada, Japan [k]

BINDWEED, *hirugao* (mid). Members of the morning-glory family (Convolvulaceae). The Japanese literally means "noon face"—thus relating in literature to the **MORNING-GLORY** (*asagao*, "morning face") of autumn and **MOONFLOWER** (*yūgao*, "evening face") of summer. **Field bindweed** (*Convolvulus arvensis*) and **hedge bindweed** (*Calystegia sepium*) commonly bloom from May to September in fields and waste places. "Bindweed" can also refer to some members of the buckwheat family (*Polygonum sp.*) blooming at about the same time, but the flowers of these plants do not have the characteristic trumpet shape of morning-glories. Also: **bindweed flowers** (*cvjetovi slaka*—Croatian).

Vruće zgarište.	Hot ashes.
Na pošteđenom plotu	In the undestroyed fence
cvjetovi slaka.	bindweed flowers.

Tomislav Maretić, Croatia [k]

MULLEIN (late). **Common mullein** (*Verbascum thapsus*) and **moth mullein** (*V. blattaria*) are both widespread in North America, with spikes of usually yellow flowers 2–6' (60–180 cm) high.

turning back—
mullein flowers higher than
the feather in her hair

Hal Roth, MD [k/s]

MOSS BLOSSOMS, *koke no hana* (mid). Family Musci. The "blossoms" are actually the spore cases of some species which lift up 1–2" (2.5–5 cm) above the very low evergreen plants, the latter ranging from 1/2–4" (1.3–10 cm) high and usually growing in dense mats or cushions in habitats ranging from active streams to dry disturbed ground. In some species the spore cases are hidden in the foliage.

zen-en to iu	Too small
niwa chiisashi	to call it a Zen garden
koke no hana	moss blossoms

Mitsui Suzuki, CA [k]

DUCKWEED, *ukikusa* (all). *Lemna sp.* The arrival of summer brings the minute free-floating leaves of duckweed to the surface of quiet waters. Typically less than one-half inch (12.5 mm) in diameter each, masses of them can cover wide areas.

haha nosete	mother aboard
fune ukikusa no	the boat goes deep
naka e iru	into duckweed

Nobuko Katsura, Japan [k]

MOREL (early). *Morchella sp.* The edible North American **black morel, yellow morel,** and **half-free morel** are available April and May, and appear later at higher elevations. (Not to be confused with the poisonous European plant *Atropa belladonna*, common name morel.) Japanese saijiki include many named mushrooms and **MUSHROOM-GATHERING** in Autumn (which see), when several edible varieties are collected. Hence the word **MUSHROOM** is an autumn topic; but other seasons also have characteristic mushrooms.

her red curls
caught on a thorn—
she reaches the morel

Randy Brooks, IL [k]

MOLD, MILDEW, *kabi* (mid). In Japan and elsewhere mold and mildew become most noticeable with the heat of midsummer on top of the early summer rains; in many climates they persist year-round.

on the porch
mold-speckled pine needles
my waiting for you

Jane Reichhold, CA [k]

AUTUMN

The following entries appear under Autumn, in the categories indicated.

------- The Season -------
Autumn
New Coolness
September
Late Autumn
Autumn Noon
Autumn Afternoon
Autumn Dusk
Autumn Evening
Long Night
Scent of Autumn
Cold Night
Autumn Deepens
------- The Heavens -------
Autumn Clarity
Autumn Light
Mackerel Sky
Moon
New Moon
Moonlit Evening
August Moon
Harvest Moon
Hunter's Moon
Starlit Night
Milky Way
Meteors
Autumn Wind
Meltemi
October Wind
Typhoon
Autumn Rain
Autumn Drizzle
Lightning
Autumn Mist, Fog
Autumn Haze
Dew
------- The Earth -------
Autumn Mountains
Flower Field
Stubble Field
------- Humanity -------
Canning
Scarecrow
Winnowing Grain
Cranberry Raking
Kelp-Bladder Popping
Mushroom Gathering
Hunting Colored Leaves
Athletic Meet
------- Observances -------
Guy Fawkes Day
Bon Festival
Grave Visiting
Welcome-Fire
Dance
State Fair
Rosh Hashanah
Yom Kippur
Halloween
All Saints' Day
-------- Animals -------
Deer
Burying Nuts
Hawks Migrate
Migrating Birds
Swallows Depart
Waxwing
Sandpiper, Snipe
Geese
Eastern Oyster
Autumn Butterfly
Dragonfly
Ephemera
Cricket
Grasshopper, Locust
Gossamer
------- Plants -------
Witch Hazel Blossoms
Eucalyptus Blossoms
Quince
Peach
Persimmon
Apple
Grapes
Chestnut
Walnut
Rose of Sharon
Lemon
Colored Leaves
Leaves Turning Color
Yellow Leaves
Leaves Start to Fall
Yellow Leaves Drop
Colored Oak Leaves
Nuts and Seeds
Acorn
Ginkgo Nut
Oak Gall
Virginia Creeper
Banana Tree
Orchid
Morning-Glory
Cosmos
Chrysanthemum
Aster
Watermelon
Winter Melon
Pumpkin
Pigeon Barley
Bush Clover
Goldenrod
Reed Plumes
Partridgeberry
Chamomile
Cocklebur
Red Spider Lily
Purple Loosestrife
Touch-Me-Not
Milkweed
Ink Caps
Lichen

Note: An asterisk at the end of an entry's text indicates that additional poems and season words on the topic may be found in Chapter 6 of The Haiku Seasons.

AUTUMN—THE SEASON

AUTUMN, *aki, Herbst*—German (all). Technically "autumn" in haikai means the period from about 8 August through about 6 November, centering on the **AUTUMNAL EQUINOX**—but commonly August through October, as it means in popular British usage (February to April in the southern hemisphere). (See entry for **SPRING**, first in the saijiki.) Poems on the season per se and on some apparent seasonal topics formed by combining "autumn" with the names of otherwise nonseasonal phenomena may be included here. In general, "autumn" seems to be preferred over **fall** in English haiku, but the underlying meaning of the **fall of the year** toward winter may be relevant, and "fall" may sound better in a particular poem. However, "fall" does not exactly coincide with "autumn", but means specifically "the season when leaves fall from trees"—*Webster's Third New International Dictionary*. In haikai terms, "fall" thus may best apply to the period from late autumn through early winter. The phrase **turning year** also usually refers to autumn, though it may be confused with the end of the year in some contexts. The word "autumn" may have a positive affect dealing with relief from the heat of summer and the quickening of commerce and academic life after the period of **SUMMER VACATION**, the bustle and fruitfulness of harvest, and the beauty of the natural world during the season. Or it may suggest the waning strength of the sun and diminished activity of plants and animals as the year moves toward winter—and the parallel weakening of humans as we age. See the discussion of the names of seasons in the introduction to the saijiki, pages 32–33.

autumn—
now the slow bee allows
stroking of fur

George Marsh, England [k]

Einkaufspassage.
Im Herbst singt die Nachtigall
auch hier, doch vom Band.

Shopping mall.
In autumn too the nightingale
sings here, on tape.

Doris Götting, Germany [s]

sheep eyes
in rear-view mirror
to fall auction

John Budan, OR [k]

NEW COOLNESS, *shinryō* (early). While **LINGERING HEAT** (*zansho*) continues from summer into early autumn, at this time we also begin to feel the **first coolness** (*shoryō*) of autumn. A great deal depends on one's immediate environment; city-dwellers in the northern hemisphere may scarcely note any difference from July into August, indeed may find August typically the hotter month. But I remember ice on the edges of lakes at dawn by the second or third week of August in northern New Jersey and southern New York state. In the high deserts of the southwestern U.S., where I now live, jackets may be needed on August evenings, however hot the day may be. Also called: **early autumn chill.**

early autumn chill
on the foreclosed farm
apples redden . . .

Sally Ann Sims, PA [k]

SEPTEMBER, *kugatsu, September*—German (mid). In September we know that autumn has truly arrived. Generally, nights are cooler, and the air takes on the color and tang of harvest time. Note that in the southern hemisphere this is mid spring.

Mitte September:	Mid September:
Kartoffelfeuerdüfte	scent of roasted potatoes
mitten in der Stadt.	in the middle of town.

Brigitta Weiss, Germany [h]

LATE AUTUMN, *banshū* (late). Commonly taken as the month of October, technically late autumn runs from about 8 October through 7 November in the northern hemisphere, from about 5 April through 5

May in the southern. This is usually the time when the **COLORED LEAVES** (which see) of deciduous trees and vines are at their peak, the **AUTUMN HARVEST** (*aki-osame*) is completed, and we grow increasingly conscious of the coming cold time of winter.

late autumn
the billboard's shadow leans
into the woods

Cor van den Heuvel, NY [k]

AUTUMN NOON, *aki no hiru* (all). In each season, the various portions of the day have their own character.

ōgoi no	a large carp
gii to megurinu	turned round with a screak
aki no hiru	on an autumn noon

Syōji Okai, Japan [k]

AUTUMN AFTERNOON (all). An autumn afternoon may be full of the activity of **AUTUMN HARVEST**, or carry a lingering sense of the lassitude of a **SUMMER AFTERNOON**. In cities the pace quickens as workers and children have come back from **SUMMER VACATION** (*natsu yasumi*, late summer).

autumn afternoon:
tossing a petal into
the Grand Canyon

Virginia Brady Young, CT [k]

AUTUMN DUSK, *aki no kure* (all). In Japanese kure normally means "close of the day", but in autumn it takes on the added meaning "close of the season" in certain contexts, as in the following poem. This refers not only to autumn per se, but also to the end of the growing season, the end of the period when living outdoors and **TRAVEL** (which see in the all-year section) are relatively comfortable. Also: **autumn heavens go dark** (*aki no ten kureyuku*). See also **AUTUMN EVENING,** next entry.

maki wari no	in the sound
oto ni kureyuku	of cutting firewood
aki no ten	the autumn heavens go dark

Shinkū Fukuda, Japan [k]

AUTUMN EVENING, *aki no yoi, herfstavond*—Dutch (all). In Japanese there are many handy, compact expressions for the time between day and night. Like crepescule, **DUSK,** and evening, each has its own flavor which changes with the seasons. The expression "autumn evening" suggests a chill absent in summer.

aki no yoi to	as autumn evening
nari no inu ga	comes on the dog
kuchun to iu	says "katchoo"

Kabon Ei, Japan [k]

alleen het haardvuur	only the hearth-fire
warmt nog haar oude lichaam	warms her old body
deze herfstavond	this autumn evening

Carla Mostert, The Netherlands [k]

LONG NIGHT, *yo naga* (all). This topic reflects the lengthening night taking over day as shadows come earlier and the year turns from summer to autumn. **ROSES,** an early summer topic, continue blooming well into autumn in many places. Note that **SHORT DAY** is a winter topic. Also: **afternoon shadows.**

the roses' shadows
farther up the white-washed walls
in late afternoon

Douglas S. Johnson, WA [k]

SCENT OF AUTUMN, *miris jeseni*—Croatian (all). The scent arising from the cuttings and dust of harvest, the burning of farm and garden waste, and the first heating fires. Related to **AUTUMN HAZE.**

kožnata jakna	a leather jacket
sva smočena od kiše	all drenched with rain
miris jeseni	scent of autumn

Rujana Matuka, Croatia [k]

COLD NIGHT, *yosamu* (late). Certainly a winter night may be colder, including a **freezing night** (see **COLD** in winter), but nights first turn cold in late autumn. Also: **first chill night.**

The first chill night:
The mother finds herself
Covering up the dolls.

Cicely Hill, England [k/s]

AUTUMN DEEPENS, *aki fukashi* (late). The feeling that autumn is over, or nearly so, as nights grow longer and we begin to feel the chill of winter. **WALNUT** is also a late autumn topic. Also: **deep autumn.**

aki fukashi	autumn deepens—
mojirianii no	the eyes of
onna no me	Modigliani's woman

Akito Arima, Japan [k]

Ever lingering
in the taste of the walnut:
deep autumn.

James W. Hackett, CA [k]

AUTUMN—THE HEAVENS

AUTUMN CLARITY, *akibare* (all). As the growing coolness of autumn reduces the relative humidity we have some of the clearest days and nights seen during the whole year. This accounts for the increased number of nighttime sky phenomena in the saijiki for autumn. Also: **autumn clearer.**

An empty plate
Smashing it

Autumn clearer

Masaya Saito, Japan [k/s]

AUTUMN LIGHT, *Herbstlicht*—German (all). In autumn the light takes on a special quality, contributed to by **AUTUMN HAZE** and the lowering angle of the sun even at midday. While such words as "dusk" and "twilight" simply mean low-light conditions, the phrase **dwindling light** suggests a consciousness of the more limited daylight hours of autumn.

Im milden Herbstlicht	In mild autumn light
der Tochter graue Strähnen—	grey strands in Daughter's hair—
bin ich schon so alt?	have I grown so old?

Richard W. Heinrich, Germany [k]

dwindling light—
a wasp clings to the warm
back of my neck

David Cobb, England [k]

MACKEREL SKY, *iwashigumo* (all). The Japanese literally says "sardine clouds". Whether from the pattern of the scales of a sardine or mackerel, it seems that in both English and Japanese the metaphor for a sky covered with a layer of mottled altocumulus clouds has its source among people familiar with saltwater fishes and the expanse of ocean sky. A mackerel sky usually indicates a coming weather system.

karuru oto	withering sound
yoshi o hanarezu	not freeing the reeds
iwashigumo	mackerel sky

Shūson Katō, Japan [k]

MOON, *tsuki, Mond*—German, *luna*—*Spanish*, *lluna*—Catalan (all). With **blossoms**, this is one of the two most important images in all haikai literature. The word "moon" by itself will always be taken as the full moon of an autumn month (August to October), unless other material in the verse clearly indicates another season. (There are a few such examples scattered through this saijiki.) The Japanese have many words, phrases, and figures of speech for the moon, most referring to autumn. Some of them are specific to the full moon of September (see **HARVEST MOON**), but many have the breadth of "moon" by itself, including some for the crescent moon. A few examples, all referring to the autumn moon but unspecified as to month: **first quarter moon** (*jōgen no tsuki*), **half moon** (*hangetsu*), **the moon's bow** (*tsuki no yumi*), **the moon's boat** (*tsuki no fune*), **rising moon** (*agari tsuki*), **waning moon** (*mochikudari*), **fifth-day moon** (*ikkazuki*)—which means the crescent moon on the fifth night after the new moon, **halo of the moon** (*tsuki no kasa*), **moon-white** (*tsukishiro*)—whiteness in the sky over where the moon will rise, **moon-mirror** (*tsuki no kagami*), **moon-sword** (*tsuki no tsurugi*), **moonlit Capitol** (*tsuki no miyako*), and so on, for more than fifty such phrases listed in the *Japan Great Saijiki*. A number of other phrases refer specifically to the moon of September. It is never necessary to say "autumn moon" in haikai. One may say **HAZY MOON**, referring to spring; **SUMMER MOON** and **WINTER MOON** are appropriate to their seasons. Regarding the last poem in this group, "Tzarskoye Selo" is a town in Poland where the Nazis took all the Jews' musical instruments and put them in one old house; the instruments sounded when the wind rose. Also: **banana moon.**

nōmen no	noh mask
kudakete tsuki no	shattering . . . this
minato kana	moon harbor

Momoko Kuroda, Japan [k]

kids skate the sidewalk
in the considered dusk
under a banana moon

Chris Torrance, Wales, UK [k]

Die Aprikosen	The apricots
sind abgeerntet. Nur mehr	all picked. Only the moon
der Mond hägt im Baum.	hangs in the tree.

Isolde Lachmann, Austria [k]

nit de lluna	night of the moon
estesa per la mar salada	extended over the salty sea
escata de sirena	scale of a mermaid

Josep Maria Junoy, Spain [h]

La luna brilla:	Bright moon:
el viento silbando	the wind whistling
a la gente que pasa.	at people who pass by.

Sergio Mondragon, Mexico [k/s]

The phantom music,
a moon, bleak, yellow,
over Tzarskoye Selo.

Ivor Garb, South Africa [k]

NEW MOON, *hatsuzuki, luna nueva*—Spanish (mid). In Japanese literally this means the "starting moon" or "first moon". In English the phrase "new moon" means two different things. In astronomers' terms, this is the time of **no moon**, when the moon has fully waned and disappeared from the night sky. (But see **STARLIT NIGHT**, below.) But many will understand this term as the Japanese do, referring to the **thin crescent moon** when it makes its first appearance at the start of a new lunar cycle. Both meanings are appropriate to international haikai, as the poems below demonstrate. Why limit this to the new moon of the coming **HARVEST MOON** of mid autumn? Because that harvest moon is so anticipated that those of a deep haikai sensibility count the days of the waxing moon, from this "starting moon" through the growing crescents of the **SECOND-DAY MOON** (*futsukazuki*), **THIRD-DAY MOON** (*mikazuki*), and so on right up to **WAITING EVENING** (*matsu yoi*) the night before the ultimate **full moon** (a season word under the topic **HARVEST MOON**) of the year.

La luna nueva.	The new moon.
Ella también la mira	She too sees it
desde otra puerta.	from another doorway.

Jorge Luis Borges, Argentina [k]

¿En la penumbra	In the shadows
algún secreto?	any secrets?
La luna nueva	The new moon

Alfonso Cisneros Cox, Peru [k]

Night of no moon
I turn on every light
To read your letter

Marco Fraticelli, PQ [k]

MOONLIT EVENING, *yūzukiyo* (all). A clear, moonlit evening. The **MALLOW** is normally a summer topic in the saijiki, but various species—including the wild, white **swamp rose-mallow** (*Hibiscus moscheutos*)—bloom into mid or late autumn. Also: **moonlit sky.**

Moonlit sky
—a white mallow petal floats
on the trap's tongue

Matthew Louvière, LA [k]

AUGUST MOON (early). This refers to the first full moon of autumn. Note that in the southern hemisphere the corresponding expression is **February moon,** which has the same early-autumn associations.

February moon
not one single flying fox snared
on its horns

Alan J. Summers, Australia [k]

HARVEST MOON, *meigetsu, pun mjesec*—Croatian (mid). The Japanese literally says **famous moon.** This is the full moon of the fifteenth night of the eighth lunar month, which is nearest the **AUTUMNAL EQUINOX**, 22 or 23 September in the northern hemisphere. During the period near the autumnal equinox the moon rises at a low angle against the horizon at nearly the same time each night. Thus it stays lower longer, appears larger, and seems to give more light than at any other time of year. For this reason folklore has it that the moon provides farmers with more light to get in the harvest; hence the name "harvest moon". Note that the term **full moon** (*mangetsu*) in haikai always refers to this phenomenon, unless some other season is named or the poem includes a seasonal topic which cannot occur at this time of year. In New Zealand the harvest moon comes in March. The angle of the rising moon near the autumnal equinox in the northern hemisphere is similar to that in the southern hemisphere at the astronomical vernal equinox—that is, the "autumnal equinox" from the southern perspective. So the same phenomenon applies in both hemispheres.

harvest moon
mice rattling
the sheaves

John Ziemba, MA [k]

full moon:
the smell of seaweed
twice as strong

Richard von Sturmer, New Zealand [k]

a full moon
cows and calves grazing
in knee-high fog

Sharon Hammer Baker, OH [k]

drvored uz put	path by the woods
u svakoj krošnji sja	in every treetop the shining
pun mjesec	full moon

Darko Plažanin, Croatia [h]

HUNTER'S MOON (late). The tenth full moon of the year, or the October full moon; from the Algonquin. The Algonquin were a powerful tribal people of what is now southeastern Canada when European colonists arrived. Since Algonquin-related languages are spoken by many tribes in eastern and central North America, it seems reasonable to assume that some still use the old name. Other tribal groups have their own names for the various moons. See also **WOLF MOON** in winter.

Hunter's moon.
A stick match lights up
a hound's eye.

Arizona Zipper, Maine [k]

STARLIT NIGHT, *hoshizukiyo* (all). The Japanese literally means "stars [like the] moon night" referring to a night of brilliant starlight with no moon, and is said to impart an air of mystery and depth to the world thus illumined. Another autumn topic that literally translates from Japanese as "moonless" (*mugetsu*) means a moon obscured by clouds, and so might best be rendered **CLOUDED MOON** in English. See also **MOONLIT EVENING** (all autumn).*

hoshizukiyo	a starlit night
ikoma o koete	crossing Mt. Ikoma
kata hiyuru	my shoulder cools

Kin'ichi Sawaki, Japan [k]

chion-in	Chion Temple
yami ni boshinu	fallen into darkness
hoshizukiyo	starlit night

Tetsunosuke Matsuzaki, Japan [k]

MILKY WAY, *amanogawa, Calea Lactee*—Romanian (early). The Japanese literally means **river of heaven**—sometimes translated **starstream**. This is the hazy white band across the night sky made by the galaxy (from Greek *gala* = milk) of which our solar system is a part. In Japan one sees it best in early autumn, when skies are at their clearest and it is associated with **TANABATA** (see **GRAVE VISITING**, below).

Air and light pollution have made it virtually invisible in heavily populated and industrialized areas, and many people have never seen the Milky Way.

Through a hole
in a borrowed tent
the Milky Way

Steve Shapiro, South Africa [h]

Casa de pe deal—
din horn se răsfiră
Calea Lactee.

House on the hill—
out of a chimney scatters
the Milky Way.

Dan Doman, Romania [h]

amanokawa
miage hoshi naki
ōsaka o omou

The Milky Way falling
I think of
starless Osaka nights

Keiko Imaoka, AZ [k]

METEORS, *ryūsei* (early). While one may see a meteor or **shooting star** year-round, the most active time for seeing meteors is during the well-known **Perseids,** a **meteor shower** that typically peaks in mid August when one can see perhaps 50 to 100 meteors an hour apparently coming from the constellation Perseus in a clear sky after midnight. Also called: **falling star** (*stea cazatoare*—Romanian).

behind the clouds
I can almost feel
the promised meteors

George Marsh, England [k]

Viata la oras—
de cand nu am vazut
o stea cazatoare?

Life in the city—
when did I last see
a falling star?

Radu Patrichi, Romania [k]

midstream halt—
the horseman looks up
at the falling stars

H. F. Noyes, Greece [k]

AUTUMN WIND, *aki kaze* (all). After the warmth of summer, the chill in an autumn wind brings news of the changing year.

fukusō wa	buried with him
kaitaku no ono	his land-clearing axe
aki no kaze	autumn wind

Seiran Yoshino, Brazil [k]

autumn wind
the back of each leaf
color of a bruise

Kristen Deming, Japan [k]

MELTEMI (early). In Greece, a strong northwind called *meltemi* comes around the latter half of August.

meltemi over—
down among cackling hens
the weathervane cock

H. F. Noyes, Greece [k]

OCTOBER WIND, *Oktoberwinde*—German (late). As autumn moves toward winter, the wind takes on a more serious chill despite the lingering warmth of the sun.

Oktoberwinde	October wind
streuen Krähen in die Luft	strews crows into the sky
Sonnenfinsternis.	solar eclipse.

Doris Götting, Germany [k]

TYPHOON, *taifū* (mid). A circular storm originating over tropical seas and growing to have winds of 74 mph (119 kph) or more. Gaining strength as it moves over water, a **hurricane** (term used in the Americas) frequently makes landfall in the temperate zone, its high winds and heavy rains causing considerable damage. Technically called **tropical cyclones,** these storms occur mainly in summer and autumn, peaking in early September.

banging away at a nail
trying to stop
the hurricane

David Gershator, VI [s]

AUTUMN RAIN, *aki no ame, ploaie de toamna*—Romanian, *lluvia de otoño*—Spanish (all). Any kind of rain in autumn, other than the **AUTUMN DRIZZLE** (next entry) that presages winter.

Ploaie de taomnă—	Autumn rain—
un şoricel sub frunză	a mouse under a leaf
ronţăie ceva.	nibbles something.

Radu Patrichi, Romania [k]

a lone man
gazes from the woolshed—
autumn rain

Hina, Australia [k]

A la deriva,	Adrift,
un bote de papel.	a paper boat.
Lluvia de otoño.	Autumn rain.

Liria Miyakawa, Argentina [k]

AUTUMN DRIZZLE, *aki shigure* (late). The famous **WINTER DRIZZLE** (*shigure*) of Japan—characteristic of many other places as well, often appears also in late autumn.

autumn drizzle—
the slow ticking
of the clock

Bruce Ross, NY [k]

LIGHTNING, *inazuma* (all). We usually see lightning a few seconds before we hear **THUNDER**, but the latter is traditionally a summer topic in haikai. This topic includes **lightning flash** (*inabikari*) and the **lord of lightning** (*ine no tono*). Note that in all these terms the Japanese begins with the character for "rice"—said to indicate that much lightning is seen during the rice harvest. (See **THUNDER** in summer for more.) **Heat lightning** is lightning so far away that one cannot hear the thunder—about 16 miles (25 km) or more distant. (Note that "lightning" is the single most-often misspelt word in English haiku; "lightening" means "becoming light".)

heat lightning
the night
jumps silently

David Gershator, VI [k]

AUTUMN MIST, FOG, *kiri*, *brouillards*—French (all). Fogs and mists become especially prominent as autumn nights cool the moist atmosphere of heavily vegetated areas. While fogs are most common in many areas through the winter, in those same areas they first become prominent in autumn, so **WINTER FOG** and **WINTER MIST** are the appropriate winter topics and **fog** by itself indicates autumn. Some Japanese haiku scholars say that what is called "haze" (*kasumi*) in spring is called "fog" (*kiri*) in autumn, but in English **AUTUMN HAZE** is a topic in itself. See "On Haze, Mist, Fog" following this entry for a discussion of these and related terms. Also called: **crawling mist** (*kruipende mis*—Afrikaans).

Kruipende mis:
die kransduif se koer
verdiep

Crawling mist:
the cooing of the rock pigeon
deepens

Deon Kesting, South Africa [k]

fog burning off . . . white of birch bark

Helen J. Sherry, CA [k]

Premiers brouillards	First fog
Dans la va et vient de vagues	In the waves' coming and going
Une étoile de mer	A starfish

Alain Kervern, Brittany [k]

kiri kizamu	carving fog
oto shite fūsha	the windmill makes a sound
mawari ori	as it turns

Toga Katsuyama, The Netherlands [k]

mountain fog
bites into my cheeks—
cedar smoke

Thomas Fitzsimmons, NM [k]

ON HAZE, MIST, FOG

In modern English the words "haze", "mist", and "fog" have fairly separate meanings with only limited overlapping. "Haze" refers to fine particles of dust, salt, or smoke possibly combined with water and suspended in air, obscuring vision somewhat less than fog. Haze is relatively dry, either blueish-gray or tinged with red, yellow, or brown and usually of more or less uniform density. Meteorologists distinguish between "haze" and "air pollution", the former naturally occurring, the latter of human origin. In North America they see haze primarily as a feature of summer or winter skies.

"Mist" involves water droplets so fine that they may hang suspended in air or may gradually fall to the ground, and is counted as a type of rain by weather professionals. Damp, and usually gray or blue, mist may be of relatively uniform density, or may appear as thin clouds of varying density. "Rising mist" may refer to fog as it lifts from ground level and evaporates. In English, mist normally has no seasonal associations but is spoken of more or less equally at all times of year, as seen in references to "mist", "mists", and "misty" in *Bartlett's Familiar Quotations* and *The Oxford Dictionary of Quotations*.

"Fog" is literally a stratus cloud formed at ground or sea level. Denser than mist or haze, fog obscures objects only a few yards or meters away. Fog tends to form at night; in the morning it appears gray or light blue. It can occur at any time of year but may be seasonal in some locales.

In English the words fog, haze, mist, and their derivatives are all used figuratively to mean vague or indistinct, with "haze" and "hazy" perhaps having a slight edge in frequency.

In Japanese the four most relevant terms are *oboro*, *kasumi*, *kiri*, and *moya*.

Taking the easiest first, *oboro* means obscure or vague, with a tinge of gloom. Thus "hazy" may be the best-suited translation, and almost all translators agree "hazy moon" is best for *oborozuki*. But for *oborozukiyo* (*oboro*—moon-night), most dictionaries and translators offer "misty moonlit night". This accords with English, in which the "hazy" of "hazy moon" refers to the obscuring quality of the atmosphere on a misty night. However, in Japan there seems to be as much haze as mist in springtime.

In the *Japan Great Saijiki,* Kenkichi Yamamoto says "The same phenomenon as the *kasumi* of daytime (morning, noon, evening) at night becomes *oborozukiyo*." For *kasumi*, the better Japanese-English dictionaries list both "haze" and "mist"—giving them equal weight in examples. Most translators seem to have agreed on "haze" as the standard equivalent, perhaps because the verb *kasumu* occurs in many figurative expressions the way "hazy" does in English. But many instances of *kasumi* look a lot more like "mist" than "haze" to this observer, and "haze" in English has few or no spring associations, so I usually specify "spring mist" or "spring haze" in my translations from Japanese, choosing one or the other as seems appropriate to the particular poem. Since *kasumi* almost always occurs together with *haru*, "spring", in classical poetry—often as *harugasumi*—it seems fair to add "spring" in translation, even though in haikai the word *haru* is unnecessary.

On the other end of the year, *kiri* presents a similar difficulty. The word means equally "mist" or "fog"—and in some contexts "spray" as in "sea spray". This seems reasonable, since a rising fog is much like a mist, and all three have to do with water droplets in the air. Just as *kasumi* occurs almost exclusively with spring in classical poems, so *kiri* appears with *aki*, "autumn"—often as *akigiri*. A poem from the *Kokinshū* (#210, anonymous) demonstrates the relationship:

harugasumi	as spring haze
kasumite inishi	obscured the wild geese
karigane wa	when they left
ima zo naku naru	so now their cries ring
akigiri no ue ni	over the autumn mist

In time the two words, *kasumi* and *kiri*, became so associated with spring and autumn, respectively, that the names of the seasons were dropped in haikai, unless one or the other occurred in summer or winter. So, in effect, *kasumi* alone means "that which hangs in the air and obscures vision in spring" and *kiri* alone means something similar for autumn.

As with *kasumi*, I tend to translate *kiri* as "autumn mist" or "fog" depending on internal clues for help. "Autumn mist" avoids confusion with "spring mist" (*kasumi*), and "fog" alone seems sufficient to suggest autumn, given that *fuyu no kiri*—"winter fog (or mist)"—is also a seasonal topic and fog at other times of year may be prefixed by the name of the season.

It is so difficult to say whether *kasumi* is "haze" or "mist" and *kiri* is "mist" or "fog" that a prominent Japanese haiku poet, Miki Saitō, says in the *Japan Great Saijiki*, "On a winter day there may be an enveloping *moya*, but between *moya* and *kiri* or *kasumi* there is no clear distinction. . . . And regarding the situations from which they originate, *kiri* has such expressions as 'stands/gushes/flows' (*tatsu/waku/nagareru*), kasumi is said to 'trail [or hang] over' (*tanabiku*), and *moya* has come to be called 'enveloping' (*tachikomeru*)." (*Moya*, unless accompanied by the name of a season, is not a season word.)

Both *kasumi* and *kiri* appear, with the names of the seasons or in compounds, at other times of year, each season presenting its special problems. Rather than attempting to create an artificial set of rigid English equivalents for all these terms, I have tried to construct a group of entries that covers the territory and allows for some flexibility in translation and interpretation. This is a tentative effort, and I am sure that poets will either choose to ignore it or perhaps construct a set of entries on these topics that makes sense for their regions.

When placing non-Japanese poems containing "mist", "haze", or "fog" (or their equivalents) in this saijiki, I have been guided either by the authors' intentions, if known, or by the content and tone of the poems. In translating such poems I have not added the names of seasons unless they were present in the originals.

To summarize, this saijiki contains the following entries involving equivalents for English "haze", "mist", and "fog" (in order of appearance):

SPRING—THE HEAVENS

HAZY MOON, *oborozuki*. Includes the season word **misty moonlit night** (*oborozukiyo*).
SPRING HAZINESS, SPRING MISTINESS, nighttime, *oboro*.
SPRING HAZE, SPRING MIST, daytime, *kasumi*.

SUMMER—THE HEAVENS

SUMMER MIST, SUMMER FOG, *natsu no kiri*.
SEA FOG, *jiri*.
SUMMER HAZE, SUMMER MIST, *natsugasumi*.

AUTUMN—THE HEAVENS

AUTUMN MIST, FOG, *kiri*.
AUTUMN HAZE. (Not in Japanese saijiki.)

WINTER—THE HEAVENS

WINTER MIST, *fuyugasumi*. Includes **cold mist** (*kangasumi*).
WINTER FOG, *fuyu no kiri*.
WINTER HAZE, *fuyu no moya*.

AUTUMN HAZE (all). Composed of a combination of water droplets with particles of soil and bits of dried vegetation, autumn haze frequently comes to farming areas during and after the harvest. At night it may take on a mistier aspect as dampness increases, resuming a kind of **golden haze** in the heat of the day. See "On Haze, Mist, Fog" at **AUTUMN MIST, FOG** for a discussion of these and related terms.

autumn haze
settles over the fields—
the brook subdued

Warren Wilburton, NY [k]

DEW, *tsuyu* (all). Autumn dew presages winter **FROST**, and images the fleetingness of this life since it is usually gone by midmorning. Also **white dew** (*shiratsuyu*), **morning dew**, **dewdrop** (*ḳapi rosa*—Serbian).

The nails leave lines
On the old morning-glory fence
Dripping dew.

Gerald Robert Vizenor, CA [k]

A circle
glistening with morning dew
no spider

Yūko Andatsu, Japan [k]

nemuritarite
tōge ḳoyu
shiratsuyu no naḳa de

slept enough
I cross the pass
through the white dew

Tohta Kaneko, Japan [k]

U ḳapi rose
Ogledaju se lica
Drvoseča

In a dewdrop
The mirrored face
Of a lumberjack

Vid Vukasovic, Yugoslavia [k]

AUTUMN—THE EARTH

AUTUMN MOUNTAINS, *aki no yama* (all). In Japan skies are clearer in autumn than at any other time of year, making even distant mountains more visible. For North Americans the point of this topic is the deciduous forests in autumn mountains and the foliage thereof. Though the topic **COLORED LEAVES** normally indicates late autumn, the trees at higher altitudes tend to turn earlier. **HILLS DRESSED UP** (*yama yosou*), another all-autumn topic, refers to this (see **HILLS SMILE** in spring).

Walking alone;
only an echo and I—
autumn mountains . . .

Eric Amann, ON [k]

FLOWER FIELD, *hanano* (all). Fields and meadows not under cultivation usually have more plants in flower in autumn than at other times of the year, accounting for this popular haikai topic.

inanaki ga	Horses call
inanaki o yobi	and answer
hanano kaze	flower field wind

Mitsui Suzuki, CA [h]

STUBBLE FIELD (late). Japanese saijiki list **STUBBLE PADDY** (*karita*) for late autumn; it seems appropriate to add comparable topics for other crops where stubble is left on the field after harvest. Also: **cornstubble.**

cornstubble
among the stalks   weeds
and the shadows of weeds

John Wills, TN [k]

AUTUMN—HUMANITY

CANNING (all). A common activity August to October, as one crop after another ripens. Products include **jelly, jam, preserves,** various kinds of **relish,** and many **canned vegetables. Cranberry sauce,** also made at this time, is associated particularly with the early winter observance **THANKSGIVING.** Also: **apple jelly.**

apple jelly poured . . .
I slip a geranium leaf
into each jar

Patricia Neubauer, PA [k]

SCARECROW, *kakashi* (all). When the harvest is brought in, the scarecrow stands revealed in all its tatters. In Japan, and in haikai, there is also a smaller **SEED SCARECROW,** *tanekagashi*, which guards seeded fields in late spring.

shadowplay
grandpa's nose perfect
for the scarecrow

Mitzi Hughes Trout, GA [k/s]

WINNOWING GRAIN (late). Closely related to Japanese *momi suri*, "winnowing rice", but normally "grain" refers to wheat. The wind shift in the poem below may indicate a coming storm.

Winnowing the grain;
the wind shifts slightly from south
to southwest—

Lorraine E. Harr, OR [k]

CRANBERRY RAKING (all). Harvesting cranberries from bogs, as in Massachusetts, New Jersey, Wisconsin, and elsewhere. **CRICKETS** is also an all-autumn topic.

In a cranberry bog
rhythm of the rakes, crying
of the crickets . . .

Virginia Brady Young, CT [k]

KELP-BLADDER POPPING (all). In autumn, along American coasts, various kelps wash up on the beach, and children love to pop their air-pockets.

no children with me
to pop the kelp bladders
ocean's salt-bitter smell

June Hopper Hymas, CA [k]

MUSHROOM GATHERING, *takegari* (late). A traditional autumn activity in Japan. Although some kind of mushroom or another is available in almost every season (see **MOREL** in summer Plants), many of the most prized edible varieties, as well as a number of poisonous kinds, are at their peak in autumn. So gathering mushrooms in autumn has become a traditional literary subject. Also: **mushroom pail.**

pail in hand
I trace the muddy path
of childhood mushrooms

Angelee Deodhar, India [k]

HUNTING COLORED LEAVES, *momijigari* (late). In Japan and most other temperate-zone regions this is a major recreation on the clear days of late autumn, when the leaves of deciduous trees have changed color from greens to reds and yellows. Also: **collecting leaves, maple viewing.**

collecting leaves
the fourth grader
sits on 'em

Raffael de Gruttola, MA [s]

Maple viewing temple
voice
of a baked potato seller.

Pat Donegan, Japan [k]

ATHLETIC MEET, *undōkai* (all). This refers to a field day for all students in a given school. In Japan, where it is a typical autumn activity, such a day features intramural sports of all kinds, large group activities, and perhaps an exhibition of acrobatics or dance.

undōkai	athletic meet
nukuna sono ko wa	don't pass that kid—
kachō no ko	the boss's kid

Piiman ("Paprika"), Japan [s]

AUTUMN—OBSERVANCES

GUY FAWKES DAY (late). Named for the infamous day of 5 November 1605, when members of the Gunpowder Plot planned to blow up the British Houses of Parliament and King James I on Parliament's opening day. The plot was to have continued with an insurrection, and failed when Guy Fawkes was arrested on trying to enter the House of Lords. In celebration of the plot's failure the British burn effigies of Fawkes (old clothes stuffed with rags, papers, straw) on bonfires and send up **fireworks**—the latter being enough to suggest the holiday in England. (Note that otherwise **FIREWORKS** is a summer topic.) Also called: **Bonfire Night**.

stuffing the Guy—
drafts of poems
long ago in print

David Cobb, England [k]

Bonfire Night:
my eyes keep straying
to the full moon.

Stuart Quine, England [k]

BON FESTIVAL, *bon* (early). Formerly held on the 15th of the Seventh [lunar] Month, now generally from the 13th to the 16th of August. One of the most important festivals celebrated in Japan, this **Festival of the Hungry Ghosts** originated in China. Families invite the spirits of departed members home for a specially prepared meal. People visit graves in preparation, and dance to traditional songs and drums. A bonfire may be lit to welcome the spirits, and another to send them on their way, or in seaside districts small lantern-boats will be set afloat on the last evening of the festival.

bon no koto	Bon Festival
tanomi kokusai	favors—overseas phone
denwa kiru	call cut off

Shōin Masago, Japan [k]

GRAVE VISITING, *haka mairi* (early). An important part of preparations for the **BON FESTIVAL** (see previous entry). People ask the spirits of departed family members to come home for the festival. In the following poem, "cowherd" suggests **TANABATA**, the festival of the **weaver maid** and the **herdsman** traditionally held a week earlier. In Tanabata, the star Altair represents the herdsman.

ushikai ni	the cowherd
michi yo keraruru	steered us off the road
haka mairi	grave visiting

Ayako Hosomi, Japan [k]

WELCOME-FIRE, *okuribi* (early). At the time of the **BON FESITVAL** people in Japan typically burn small bonfires at their gates to light the way for the spirits of departed family members as they return for the holiday. Also called: **gate-fire** (*kadobi*).

amerika ni	in America
kadobi taki haha	a welcome-fire lights the gate
mukaekeri	for mother's soul

Mikako Jones, USA [h]

DANCE, *odori* (early). The power of the **BON FESTIVAL** and its dancing is so great that in haikai the simple word "dance" (*odori*) means Bon Festival dancing. Other named dances, of course, would have their own seasons or be common all year. Also: **Bon odori dancers.**

Circle of bon odori
dancers are turning
a puppy also

Hajime Ichinose, Japan [k]

STATE FAIR (all). An annual competitive exhibit of farm and home products, with prizes awarded for the best produce and livestock, best pies and canned goods, etc. Dates vary by state. There are also **county fairs,** which usually precede state fairs.

Alaska State Fair
ninety-four pound cabbage
only second place

Mark Arvid White, AK [s]

ROSH HASHANAH (mid). **Jewish New Year,** the first two days of the seventh lunar month (*Tishri*) in the Hebrew calendar (falling in September or early October, Gregorian), beginning at sunset the day before—as do all Jewish holy days. Features gatherings of family and friends at home, with candle-lighting and prayer, followed by congregational services at a temple. Special prayers asking that God note the efforts and hopes of the people mark this **Day of Remembrance, Yom Hazikkaron.** Scripture commands the blowing of the **shofar** or **ram's horn,** on this, the **new moon of Tishri,** making the horn a primary symbol of the holiday. Observances of the first day often include going to a river, lake, or ocean and emptying one's pockets of lint and crumbs in a symbolic cleansing. Thus begins the ten-day period of renewal, the **High Holy Days,** that ends in **YOM KIPPUR** (see following entry).

Sound of the Ram's horn—
chanting . . . bearded patriarchs
wail in the New Year.

Leroy Kanterman, NY [h]

YOM KIPPUR (mid). Also **Day of Atonement** or **Sabbath of Sabbaths**, the 10th day of the seventh lunar month (*Tishri*) in the Hebrew calendar (usually between mid-September and mid-October, Gregorian). From the previous evening until sundown on the day of Yom Kippur, one abstains from food, drink, washing or anointing the body, wearing leather shoes, sexual intercourse, and any sort of work. The philosopher Philo of Alexandria likened the fast of Yom Kippur before the harvest to the pause for a blessing before a meal. The purpose of the fast is not to chastise the body, but to give all attention to prayer, asking for the Lord's forgiveness for the sins of the past year and to have one's name written in the **Book of Life** for the coming year. This concludes the **High Holy Days** or **Days of Awe** that began with **ROSH HASHANAH** ten days earlier (see above). The end of Yom Kippur may be celebrated with a party to break the fast. **SUKKOT**, a festival of thanksgiving for the harvest, follows at the full moon five days after Yom Kippur—and was no doubt part of the inspiration for **THANKSGIVING DAY** (see winter).

Yom Kippur—
round and round
the lake.

Alexis Rotella, CA [k/s]

breaking the fast
with pizza and soda
on Yom Kippur

Sydell Rosenberg, NY [k/s]

HALLOWEEN, *harowiin* (late). Some 2,000 or more years ago, Celtic priests (Druids) in what is now France celebrated the beginning of winter with the feast of **Samhain**, the Lord of the Dead, early in November—probably at the full moon nearest the midpoint between the autumnal equinox and the winter solstice. (Observed today on 1 November.) They thanked the sun spirit for the harvest, and prepared for winter, and Samhain gathered the souls of the dead and decided their fate for the coming year. Ghosts visited their living relatives briefly to ask for comfort; frustrated spirits sometimes played pranks on the living. To replace non-Christian rites with Christian observances, Roman Catholic popes moved **ALL SAINTS' DAY** from May to 1

November, and called it "Hallowmas" or "All Hallows' Day". This made 31 October **All Hallows' Eve, Hallowe'en,** or **Halloween,** the vigil of the holy day, but early customs persisted. The Scots and Irish people brought Halloween to North America, along with the associated **witches, black cats, bats,** devils and demons, **goblins** and **ghosts, bobbing for apples,** fortunetelling, and **jack-o-lanterns** (pumpkins carved with a face and illuminated). **Trick-or-treating** (children going from door to door, in costume, asking for treats) seems to be a North American addition based on old pre-Christian customs.

Halloween eve . . .
white limbs
of the sycamore

Sharon Lee Shafii, KY [k]

Masked streetcorner witch
kisses me—I wonder if
she's someone I know

Kam Holifield, NY [s]

ALL SAINTS' DAY, *banseisetsu* (late). 1 November. Solemn holy day for Roman Catholics, who attend a mass celebrating the company of the Church Eternal (the saints, who have been accepted into Heaven), and observed by many other Christians. Originally in May, but moved to its present date by Pope Gregory III in the 8th century. Followed by **All Souls' Day,** 2 November, when the church prays for the deliverance of all souls from Purgatory. **HALLOWEEN** (previous entry) is the eve of All Saints' Day. Also called: **Hallowmas, All Hallows' Day.**

All Saints' Day
the Jack-o-lantern
full of gnats

Jane Reichhold, CA [k/s]

AUTUMN—ANIMALS

DEER, *shika* (all). The Japanese or **sika deer** (*Cervus nippon*; "sika" is an internationally recognized common name, though the Japanese word is pronounced *shika*) has been a classical symbol of autumn since the *Kokinshū*. The deer are noted for their mating calls, which begin in September or October when they come down to the lowlands after summering in the mountains. In almost all species the antlers of the male deer, or **buck**, harden in early autumn, making them ready for the competitive battles of the mating season. (Some deer in tropical habitats have no fixed breeding season.)

The lake in moonlight.
The mild muzzle of a deer
touches the water.

Stefan Benea, Romania [h]

BURYING NUTS (all). Squirrels, mainly North American gray tree squirrels (*Sciurus carolinensis*), are seen year-round, but their winter preparations take place in autumn, when they collect acorns and other tree seeds and bury them for later consumption. Also: **squirrel hides nuts.**

the old fort
a squirrel hides something
in its walls

Doris Heitmeyer, NY [k]

HAWKS MIGRATE, *taka wataru* (late). Of the eighteen species of hawks seen in Japan, about half migrate there for winter. **HAWK** (*taka*) by itself is a winter topic.

fun-en no	the chimney-smoke
sora taka wataru	sky has become the path
michi to naru	hawks migrate

Akiko Koga, Japan [k]

MIGRATING BIRDS, *wataridori* (all). From the many species of **SANDPIPER** and **snipe** that begin passing through Japan's estuaries and inland waters in late summer on the way further south (one variety or another transient all autumn and into winter), through the several kinds of **SMALL BIRDS** (*kotori*) that appear in mid autumn, to the **FIRST DUCKS** (*hatsugamo*), **GEESE,** and **ARRIVING CRANES** (*tsuru kitaru*) of late autumn, Japan's skyways have always been rich in birdlife. As this topic suggests, it is often difficult to see just what kinds of birds are on the move. Phrases like **birds migrate** (*tori wataru*), **birds of passage** (*kōchō*), and **traveling birds** (*ryochō*) may be used throughout autumn. In Japanese haikai the word *wataru* (usually translated as "migrate") is reserved for birds coming here—whether to breed or overwinter—or just passing through, while *kaeru* (often translated as "return") means to go from here back to some other place, whether north for the summer to breed, or south for the winter after breeding here. Also: **chains of birds** (*Vogelkette*—German). See the "Note on 'Return'" at the entry for **DEPARTING GEESE** in spring.

Nahe den Wolken	Close to the clouds
die Vogelkette schlängelt	chains of birds twist and turn
gegen den Seewind.	against the sea-wind.

Margret Buerschaper, Germany [k]

SWALLOWS DEPART, *tsubame kaeru, odlaze laste*—Croatian (mid). **SWALLOW** (*tsubame*) in Europe and Japan, **barn swallow** in North America, **house swallow** in some areas, **European swallow** in Africa, **common swallow** in India and the Himalayas, all refer to *Hirundo rustica*—a mid-spring topic, which see for more information. This is one of the most strikingly migratory birds, known almost worldwide for journeys of up to 7,000 miles (11,000 km), from breeding ranges in northern Canada and Alaska and throughout much of North America in summer to non-breeding territories from Central America to Argentina during the northern winter—summer in the south. Similar migrations take place from virtually all of Europe to southern Africa, from the Himalayas to Sri Lanka, from Siberia, China, and Japan to Southeast Asia and Oceana. (Only a few make it to Australia and New Zealand, however, where the welcome swallow, a race of the Pacific swallow [*H. tahitica*], dominates and is only partially migratory.)

Swallows begin leaving the northern hemisphere in August and continue to depart through October, peaking in many areas in September. **CLIFF SWALLOWS DEPART** a little later, making their leave-taking a late-autumn topic. As with other migratory birds, the Japanese phrase *tsubame kaeru* literally means "swallows return"—to that other place. (See the "Note on 'Return'" at the spring entry for **DEPARTING GEESE**.)

odlaze laste—	swallows departing—
u kosi mog oca	in my father's hair
nove sjedine	new grey

Robert Bebek, Croatia [k]

WAXWING, *renjaku* (late). The **Japanese waxwing** (*Bombycilla Japonica)* and **Bohemian waxwing** (*B. garrulus*) common to Japan, continental Europe, and western North America look much alike, and share habits with the **cedar waxwing** (*B. cedrorum*) found in most of North America. In much of central Europe and the southern and western U.S.—and all of Japan—these birds arrive in autumn, as the Japanese saijiki placement suggests. But in large portions of northern Europe and North America, their summer and winter ranges overlap. Generally, they are more noticed in autumn when flocking increases and the foods of the season are berries and fruits which are more likely to be close to humans than the insects, flowers, and sap that make up their summer diet. So it seems to make sense to accept the traditional Japanese position of late autumn, when most people first notice increasing numbers of waxwings. (But note that Japanese waxwings move to mainland Asia for the summer. See also the "Note on 'Return'" at **DEPARTING GEESE**, spring.)

memory loss
but she knows the cedar waxwings
return next week

Nasira Alma, OR [k]

SANDPIPER, SNIPE, *shigi* (all). Sandpipers, curlews, and snipes (family Scolopacidae, about 80 species world-wide) are mainly wading birds found along lake and ocean shorelines and mudflats. In mid-temperate zones we may notice many species only during migrations, but milder temperate zones find some species overwintering. The bird name by itself has traditionally been autumnal, indicating arrival in the poet's region, while "returning" (the usual translation for kaeru) indicates the spring migrations to summer breeding grounds closer to the pole. (See **GEESE**, following.) Some notables include: **sharp-tailed sandpiper** (*uzura-shigi*), **green sandpiper** (*kusa-shigi*), **common sandpiper** (*iso-shigi*), **spotted redshank** (*tsuru-shigi*), **redshank** (*aka-ashi-shigi*), **ruddy turnstone** (*kyōjo-shigi*), **jack snipe** (*ko-shigi*), **common snipe** (*ta-shigi*), **wimbrel** (*chūshaku-shigi*).

ebb tide
sandpipers skitter
across her ashes

Jerry Kilbride, CA [k]

the turnstone's cry
amidst the beach-wrack
his cinnabar legs

June Hopper Hymas, CA [k]

GEESE, *kari* (late). Many geese fly into Japan to overwinter. Also called **wild geese** (*karigane*) and **geese migrate** (*kari wataru*). See **DEPARTING GEESE** in spring, and the "Note on 'Return'" at that entry.

hashi kurete	dusk on the bridge
karigane no sora	the sky still left
nokorikeri	for the wild geese

Tokihiko Kusama, Japan [k]

kari no kazu	a number of geese
watarite sora ni	were migrating—in the sky
mio mo nashi	not even a wake

Sumio Mori, Japan [k]

isshun no	a moment when
kari no tsubasa ga	wings of wild geese
kumo o kesu	erase the clouds

Jack Stamm, Japan [k]

FIRST OYSTER (late). **OYSTERS** form an important part of the diet all winter in many parts of the world, but when the first oysters arrive in the markets in late autumn oyster-lovers rejoice. The topics and season words that follow all belong in winter. The **eastern oyster** (*Crassostrea virginica*; "eastern" refers to eastern U.S.) is the preferred variety for **OYSTERS ON THE HALF-SHELL**, an excellent seafood served raw. (As a way of preparing and serving food this is a topic in the Humanity category rather then a season word under Animals.) The **Japanese** or **giant Pacific oyster** (*C. gigas*, Japanese *kaki*) has been cultivated along the U.S. Pacific coast, where we also have a native **Pacific oyster** (*Ostrea lurida*), a bit smaller and said to have better flavor. A number of different commercial oysters are canned and used in soups and **OYSTER STEW**, another all-winter dish.

first oysters
  shadows of sea gulls reel
on the market wall

Ellen Compton, DC [k]

AUTUMN BUTTERFLY, *aki no chō* (all). Some Japanese saijiki note that there are no butterflies with first flights in autumn, so the common Japanese image in autumn is of a bedraggled **old butterfly** (*oichō*) that survives from one of the summer flights. In fact, there are a number of butterflies with spring or summer flights that have new flights in autumn. There are also a few prominent butterflies that fly only in autumn; among the Lycaenidae these include Britain's **brown hairstreak** (*Thecla betulae*) and the Eurasian **long-tailed blue** (*uranamishijimi, Lampides boeticus*)—which does appear in Japan. (Confusingly, the Japanese apply the same common name to both the long-tailed blue and the **common blue**, which see under **SUMMER BUTTERFLY**.) Two kinds of **angled sulphur** (*Anteos sp.*) represent the Pieridae in North American autumns. Autumnal skippers in North America include the **Leonardus skipper** (*Hesperia leonardus*) of the eastern U.S. and Canada, and the **Pawnee skipper** (*H. Pawnee*) of the plains states, both found August to September.

The migratory monarch (*Danaus plexippus*) is noted in autumn in the phrase **monarchs leaving**, that is, heading south. Another interesting case is the **Camberwell beauty** (*Nymphalis antiopa*), seen only in autumn in the British Isles, where it therefore signifies autumn. But the very same species, known in North America as the **MOURNING CLOAK**, flies year-round in most of the U.S., yielding an entry in the all-year section of this saijiki. See also the entry for **BUTTERFLY** in spring and the essay "Butterflies Throughout the Year" that follows it, as well as entries for **SUMMER** and **WINTER BUTTERFLY**.

Note: The poem below echoes a phrase from the *Manyōshū*, *iyoyo*, where it is found in the famous lament by Ōtomo no Tabito for his wife (poem number 793): "Come to know/ what an empty thing/ this world is—/ still more and more/ deeply have I sorrowed." (*Yo no naka wa munashiki mono to shiru toki shi iyoyo masumasu kanashikarikeri.*)

iyoyo ki ni	more and more yellow—
iyoyo isogeri	more and more hastened
aki no chō	the autumn butterfly

Yoshiko Yamashita, Japan [k]

DRAGONFLY, *tonbo*, *libel*—Dutch (all). Order Odonata, suborder Anisoptera. The dragonfly is a powerful image with its large eyes, thick body, and wings reaching a spread of 5" (12.5 cm) in some species, though 2-3" (5-7.5 cm) is more usual. Emerging in mid summer but most prominent in autumn, a number of species are called **darners, darning needles,** or **skimmers.** They come in many colors and sizes. **RED DRAGONFLY**, referring to a group of red-bodied skimmers with about 2" (5 cm) wingspans (Japanese *akatonbo* or *akane*; *Sympetrum sp.*), is often given status as an autumn topic on its own. A number of skimmers appear in summer, as recognized in the topic **SUMMER SKIMMER** (*natsu-akane*). Dragonflies hold their wings spread to the side when at rest. The dragonfly may be distinguished from its more slender, smaller, and usually jewel-like cousin the **DAMSELFLY** (a summer topic), which usually holds its wings together next to or over the body when at rest.

spot of sunlight—
on a blade of grass the dragonfly
changes its grip

Lee Gurga, IL [k]

libellenogen	dragonfly eyes
aan weerskanten van een halm	on both sides of a blade
bedacht op rivalen	watching for rivals

Marianne Kiauta, The Netherlands [k/s]

EPHEMERA, *kagerō* (early). An order of insects that live only a day or so as adults; associated with fresh water. Called "mayflies" in the British Isles and North America, they are also common in Australia and New Zealand, where they provide food for trout introduced from North America, especially in early summer and early autumn. Japanese varieties appear mainly from July to September, and have been recognized as an early autumn phenomenon since Bashō's day. Though the words refer to the same group of insects, I suggest that in haikai "ephemera" be reserved for early autumn and "mayfly" for summer, and that the Japanese insect *kagerō* always be translated as "ephemera". (Not to be confused with the spring topic **HEAT SHIMMER**, Japanese *kagerō*, visual distortion over a heated surface; or with the autumn topic **GOSSAMER**, also sometimes called *kagerō* in Japanese.) More on ephemera at **MAYFLIES** (summer). Also called **dayflies**.

kagerō no	the ephemera
setsuna setsuna no	moment by moment
kage nagaru	shadows flow

Ōran Shimizu, Japan [k]

CRICKET, *kōrogi*, *zrikavac*—Croatian (all). *Gryllus sp*. All crickets are noted for males that "sing" by rubbing special organs on their fore wings together. The common **field cricket** of North America (G. pennsylvanicus) and **Chinese cricket** of Asia (*G. mitratus*) are representative. Classified separately and each accorded a topic on its own are the **TREE CRICKET** (Japanese *kantan, Oecanthus sp.*), the **BELL**

CRICKET (*suzumushi, Homoeogryllus japonicus*) and the **PINE CRICKET** (*matsumushi, Madasumma marmorata*), all specific to early autumn. The latter pair provides an interesting example: According to Edward G. Seidensticker in his translation of *The Tale of Genji*, "The bell cricket of the Heian Period [794–1185] seems to have been what is today called the pine cricket . . . and the Heian pine cricket has become the bell cricket." Thus the difficulty of identifying anything solely by its common name. Today the Japanese describe the singing of the Chinese cricket as *korokoro*; that of the tree cricket as *fuhi, ro—fuhi, ro*; with *riin-riin* representing the bell cricket; and *chinchirorin* for the pine cricket. They say the songs of the last two are especially beautiful. Crickets are also called *chichiro* and other common names in Japanese.

Mali zrikavac	Little cricket
sjetio se ljubavi	remembered love
u samo podne.	just at noon.

Dragan Vučetć, Croatia [k/s]

chichiro naku	a cricket chirps
koki de hajimeshi	my seventies begun
kuriyagoto	with kitchen chores

Meiga Higashi, Japan [k]

GRASSHOPPER, LOCUST, *batta*, *inago*, *skakavac*—Croatian (all). Family Acrididae. Closely related to the nocturnal crickets, grasshoppers are mainly diurnal. Like crickets, they "sing" by rubbing together wings or wings and legs; their songs are lower pitched than those of crickets. As their name suggests, grasshoppers move from place to place mainly by hopping. Japanese saijiki include *batta* and *inago* and a number of related kinds as separate autumn topics. Batta refers to the larger of the **short-horned grasshoppers**, particularly the brown-to-black **lubber grasshoppers**, also called **locusts**, which reach 2–3" (50–75 mm) long, and can be very destructive of crops. If sufficient numbers arrive at maturity at the same time in the same region, they may form swarms of millions and fly over great distances, descending on crops along the way and stripping every living plant of flower, fruit, and leaf. This was one of the great plagues of Egypt in the account of the Exodus of the

Jews. *Inago* includes medium-sized green grasshoppers of the short-horned family, about 1.5" (3 cm) long. The **PYGMY GRASSHOPPERS** (family Tetrigidae)—a half-inch (13 mm) or shorter—which are seen mainly in spring and early summer, have not made it into traditional saijiki, though at least one species, *Acrydium japonicum*, is known in Japan. The order Orthoptera includes more than 23,000 species of grasshoppers, crickets, and katydids. Since common names frequently differ from place to place or over time (see **CRICKET**, above), and types plentiful in one part of the globe do not appear in others, I have made no attempt to include all the varieties listed in Japanese saijiki. Comparing traditional saijiki with North American field guides indicates that the more obvious grasshoppers in both regions appear in late summer and become prominent in autumn, so the placement in the Japanese saijiki seems universal enough to adopt here.

Utoploj livadi	On a warm meadow
nadskakuju se	compete in jumping a boy
dječak i skakavac.	and a grasshopper.

Ivan Kovačeveć, Croatia [k]

GOSSAMER, *yūshi* (mid-late). The Japanese literally says **wandering threads.** Gossamer is **spider silk** that has been let out into the breeze by the young of small spiders—particulary members of the family Linyphiidae. Clinging to their threads, the spiderlings let go of their perches to drift on air currents, and are occasionally carried as high as 10,000' (3,000 m) or more and perhaps for miles before landing to find new homes. The phenomenon occurs on warm, sunny days from early spring to late autumn over grasslands and meadows. Most Japanese saijiki include *yūshi* under **HEAT SHIMMER** (*kagerō*) in spring, and gossammer is sometimes called *kagerō* in Japanese, but the most careful authorities show *yūshi* in late autumn. In North America it is most prominent in mid and late autumn. Also called: **ballon spiders, wild horses** (a literal translation of the Japanese *yaba*).

Blue sky . . .
higher and higher
goes the spider silk

Robert Mainone, MI [k]

AUTUMN—PLANTS

WITCH HAZEL BLOSSOMS (late). (*Hamamelis sp.*) One of the last shrubs or small trees of eastern North America to blossom, with small, thin-petalled yellow flowers. **JAPANESE WITCH HAZEL,** or *mansaku* (*H. japonicus*), is an early-spring topic.

leaves turning . . .
the witch hazel's new
hidden blossoms

William J. Higginson, NM [h]

EUCALYPTUS BLOSSOMS (all). *Eucalyptus sp*. Many types are called **gum tree**. This genus of more than 500 substantial broad-leafed evergreen trees in the Myrtle family originates in Australia. Many species are now widely introduced in tropical and sub-tropical regions around the globe, including parts of Africa, Asia, Europe, and the Americas, where they are found in California, Florida, Puerto Rico, and many Central and South American countries. The well-known **bluegum** or **Tasmanian bluegum** (*E. globulus*) grows to 120' (37 m) and has creamy white blossoms autumn through spring, depending on locale; it is the official flower of the Australian state of Tasmania, and is widely grown in California. The **red flowering gum** (*E. ficifolia*, to 40' [12 m]) and **beakpod eucalyptus** (*E. robusta*, to 90' [27 m]) have striking flowers of crimson and cream, respectively, blooming late summer to spring.

Flower buds of all three of these species release an operculum or "lid" (outer tip of the calyx) as they begin to blossom. The lids are also called: **eucalyptus caps** (*sombreritos de eucaliptos*—Spanish).

Desde los eucaliptos,	From the eucalyptuses,
enanos invisibles	invisible dwarfs
dejan caer sus sombreritos.	let their caps fall.

Fernando Alegria, Chile [h/s]

QUINCE, *boke no mi* (early). *Chaenomeles sp*. The **Japanese flowering quince** or **japonica** (*C. japonica*) and the **common quince** (*C. vulgaris*) share the same timetable, with bloom starting in late spring and fruit ripening in early to mid autumn. Both fruits are rather bitter for eating out of hand, but add tang to cooked apple dishes and make excellent jams and jellies. (Until recently the genus was called *Cydonia*; at one time quinces were thought to be part of the *Pyrus* genus along with pears.)

boke no mi o	setting down the quince
yotabi oki naoshi	for the fourth time
mite mo	but still . . .

Dhugal Lindsay, Australia [k/s]

PEACH, *momo* (early). A most popular fruit, peaking in early autumn. In Japan it brings to mind the famous legend of Momotarō, a child born of a peach found floating in a river. The **nectarine** is included under this topic.

slicing
longitude and latitude
into the peach

Suezan Aikins, NS [k]

nectarine
warm and sweet
down to the stone

Susan Rowley, England [k]

PERSIMMON, *kaki* (late). The bright pinkish-orange fruit of the **Japanese persimmon** (*Diospyros kaki*), also now called **kaki** in English, is highly prized world-wide for its tangy pulp, which is quite astringent until fully ripe and a bit soft. Waiting for persimmons to ripen is a classic test of patience in Japan. The American **common persimmon** or **wild persimmon** (*D. virginiana*) provided a popular fruit in colonial times and still grows wild throughout the southeastern U.S., but has now been generally replaced at the market by the kaki. Israeli farmers have developed a variety called **sharon fruit,** seedless and ripe while still firm. Kaki may be the most frequently mentioned fruit in haikai, especially associated with the poet Shiki Masaoka.

kaki o mogu	I pluck persimmons
ittō ittō	like dousing lamps
kesu gotoku	one by one

Yoshiko Yoshino, Japan [k]

kaki kueba	Eating a persimmon
kaki no suki naru	I remember the one
hito omou	who loved this taste

Mitsui Suzuki, CA [k]

wild persimmons . . .
a woman at the roadside
wiggles her last tooth

Peggy Willis Lyles, SC [k/s]

APPLE, *ringo* (late). The main group of domestic apples, *Malus sp.*, comes from Eurasia, while native North American **crabapples** are sometimes placed under the *Pyrus* genus. The apple is probably the first autumn fruit one thinks of, its many varieties eaten raw, cooked in pie and cobbler, made into jelly, pressed into **cider**, and featured in games associated with **HALLOWEEN** (see under autumn Observances). In the second poem below "scrumping" means stealing apples, usually a childhood activity.

A piece of
apple lying on the lawn
the baby's first step

Ken'ichi Yamamoto, Japan [k]

Apple boughs heavy
Old men go scrumping again—
So many summers

Cicely Hill, England [k]

a crab apple
from the highest branch
rattles down the rain spout

Michael Dylan Welch, CA [k]

GRAPES, *budō*, *les raisins*—French (mid). Modern global markets enable us to buy grapes most of the year, but their season is mid autumn. The word "grape" also suggests its most famous product, wine.

moonlight gleaming
on the grapes—the lovers
can't stop laughing

Penny Harter, NM [k/s]

D'avoir trop goûté	Having too much
Les raisins d'automne amers,	tasted autumn's bitter grapes
Ivre mort je rêve.	dead drunk I dream.

Georges C. Friedenkraft, France [k/s]

CHESTNUT, *kuri* (late). The edible fruit of the chestnut tree (*Castanea sp.*). **ROASTING CHESTNUTS** is a late autumn activity in Japan, though Americans may associate it with winter because of "A Christmas Song", which begins "Chestnuts roasting on an open fire . . ." The American chestnut (*C. dentata*) is now virtually extinct, but replaced by Asian species. Not to be confused with the poisonous **horsechestnut** (*tochi no mi, Aesculus sp.*), available late autumn and used in the children's late-autumn game of **conkers**.*

reirō to	brilliantly
daichi ni zaseri	on the earth there sits
kesa no kuri	this morning's chestnut

Sonō Uchida, Japan [k]

Between tombstones
eagerly gathering
chestnuts.

Gusta van Gulick, The Netherlands [k]

WALNUT, *kurumi*, *Walnuß*—German (late). *Juglans sp.* The most common American walnut, the **black walnut** (*J. nigra*), and that native to Japan, *J. mandshurica*, both yield their prized fruit in late autumn.

te ni miteri	a palm-full
oto no samishiki	their sound so desolate
kurumitachi	these walnuts

Tokihiko Kusama, Japan [k]

Lau noch der Abend.	Still mild, the evening.
Der Baum wirft mir die Walnuß	The tree flings me a walnut
direkt vor den Fuß.	right to my foot.

Margret Buerschaper, Germany [k]

ROSE OF SHARON, *mukuge* (early). *Hibiscus syriacus.* Another common name in English is **hibiscus.** Blossoms white, pink, or bluish mauve, on a substantial bush or shrub sometimes used for hedges. Note that in some areas "rose of Sharon" is also a common name for the yellow-flowered, low-growing plant known as **ST. JOHNSWORT** (Japanese *otogirisō, Hypericum sp.*), a healing herb also of early autumn, and that *Hibiscus syriacus* is called **althea** in some areas, where it may be confused with the mid-summer hollyhock (*Althaea rosea*). Also, the foreign-derived Japanese word *haibisukasu* refers to the related **CHINA ROSE** (*Hibiscus rosa-sinensis*), blooming in late summer. With all that, is it any wonder that translations of Bashō's famous verse on the horse eating the *mukuge* vary so? For those interested, Bashō painted a color portrait of a flowering plant to accompany the poem; it appears to be *Hibiscus syriacus.*

in its voice
a fledgling hummingbird finds
the hibiscus' depth

Phyllis Walsh, WI [k]

LEMON, *remon* (late). *Citrus limon*. The familiar yellow fruit of a 10–20' (3–6 m) evergreen tree typically grown in the subtropics and milder portions of the temperate zones. Lemon trees may bloom year-round under suitable conditions, but more commonly bloom in spring and autumn, bearing fruit in summer and late autumn into winter. High in vitamin C, lemons are sour to taste. They provide the basis for the refreshing summer drink **LEMONADE** (*remonsui, remonēdo*) and flavoring used in preparing foods ranging from meats to preserves and desserts.

remon kajiru	nibbling a lemon
tsuma ni wakare o	a segment to my spouse
iidasezu	to shut him up

Mariko Nishide, The Netherlands [k/s]

COLORED LEAVES, *momiji* (late). In Japanese the most common characters for *momiji* suggest **red leaves**, but the term may also be written with characters meaning **yellow leaves**. Written as "red leaves" the characters refer to the red-turned leaves of some maples, but can be applied collectively to all leaves that are most noted to change color in late autumn. Other colors may be included under this topic, such as **copper leaves**, and so on.

This is a very popular topic, the autumnal equivalent of **BLOSSOMS** in late spring. In the *Japan Great Saijiki* the entry for *momiji* is one of the most extensive, detailing its history as the epitome of autumn from the *Manyōshū* to the present. This is immediately followed by a four-page photo essay on the theme in the visual arts and textiles for kimono.

There are also numerous other entries on closely related topics. In addition to those noted below we have **FIRST COLORED LEAVES** (*hatsu momiji*, mid autumn); **SHINING LEAVES** (*teriha*, late); and **ASSORTED COLORED LEAVES** (*zōki momiji*, late), which suggests the leaves of a grove or woods of mixed trees. The single word **MAPLE** (*kaede*) in haikai means the red leaves of maples in late autumn. (Compare the phrase "full moon" referring specifically to the full moon of mid autumn.) And many other trees are named with the colors of their leaves in mid or late autumn.

no tree, no yard
but from my walk colored leaves
  to hold and press

L. A. Davidson, NY [k]

Copper leaves,
tier on top of tier,
tinkling, tinkling.

Stephen C. Maassen, MO [h]

LEAVES TURNING COLOR, *usumomiji* (mid). The Japanese literally says **thinly colored leaves.** While colored leaves dominate the October woods in the north temperate zone, many people living in such an area keep a sharp lookout for the earliest turning leaves of September, which while colorful still retain some of their original green. The closely related topic **FIRST COLORED LEAVES** (*hatsu momiji*, mid autumn) indicates leaves that have just fully turned color.

leaves turning color
I grab all the words I can
to end my novel

Leatrice Lifshitz, NY [k]

YELLOW LEAVES, *kōyō* (late). The yellows of ash, aspen, beech, birch, some cherries, chestnut, elm, hickory, and so on. Also, some North American maples turn yellow instead of red. (See also **YELLOW LEAVES DROP,** below.) Since **COLORED LEAVES** (above) is usually understood to mean "red leaves" or all colored leaves collectively, "yellow leaves" can be a topic in its own right. Also: **yellowing woods.**

yellowing woods—
sapling shadow stripes
on the bent grass

Sharon Hammer Baker, OH [k]

LEAVES START TO FALL, *momiji katsu chiru* (late). The Japanese literally says **leaves colored and falling,** and often effectively means **col-**

ored leaves start to fall. The leaves of most deciduous trees begin falling while still colored—in late autumn—the phenomenon indicated here. A famous song provides the appropriate title for this topic: "When autumn **leaves start to fall**" (*konoha katsu chiru*). Note, however, that **COLORED LEAVES FALL** (*momiji chiru*, written with the characters for and assuming the meaning "red leaves fall") is an early-winter topic.

In effect, while we normally think of "falling leaves" as autumnal, in haikai one must somehow specify that the leaves in question are just beginning to fall or are falling early to keep the image in autumn. Otherwise the leaves must be specified as yellow (see the entry **YELLOW LEAVES DROP** immediately below), or must be specific kinds of leaves falling or fallen in their appropriate seasons, such as **FALLEN EVERGREEN LEAVES** (*tokiwagi ochiba,* early summer), **ONE PAWLONIA LEAF** (*kiri hitoha,* early autumn), and **WILLOW LEAVES FALL** (*yanagi chiru,* mid autumn). Note that **FALLEN LEAVES** (*ochiba*) is an all-winter topic.

momiji katsu	colored leaves
chirinu jizai ni	have started to fall—freely
mizu hashiri	the water runs

Aya Shōbu, Japan [h]

momiji katsu	leaves colored
chiru ya kōji no	and falling . . . the weighing
hakari-uri	and selling of yeast

Akane Yamamoto, Japan [k]

YELLOW LEAVES DROP, *kōraku* (late). Typical images of "yellow leaves" in Japan include the foliage of various oak, zelkova, and gingko trees. In North America we would add elm, beech, birch, hickory, black walnut, honeylocust, aspen, and cottonwood, at least. "Gold leaves" is a frequent alternative for "yellow leaves", especially for aspens. In Japanese haikai this topic brings to mind particularly falling gingko leaves. Also called: **trees toss gold.**

Autumn trees
toss gold
on the poor man's grave

Veronica Haughey, New Zealand [k/s]

COLORED OAK LEAVES, *kashiwa momiji* (late). Colored oak leaves (*Quercus sp.*) rate their own topic. In Japan most of the well-known oaks turn yellow, but **flaming oak** suggests one of the many North American species that turn red.

twigs and leaves crackle
wind rising on the hilltop
a flaming oak

Marshall Hryciuk, ON [h]

NUTS AND SEEDS, *ko no mi* (all). Literally, the "fruits of trees" in Japanese; once a mainstay of human life, they still provide many of the delicacies enjoyed in autumn and winter.

ko no mi hirou	as I gather nuts
ware tōmaki ni	around me in distant circles
yūgarasu	evening ravens

Yoshiko Yoshino, Japan [k]

ACORN, *donguri*, *eichel*—German, *eikel*—Dutch (late). Famed for the size and strength of the oak tree that grows from this small seed. The following poem includes a haikai twist: in German slang *eichel* also refers to the glans penis.

dämmern	shimmer
im tropfen	in the drop
an der eichel	on the acorn

finley m taylor, FL [k/s]

op eigen tijden	in their own time
breken eikels de stilte	acorns break the stillness
van een leien dak	of a slate roof

Anton Gerits, The Netherlands [k/s]

GINKGO NUT, *ginnan* (late). This bitter astringent fruit, slightly toxic, is used in Chinese medicine. Also called **ginkgo fruit** or **fruit of the ginkgo** (*ichō no mi* or *ginnan no mi*).

ginnan no	ginkgo nuts'
kara waru oto ya	shells cracking sound . . .
yoru no ame	night rain

Yasuaki Matsuo, Japan [k]

ginnan no	fruit of the ginkgo
mi no tera-tera to	so bright and shiny
tsukiyo kana	this moonlit night

Ryūta Iida, Japan [h]

OAK GALL, *hyon no mi* (late). These are the leaf galls of a type of live oak (Japanese *isunoki, Distylium racemosum*) found in southwestern Honshu, Shikoku, Kyushu, and Okinawa. The galls dry out in autumn after the gall wasps vacate, leaving their tunnels behind. Children pick the leaves and blow through the galls, making a "hyuu-hyuu" sound. Also called: **oak-gall flute** (*hyon no fue*), **monkey-flute** (*sarubue*).

hyon no fue	when you blow
fukeba nami-oto	a gall-flute sound of waves
kaze no oto	the sound of wind

Teiko Inahata, Japan [k]

VIRGINIA CREEPER (all). (*Parthenocissus quinquefolia*) Also called **five-fingered ivy.** A woody climbing vine of the grape family common in North American woods, especially among evergreens, and on disturbed ground at woods' and fields' edges, it is cultivated in Europe. Its leaves turn a brilliant red in autumn. Innocuous greenish blossoms appear in summer, followed by small berries ripening to blue-black in late autumn. Sometimes called **woodbine**, but this is also a common British name—used by Shakespeare and other authors—for **HONEYSUCKLE** (Japanese *suikazura no hana, Lonicera sp.*), an early summer topic.

A morning moon, too,
westering along the stream;
woodbine turning red

Robert Spiess, WI [k]

BANANA TREE, *bashō*, *bananier*—Romanian (all). *Musa sp.* In Japanese poetry "banana tree" refers to a variety of banana or **plantain tree** bearing inedible fruit and cultivated for its aesthetic value. The 10' (3 m) long **banana leaves** easily tear in wind and rain, and tattered strips hang from the central veins; they make a pleasing rustling sound in a breeze. By the end of autumn the leaves are usually quite ripped and dried out, giving **TORN BANANA LEAVES** (*yare bashō*) its own status as a late-autumn topic. The related topics **GREEN BANANA LEAVES** (*aobashō*, mid summer) and **BANANA BLOSSOMS** (*bashō no hana*, late summer) appear less often. The banana tree was especially prized by the poet Bashō who elevated haikai from doggerel and made it the major genre of Japanese poetry for the next three hundred years. Knowing his fondness for it, his disciples kept a banana tree planted next to his cottage on the bank of the Fukagawa river in Edo. Over the years he occupied three different cottages, each of which became known as the "Banana Tree Cottage" (*bashō-an*). Bashō eventually took his name from the cottage and its plant. Whether speaking of this or another variety, a haikai poet who mentions the banana tree draws on this heritage. Note that the **BANANA** fruit is an all-year topic, and carries little of this association.

Din bananier	Of the banana tree
au făcut o statuie:	they have made a statue:
gaiţ-n sobor.	jays gathering.

Manuela Miga, Romania [k]

ORCHID, *ran*, *orkhidei*—Russian (mid). Members of the family Orchidaceae, which contains over 17,000 species and varieties. Many orchids have been long cultivated; many more grow wild. In haikai "orchid" by itself refers to varieties that bloom in mid autumn. Some Chinese orchids are noted for their sweet fragrance, making **orchid scent** (*ran no ka*) also a season word. Several orchids are prominent enough to be topics themselves, each with its own blooming time, such as the **LADY'S SLIPPER** (Japanese *atsumorisō*, *Cypripedium sp.*) of mid summer.

Orkhidei! Sred' nikh—	Orchids! Among them—
devitsa v ochkakh, pytajushchajasja	a girl with glasses, attempting
perepisat' vse nazvanija!	to copy all the names!

Alexey V. Andreyev, Russia [s]

MORNING-GLORY, *asagao, purperwinde*—Afrikaans (early). *Ipomoea sp.*. Most garden and wild varieties bloom July to October, with the common bright blue morning-glory peaking in August.

just as it closes . . .
a small bug enters
the morning-glory

Geri Barton, NY [k]

Uit buurman se tuin	From a neighbor's garden
kom ellelang lote van	come yard-long lots of
sy purperwinde.	his morning-glory.

Eisina Callard, Namibia [k/s]

COSMOS, *kosumosu* (mid). *Cosmos bipinnatus*. The common garden cosmos, originally from Mexico; most effectively planted in early summer for fall bloom. The plants grow 2–4' (60–120 cm) tall, with bright pink, cerise, and white daisylike blossoms.

This remote classroom
where my father taught when young
—the cosmos flowers

Kōko Katō, Japan [k]

CHRYSANTHEMUM, *kiku* (all). A favorite flower of the Japanese; a design based on it forms the Imperial crest. In Japanese the word is likely to refer to white chrysanthemums unless **yellow chrysanthemums,** *kigiku*, is specified.

every way
the wind blows
chrysanthemums

Gary Hotham, MD [h]

ASTER, *shion* (mid). The asters make up a large part of the family Compositae, including a number of cultivated and wild plants. Among fall-blooming garden asters are the many hybrids developed from *Aster novae-belgii*, most with blue flowers, called the **New York aster** in the U.S. and the **Michaelmas daisy** in England. There are also several blue and lavender-to-purple flowered wild species in Japan, England, and the U.S. that bloom in autumn. The cultivated **CHINA ASTER** (Japanese *ezogiku, Callistephus sinensis*) is a late-summer topic with single, double, and pompom-shaped flowers in several colors; this is the flower sometimes called *asutā* in Japanese.

grandmother knitting
silver bowl of blue asters
on a lace doily

Charles B. Dickson, GA [h]

WATERMELON, *suika* (early). Renowned for their sweet juice and black seeds, watermelons are available from late summer through early autumn. **WATERMELON BLOSSOM,** *suika no hana*, belongs to mid summer; the popular Japanese game of **WATERMELON SPLITTING,** *suika wari*, and **CHILLED MELON,** *hiyashi uri* (which includes **watermelon cooling,** *suika hiyasu*), go with late summer.

family reunion
child's face lost
in watermelon

Addie Adam, FL [k]

WINTER MELON (all). *Cucumis melo* varieties. Usually refers to **casaba, crenshaw,** and **honeydew** melons, varieties of the *inodorus* melon group. Harvested in autumn and stored properly, they can be enjoyed through the winter. See also: **MELON** in Summer.

Admiring
the honeydew . . . still
she won't cut it.

S. T. Malthorne, Australia [s]

PUMPKIN, *kabocha* (all). Perhaps the most typical fruit of autumn after the **APPLE**, the pumpkin belongs to the large genus *Cucurbita*, which includes numerous squashes. In North America the word "squash" is sometimes used for pumpkin, though **squash** by itself is usually a synonym for **SUMMER SQUASH**, a late-summer topic.

Laughing loudly
As they harvest pumpkins—
The homely couple

Marco Fraticelli, PQ [k/s]

PIGEON BARLEY, *hatomugi* (late). This grain was introduced into Japan from the tropics in the early eighteenth century, and is an edible variety of the grass known in English as **JOB'S-TEARS** (*Coix lacryma-jobi*), and in Japanese as **rosary beads** (*juzudama*)—also a late-autumn topic.

hatomugi ya	pigeon barley . . .
naishobanashi no	those secret whisperings
kikitorezu	cannot be caught

Sumiko Takahata, Japan [k]

BUSH CLOVER, *hagi* (early). *Lespedeza bicolor.* In haikai this refers to **mountain bush clover** (*yamahagi*), which yields bright pink blossoms on bushy plants up to 6' (2 m) high from July through September. From the earliest times, bush clover has been counted one of the **SEVEN HERBS OF AUTUMN** (*aki no nanakusa*, an all-autumn topic) by Japanese poets. The others are: **WILD PINK** (*nadeshiko*, now considered late summer; it blooms July to October), **CHINESE AGRIMONY** or **agueweed** (*fujibakama*, early autumn), **"MAIDENFLOWER"** (*ominaeshi*, early), **CHINESE BELLFLOWER** (*kikyō*, early) **KUDZU BLOSSOMS** (*kuzu no hana*, early), and **PAMPAS GRASS** (*susuki*, all).

iete ima	all better now
hashitte mitashi	ran out to see
hagi sakinu	bush clover blooming

Yasuko Nederkoorn, The Netherlands [k]

GOLDENROD, *awadachisō* (early). There are many *Solidago* species in North America and Eurasia, most blooming August to October, but several earlier or later. A common sign of autumn's arrival.

escaped canary—
hearing his song somewhere
in the goldenrod

Patricia Neubauer, PA [k/s]

REED PLUMES, *ashi no howata*, *rietpluimen*—Dutch (late). When the **REED BLOSSOMS** (*ashi no hana*) of mid autumn have gone to seed, cottony tufts shine above the brown of the dried reeds.

Rietpluimen buigen	Bowing reed plumes
de zonsondergang tegemoet	encounter the sunset
in de waterspiegel.	in the water's surface.

Lieve Mignon, Belgium [k]

PARTRIDGEBERRY (all). *Mitchella repens.* After its twin-blossoming white or pinkish flowers from May to July, the partridgeberry produces a scarlet (sometimes white) edible berry with two blossom-scars. This trailing creeper is common in the woods of eastern Canada and U.S. south to the mid-Atlantic states. Also called **running box** because its round, shiny leaves resemble those of the box hedge. The name **TWIN-BERRY** is sometimes applied to this and other plants producing berries with two blossom-scars, but is correctly the common name of some members of the honeysuckle family (*Lornicera sp.*) found in the mountains of the western U.S. and Canada and ripening at about the same time.

slant of sun across the forest floor to a partridgeberry

Anita Virgil, VA [k]

CHAMOMILE, *kamilice*—Serbian, (early). *Anthemis nobilis*. Also spelled **camomile**, this well-known medicinal plant blooms in August and September.

Zagledan u cvet	Absorbed by blooming
kamilice. Nešto me	camomile. The old woman
pitala starica.	asks me something.

Milijan Despotović, Yugoslavia [k/s]

COCKLEBUR, *onamomi* (early). *Xanthium strumarium*. Known in England as **bur-weed** this 2' (60 cm) high plant has minute flowers and small, prickly fruits—**burrs** or **burs**—August to October that easily stick to fur and cloth, thus helping to strew the plant far and wide on waste and disturbed ground. Also called **cockle burr**.

In the dog's coarse fur,
A few yellow cockle burrs
And the dusty heat.

Christopher Thorsen, CA [k]

RED SPIDER LILY, *manjushage* (mid). *Lycoris radiata*. This bulb of the Amaryllis family blooms around the time of the autumnal equinox, and is also called **Higan flower** (*higanbana*) and **dead-person flower** (*shibito-bana*) in Japanese. After the bright red-orange flowers, which rise on straight stalks to about 16" (40 cm) and then die down, the leaves appear.

AUTUMN HIGAN (*akihigan*), the week surrounding the **AUTUMNAL EQUINOX** (*shūbun*) on 22 or 23 September, like the similar week of mid-spring **HIGAN**, is a time of grave-visiting and offering respect, including Buddhist ceremonies, to one's forebears. An old saying that no heat or cold lasts through Higan, recognizes that the seasonal cycle has shifted to the mid-point between the extremes.

manjushage	red spider lily—
ishiku wa shisha no	the stonecutter carves only
na-nomi horu	the names of the dead

Masae Izawa, Japan [k]

PURPLE LOOSESTRIFE, *misohagi* (early). *Lythrum salicaria*. Purple loosestrife has brilliant pinkish-lavender flowers blooming on crowded 2–4' (60–120 cm) spikes for a month or two June to September, depending on locale, and is known throughout the northern hemisphere.

election rally
purple loosestrife spreads
along the river

Winona Baker, BC [k]

TOUCH-ME-NOT, *tsurifunesō* (early). *Impatiens sp*. The common name and the Latin both derive from the famous pods of these plants of the balsam family known throughout Eurasia and much of North America. Once a pod is ripe, a touch or even a gust of wind suffices to split it into five springlike coils which broadcast the seeds well around the area. All species have orchidlike, brightly colored blossoms. In the U.S. the plant is also known as **jewelweed**, since one of its lozenge-shaped, bright green leaves holds air bubbles when under water, giving it a gemlike appearance. The most common eastern species, **spotted touch-me-not** (*I. capensis*), has orange flowers enjoyed by hummingbirds; the juice of its hollow stems has been scientifically confirmed as a fungicide and is a folk remedy for poison ivy. **Pale touch-me-not** (*I. pallida*) with yellow flowers ranges all across southern Canada and the northeastern and central U.S. A purple-flowered species called **Indian balsam** (*I. glandulifera*) is common in Europe and the Saint Lawrence area of Canada and the U.S.; the Japanese touch-me-not (*I. textori*) has pinkish-purple blossoms. Plants range from 16" to 6' (40–180 cm) high, and usually grow along the banks of streams, blooming from June or July to September or October, with the first seed pods maturing in August.

to sail
above the jewelweed
to settle

John Wills, TN [k]

MILKWEED (all). *Asclepias sp*. A large genus of North American plants that have a milky fluid in their hollow stalks. "Milkweed" in haikai refers to the seed-bearing **milkweed pods**—with bright white, silky hair—of **common milkweed** (*A. syriaca*, eastern) and **showy milkweed** (*A. speciosa*, Pacific coast). Both form large pods after the summer bloom period, sending their seed aloft when the pods split open in autumn.

the wind
along the old railroad tracks
a milkweed pod opens

Cor van den Heuvel, NY [k]

INK CAPS (all). *Coprinus sp*. Edible mushrooms with gills that self-digest into a black "ink" as the spores mature. Because of the dissolving gills, ink caps must be harvested at just the right time to avoid a mess. The **alcohol inky** or **ink coprinus** (*C. atramentarius*) and **shaggy mane** (*C. comatus*) both appear throughout autumn, though some may be seen earlier; the latter is quite prized for edibility. Some ink caps show up at other times, most notably the **COMMON INKY CAP, glistening coprinus,** or **mica cap** (*C. micaceus*) which can be found in many areas April through October and year-round in southern California, making it an all-year topic. Also called: **shaggy ink caps.**

Shaggy Ink Caps!
huge and good to eat
yesterday

Susan Rowley, England [k/s]

LICHEN, *iwatake* (late). A "lichen" is actually a symbiotic pairing of a fungus and an alga. Most live on rocks or trees (the Japanese literally means "rock fungus"); many change color with the seasons.

lichen grow
in the crevice of her smile—
the old stone goddess

John Thompson, CA [k]

WINTER

The following entries appear under Winter, in the categories indicated.

------- The Season -------
Winter
Indian Summer
Winter Solstice
July
Close of the Year
New Year's Eve
January
Great Cold
Winter Day
Winter Morning
Winter Evening
Short Day
Winter Night
Cold
Freeze
Deep Winter
------- The Heavens -------
Winter Sky
Winter Clouds
Winter Sun
Winter Moon
Wolf Moon
Winter Stars
Orion
Winter Wind
Withering Wind
North Wind
Winter Drizzle
Winter Rain
Months of Rain
Snow Pellets
Frost
First Snow
Snow
Snowflakes
Snowstorm
Winter Mist
Winter Fog
Winter Haze
Winter Rainbow
------- The Earth -------
Winter Mountain
Snow-Capped
Withered Field
Winter Field
Withered Garden
Pothole
Winter Beach
Winter Harbor
Frozen Ground
Ice
Icicles
January Thaw
------- Humanity -------
Long Underwear
Sweater
Overcoat
Blanket
Muffler
Hot Cereal
Soup
Sea-Devil Stew
Snow-Shoveling
Cardboard House
Fireplace
Hearth
Firewood
Hunting
Tracking
Logging
Snow-Viewing
Cat's Cradle
Snow Throwing
Snowman
Ski
Ice Hockey
Soccer
Rugby
Basketball
Common Cold
Cough
Sneeze
Breath is White
Freezing Shadow
Basking in the Sun
Old Diary
Winter Vacation
— Observances —
Groundhog Day
Armistice Day
Election Day, U.S.
Thanksgiving Day
Advent
Hanukkah
Christmas
Boxing Day
Bashō's Day
Nick's Day
------- Animals -------
Fox
Hare, Rabbit
Owl
Northern Wren
Swan
Duck
Grebe
Whale
Dolphin
Codfish
Winter Butterfly
Winter Mosquito
------- Plants -------
Early Plum Blossoms
Remaining Wildflowers
Buddha's-Hand Orange
Winter's Colored Leaves
Colored Leaves Fall
Leaves
Dry Leaves
Fallen Leaves
Winter Grove
Bare Tree
Narcissus
Hellebore
Withered Roses
Leeks
Withered Grass
Winter Violets

Note: An asterisk at the end of an entry's text indicates that additional poems and season words on the topic may be found in Chapter 6 of *The Haiku Seasons*.

WINTER—THE SEASON

WINTER, *fuyu, winter*—Dutch, *zima*—Russian (all). Technically, in haikai "winter" means the period from about 7 November through about 3 February and centering on the winter solstice, but commonly November through January (May to July in the southern hemisphere). Generally, the word "winter" adds a sense of cold, gloom, and isolation to a poem. See the discussion of the names of seasons in the introduction to the saijiki, pages 32–33.

Mimosa-geuren	Scent of mimosa
komen de winter binnen	comes into winter through
door het open raam	the open window

Roel Houwink, The Netherlands [h]

Zima. U menja na stene	Winter. On my wall
"Bol'shaja Volna" Khokusaja	Hokusai's "Great Wave"
visit nepodvishno.	hangs motionless.

Alexey V. Andreyev, Russia [k]

INDIAN SUMMER, *koharu* (early). The Japanese literally means "little spring"—a period of mild weather in early November before the cold of winter digs in. Also: **Indian summer day** (*koharubi*).

koharubi ya	Indian summer day . . .
rinrin to naru	I want some earrings
mimiwa hoshi	that go jingle-jingle

Momoko Kuroda, Japan [k]

a red-tailed hawk
stuck on the sky—
Indian summer haze

Kay F. Anderson, CA [k/s]

WINTER SOLSTICE, *tōji* (mid). About 21 or 22 December. The **shortest day of the year,** astronomically defined as the time when the sun stands directly overhead at the Tropic of Capricorn and the axis of the earth is at an angle of 23.4 degrees with respect to the plane of the earth's orbit around the sun. The solstice marks the beginning of the shift that eventually results in spring and our awareness of longer days, but because of heat lag the coldest days of the year usually come four to six weeks after the winter solstice. Southern hemisphere residents experience their winter solstice in June, though astronomers adhere to the December date regardless of their location.

shorter kisses
longer quarrels—
winter solstice

Eric Amann, ON [s]

JULY (late). As July is **LATE SUMMER** in the haikai calendar for the northern hemisphere, so it is **LATE WINTER** in the southern. In the following poem **pipiwharauroa** is the Maori name for the **SHINING CUCKOO** or **whistler** (*Chalcites lucidas*), a sparrow-sized bird normally heard rather than seen, an early-spring topic in New Zealand.

July—
the pipiwharauroa
its shrill cry so soon

Jeanette Stace, New Zealand [k]

CLOSE OF THE YEAR, *toshi no kure* (mid). The **end of the year** (*saimatsu*) takes on a special frenzy as we try to finish all our projects and meet obligations. As the year ends we often have mixed feelings: something is over, something perhaps not completed, but we must go on to the new. Also: **year end, almost the New Year, end of the year** (*fin de l'année*—French), the **year is closed** (*toshi kururu*), and a number of other related expressions in Japanese.

almost the New Year . . .
instead of lighting, crumbling
my last cigarette

Rengé / David Priebe, CA [k/s]

na o kukuru	the green of the straw
wara no aokute	binding together the herbs . . .
toshi kururu	the year closes

Masako Takahashi, Japan [h]

year-end gift giving—
five new calendars, but
only one year!

Kristen Deming, CA [s]

Je n'ose abandonner	I dare not give up
Ce dictionnaire loqueteux	This tattered dictionary
La fin de l'année	The end of the year

Megumi Fukushima, Japan [k]

NEW YEAR'S EVE, *toshi no yo*, *Stara Godina*—Serbian (mid). The Japanese literally reads "the year's night". Whenever the caprices of religion, politics, and commerce have set the beginning of the **NEW YEAR** with respect to the earth's orbit around the sun, people have noted the end of each year in a reflective spirit. Often we celebrate the end of the year with a **NEW YEAR'S EVE PARTY** (*toshiwasure*) the day or evening before. On the one hand, we commemorate the end of one year, perhaps by reminiscing about its good and bad times and rejoicing in having survived another cycle of the seasons. On the other, such parties frequently continue into the next day, affording a chance to greet the first day of the New Year at its very beginning.

Stara Godina—	New Year's Eve—
moje mišli lutatu	my mind wanders over
grobljem predaka.	ancestors' graveyard.

Kretić Milivoje, Yugoslavia [k]

JANUARY, *ichigatsu*, *enero*—Spanish (late). Like the name of a season, the name of a month may be used to shift the time of a poem containing an image that would otherwise be understood as pertaining to another time period. In the following poem, "dew" would normally be understood as an autumnal topic, but "January" shifts it to the coldest time of year. Though it may not usually be freezing in January in Cuba or Florida—the author's original home and present residence, respectively—there is still a chill in the January air lacking at other times of the year.

Aquí y allá en el cementerio	Here and there in the cemetery
el rocío	dew
como huesos de Enero.	like the bones of January.

Ana Rosa Núñez, FL [k]

GREAT COLD, *daikan* (late). One of the traditional Chinese fortnightly periods, at the end of January and the first few days of February in our calendar. In various parts of the north temperate zone this is indeed the coldest time of the year.

nawatobi ya	a jump rope . . .
daikan no chi o	beats the ground
tatakitsuke	of the Great Cold

Seiichirō Fujita, Japan [k]

WINTER DAY, *fuyu no hi* (all). For the Japanese haikai community, this refers to both a winter day and the winter sun, since *hi* means both "day" and "sun"; the topic includes, **winter sunshine** (*fuyu hinata*). **SNOW** will not be part of the picture unless directly mentioned or implied, in which case the poem would be classified under that late-winter topic.

fuyu no hi ya	a winter day . . .
fushite miaguru	the length of the koto
koto no take	I kneel to admire

Setsuko Nozawa, Japan [h]

WINTER MORNING, *fuyu no asa*, *zimsko jutro*—Croatian (all). The typical winter morning is cold and clear, unless in the middle of a late-winter **SNOWSTORM**.

A winter morning:
the police biker needs
his leather jacket.

Dick Pettit, Sultinate of Oman [k]

U zimsko jutro	On a winter morning
pralje na potoku.	laundresses at the brook.
Udarci platna.	Linens clapping.

Katarina Pšak, Croatia [k]

WINTER EVENING, *fuyu no kure, winteravond*—Dutch (all). In winter evening comes early, and usually brings a chill. In parts of the temperate zones it may be dark well before the close of the business day in the middle of winter, in which case "evening" suggests the time after five or six p.m., when people have left work.

winteravond	winter evening
de schapen staan stil bijeen	the sheep stand still together
te verdonkeren	in the darkening

Marcel Smets, Belgium [k]

SHORT DAY, *tanjitsu* (all). The shortest day of the year is the **WINTER SOLSTICE,** a mid-winter topic, but we begin feeling the **LONG NIGHT** (*yo naga*) in autumn and the shortness of daylight throughout winter. The topic "short day" includes **early dusk** (*kure hayashi*) and **darkness at five** (*Dunkelheit um Fünf*—German).

In der fremden Stadt	In the strange city
plötzlich den Weg verloren.	suddenly we lose our way.
Dunkelheit um Fünf.	The darkness at five.

Günther Klinge, Germany [k]

WINTER NIGHT, *fuyu no yo, nuit d'hiver*—French (all). Even indoors, we feel the chill in our bones, in our minds, on a winter night.

winter night—
the cat sitting in a drawer
filled with letters

Kenneth Tanemura, CA [k]

Longue nuit d'hiver	Long winter night
les hommes au comptoir du bar	the men leaning at the bar
ont les yeux qui brillent	have shining eyes

Patrick Blanche, France [k]

COLD, *samushi*, *froid*—French (all). This is the cold of air, weather, and the like. This topic includes **freezing night** (*kanya*). Note that in Japanese there is another word, *tsumetashi*, also a seasonal topic, for the cold of things, as to the touch. I have placed the poem with the phrase **blow on hands** here, for the context makes clear that this is a reaction to the cold.

four a.m.
the cold of space pours down
from distant stars

Ruth Holter, OR [k]

The artist's model
hangs her clothes over the screen
he blows on his hands.

Patricia V. Dawson, England [s]

a cold room
the shape of the last guest
in the empty chair

Martin Lucas, England [k]

À cheval	On horseback
Soleil et pluie se marient	A marriage of sun and rain
Froid mouillé sur ma peau	The wet cold on my skin

Alain Kervern, Brittany [k]

After washing up
putting a warm plate back
in the cold cupboard

David Burleigh, Japan [k]

FREEZE, *itsuru* (all). Everything freezes when the temperature drops below 32°F (0°C). In early winter the thermometer drops overnight, later it remains below freezing all day. **Icy** or **freezing** (*ysige*—Afrikaans) may be used as adjectives to express this feeling.

Ysige skemer
in die kaggelhoutmandjie
slaap 'n slangetjie

Freezing twilight
in the firewood basket
a field snake sleeps

Deon Kesting, South Africa [k]

waiting for crumbs
the blackbird's gold-rimmed eye
on my freezing fingers

Ruth Robinson, England [k/s]

cat, if only
you could sip Earl Gray with me
this iced night

Geraldine C. Little, NJ [k]

DEEP WINTER, *fuyu fukashi* (late). By late winter in most parts of the temperate zones we feel the **COLD TIME** in our bones. The "deep" in "deep winter" suggests how far winter has penetrated into our bodies and our minds. Also: **winter is long** (*iarna e lungă*—Romanian).

deep winter:
a woodpecker tapping
into its own sound

Adele Kenny, NJ [k]

toate bărcile	all the boats
scîrţîie în surdină . . .	creak in a low tone . . .
iarna e lungă	winter is long

Ion Codrescu, Romania [k]

WINTER—THE HEAVENS

WINTER SKY, *fuyu no sora* (all). This refers to the daytime sky in winter, paler than at other times of the year with a sun that has less force.

giant contrails
fan out against
the cold winter sky

Mary E. Durham, TX [k]

WINTER CLOUDS, *fuyu no kumo* (all). Clouds have a different meaning in each season; in winter they may presage a cold rain, sleet, or snow.

kaihyō no	the roar of seals
hōkō fuyu no	calls out to
kumo o yobu	the winter clouds

Tanzan Sunami, Japan [k]

WINTER SUN (all). Japanese *fuyu no hi*, usually taken as **WINTER DAY** (The Season category), may also be read as "winter sun"; in English "winter sun" must have its own place in The Heavens category. **Winter's Old Sol** (*fuyu no taiyō*) or **wintry Sol** (*tōyō*) suggests the weakness of the winter sun. The winter sun is highly valued despite its weakness. See the winter topic **BASKING**. Note that a **tiercel** is a male peregrine falcon or goshawk used in **FALCONRY** (*takagari*), another winter topic. Also: **winter sunshine**.

Winter sun.
shadows of my earrings
on the sketchbook

Kris Kondō, Japan [k]

sinking into the ice—
the willow branch
with the pale winter sun

Jeff Witkin, MD [k]

winter sun
in the eye of her tiercel
returns to her glove

Harvey Hess, IA [k]

pencil marks
in the book of a dead friend;
winter sunshine

Ruby Spriggs, ON [k]

chawan-ichi	chinaware sale—
hitotsu hitotsu ni	on one after another
tōyō kana	wintry Sol

Shugoe Miyamoto, Japan [k]

WINTER MOON, *fuyu no tsuki* (all). By turns beautifully crystalline and shrouded in cold mist or clouds, the winter moon offers either stark or meager light. For those clear, cold moonlit nights, **cold moon** (*kangetsu*) may be the better season word to use.

winter moon
nudge of the unborn child
between us

Jean Jorgensen, Alberta [k]

WOLF MOON (late). Algonquin name for the first full moon after the winter solstice, usually in January. See also **HUNTER'S MOON** in autumn.

the power out—
through deep windows
wolf moon

K. G. Teal, NY [k]

WINTER STARS, *fuyu no hoshi* (all). The clarity and chill of winter skies bring the stars closer. The opening lines of the following poem suggest early winter.

one more ride
with the top down—
winter stars

Yvonne Hardenbrook, PA [k]

ORION, *orion* (all). The constellation Orion governs the winter sky with its bright red star, its blue-white star, and its belt of three stars straight-across. In the northern temperate zone it appears in November and falls out of view in April.

Orion's belt . . .
three sparks
in a curl of woodsmoke

Mark Evans, IA [k]

the Greyhound's
running lights
under Orion

Gene Doty, MO [k]

WINTER WIND, *fuyu no kaze* (all). Winter is known for its winds; see **WITHERING WIND** and **NORTH WIND**, following. A "winter wind" will simply suggest a cold wind during the winter months. A more intense expression: **freezing wind** (*itekaze*).

archery practice:
sound of a bowstring quivers
in the freezing wind

Zhu Hao, China [k]

WITHERING WIND, *kogarashi* (early). Literally "tree-witherer", in Japan a most-feared windstorm that takes remaining leaves from the trees and pierces the body, numbing the spirit.

kogarashi ya	withering wind . . .
uma arawarete	a horse coming into view
umi no ue	on the ocean

Akira Matsuzawa, Japan [k]

NORTH WIND, *kita* (all). In the northern hemisphere, the characteristic cold north wind of winter.

naki fubo e	when I give back
tsuma kaesu toki	my husband to his late parents
kita sumite	the north wind clearing

Sachiko Hirai, Japan [k]

WINTER DRIZZLE, *shigure* (early). This is the special name for the chill drizzling showers of early winter in Japan, one of the most prominent topics in haikai and dating back to the earliest Japanese poetry. The entry for *shigure* in the *Japan Great Saijiki* is more than twice as long as those for **BLOSSOM** (*hana*), **CHERRY BLOSSOM** (*sakura*), or **MOON** (*tsuki*). By this time the northern temperate zone has lost the bright colors of the growing year and harvest, and we feel and see the "wailing winds, and naked woods, and meadows brown and sere . . . the cold November rain" (William Cullen Bryant, "The Death of the Flowers"). Since the following poems, from widely separated areas, seem to embody the mood of *shigure*, I propose **November rain** (*chuva em novembro*—Portuguese) as a season word under this topic. Of course "November rain" poems from the south temperate zone would find themselves in early summer.

November rain—
long ropes of the window washers
float in the wind

Judson Evans, MA [k]

chuva em novembro	november rain
para pe lado corre	which way
o nosso amor	shall our love run

Yvette Kace Centeno, Portugal [k]

WINTER RAIN, *fuyu no ame* (all). Any rain in winter suggests a chill dampness.

winter rain
at dusk the darkness
of stones

George Ralph, MI [k]

dango tsukuri	as the farmer's wife
oshieru nōfu ni	teaches dumpling-making
fuyu no ame	the winter rain

Kinuko A. Jambor, Japan [k]

MONTHS OF RAIN (late). In Wales, where the poem below was written, and in the tropics (see the discussion in the introduction to the saijiki, pages 21–23), long months of rain are typical of "winter".

After months of rain
surprised
by my shadow

Ken H. Jones, Wales [k/s]

SNOW PELLETS, *arare* (all). "Snow pellets", **snow grains, soft hail,** and **tapioca snow** are all terms for what meteorologists call **graupel.** Composed of crisp white opaque pellets, the phenomenon is common in Japan, where graupel frequently mixes with snow or rain, and is therefore the first image of hard precipitation that comes to mind, accounting for the fact that *arare* occupies the figurative niche in Japanese that is occupied by "hail" in English. *Arare* is therefore frequently translated as "hail". Note, however, that **HAIL** (*hyō*), composed of hard ice pellets, is a summer topic. A related season word in Japanese, **ice rain** (*hisame*), includes both graupel and **SLEET** (*mizore*)—which is a winter topic on its own. And **spring graupel, spring snow pellets** or **CORN SNOW** (*haru no arare*) represent a spring topic.

wadanaka ni	in the landscape
kyōkai no kane	sound of a church bell
arare furu	snow pellets fall

Yatsuka Ishihara, Japan [k]

FROST, *shimo*, *Frost*—German (all). Frost is winter's **DEW** (autumn). Both are classified as "falling things" under The Heavens in haikai, though we usually see them on the ground, on plants, and so on. **Ground frost**—also called **hoarfrost** or **white frost**—forms on cold, clear nights when heat quickly leaves the ground, making it colder than the surrounding air (and below freezing). **Window frost** results from window glass chilled by outside air to the point where water vapor inside sublimates on the glass. (Note that "frosted window" may refer to window frost or to a window with glass that has been manufactured as translucent, rather than transparent.) **Rime** (*inje*—Croatian) is frost on exposed objects such as wires and trees, formed through contact with supercooled **FOG** (an autumn topic). **Black frost** occurs when cold air freezes plants to the point where the leaves turn black but there is not enough water vapor in the air to form fog.

creaking
under the crowded last train
frosted rails

Kohjin Sakamoto, Japan [k]

Der Frost der Mythen	The frost of the myths
im Wind über Argolis	in the wind over Argolis
macht richtig hungrig.	makes me really hungry.

Gustav Rödler, Austria [k/s]

Jutarnje inje—	Morning rime—
svaka iglica bora	every pine needle
nakostriješena.	bristling.

Zvonko Petrović, Croatia [k]

a tiny puff
of frost as the mudlark's song
peals through the dawn

Alex McQueen, Australia [k]

FIRST SNOW, *hatsu yuki*, *prvi snijeg*—Croatian (mid). Comes a month before the storms that bring quantities of snow to field and town, and therefore, in Japanese terms, mid winter.

Dijete stresa
prvi snijeg s ljuljačke.
Tiho je jutro.

A child shakes
the first snow from the swing.
A quiet morning.

Tomislav Maretić, Croatia [k]

SNOW, *yuki*, *zăpada*—Romanian, *sneg*—Serbian, *snijeg*—Croatian (late). Equal to the cherry blossoms of spring and the moon of autumn in imagistic power, snow is traditionally associated with late winter in Japan's mild climate, but of course is seen earlier and later, in both Japan and most of the rest of the temperate zones. Also: **falling snow** (*furu yuki*), **snow falls** (*yuki furu*), and so on. In the last poem in this group the pronoun refers to the title and "B&H" to Bosnia and Herzegovina. At first glance the "snow" seems to mean electronic interference; for me this is also the snow of winter in Sarajevo in the mid 1990s. (While haiku usually have no titles, in Japanese a "preface" may be given, indicating the place and circumstances of composition.)

furu yuki ni
chikara nukitaru
migiwa kana

in falling snow
strength has slipped away—
the water's edge

Mizue Yamada, Japan [k]

yuki suki de
parii ga suki de
hitori tabi

for love of snow
for the love of Paris
a solitary voyage

Shunsō Machi, Japan [k]

sugatami ni
furu yuki utsushi
kigaekeri

as the long mirror
reflects the falling snow
I change clothes

Chie Kamegaya, BC [k]

in Gauguin's hut
his last picture
Breton snow

Tony Quagliano, HI [k]

după concert	after the concert
curăţînd tăcut zăpada	clearing the car of snow
de pe maşină	not a word is said

Ion Codrescu, Romania [k]

Sneg pada—	Snow falls—
ljudi prolaze i odnose	people pass by carrying
ničije pahulje.	nobody's flakes.

Dušan Mijajlović Adski, Yugoslavia [k]

Mala stopa u	A small footprint
utabanom snijegu	in the stamped snow of
velike stope.	the big footprint.

Anica Gečić, Croatia [k]

EUROPA	EUROPE
Gledajući vijesti o BiH	Watching the news about B&H
jedino je uznemiri	all that bothers her
snijeg na ekranu.	is snow on the screen.

Enes Kišević, Croatia [s]

SNOWFLAKES, *kazahana* (late). Literally "wind-flowers" in Japanese; like the English "snowflakes" the term suggests lightness, the joyous aspect of falling snow.

confetti-colored
by city neon, snowflakes
melting in his hair

Dianne Borsenik, OH [k]

SNOWSTORM, *fubuki* (late). The Japanese literally means **blowing snow**; more snow and wind than just "snowing". Note that Japanese poets avoid such redundant expressions as "late winter snowstorm", since "snowstorm" is a late winter topic; in other languages and regions such expressions may clarify the image for those unfamiliar with the Japanese tradition.

Late winter snowstorm:
a button pops off & clicks
on the wooden floor

Clark Strand, NY [k]

WINTER MIST, *fuyugasumi* (all). Also: **cold mist** (*kangasumi*). See "On Haze, Mist, Fog" at **AUTUMN MIST, FOG** for a discussion of these and related terms.

cold mist on the sea,
smoke pours from the mouths of fish
cooking on the fire

Rebecca Rust, NC [k]

WINTER FOG, *fuyu no kiri* (all). While some coastal areas experience tremendous amounts of **SEA FOG** (which see) in summer, winter is the foggier season most places. In densely populated areas, winter fog frequently combines with smoke to create a winter **SMOG** (*sumoggu*). Smog and its close relative **AIR POLLUTION** (another winter topic) can create breathing problems. Of course there is also **SUMMER AIR POLLUTION**, both types being held in place by heat inversions (warmer air above cooler air) which tend to stay in place longer during summer and winter than in spring or autumn. See "On Haze, Mist, Fog" at **AUTUMN MIST, FOG** for a discussion of these and related terms.

sensha sarishi	the tank leaves
ato fuyugiri ni	behind in the winter fog
hitsuji ou	driven sheep

Ryūsai Takeshita, Japan [k]

WINTER HAZE, *fuyu no moya* (all). Some Japanese critics see little difference between *moya* and *kasumi*, which may both be translated as "haze" or "mist". Parallel with **cold mist** under **WINTER MIST** (*fuyu-*

gasumi), above, we have also **cold haze** (*kan-ai*), a season word under the current topic written with characters for "cold" and *moya*. Other critics include what I have called "winter haze" (*fuyu no moya*) under **WINTER FOG** or vice-versa. See "On Haze, Mist, Fog" at **AUTUMN MIST, FOG** for a discussion of these and related terms.

The sheen of silver
through cold haze—
refinery tanks.

Alice Dartley, NJ [k]

WINTER RAINBOW, *fuyu no niji* (all). Rainbows can be seen at any time of year, when an observer stands between the sun and a rain-shower cloud—provided the angles are right and the sky is clear in the right place. The droplets in the cloud act as prisms, dividing the light into different color bands as seen by the observer. Conditions for seeing rainbows are more common in summer in most of the temperate zones, accounting for the assignment of **RAINBOW** (*niji*) to summer in the saijiki. But they also occur at other times, so the topics **SPRING RAINBOW** (*haru no niji*) and **AUTUMN RAINBOW** (*aki no niji*) are recognized as well as winter rainbow.

Thou too Brutus!	*Et tu, Brute!*
ima mo fuyu niji	even now a winter rainbow
kieyasuku	ready to disappear

Shūson Katō, Japan [k]

WINTER—THE EARTH

WINTER MOUNTAIN, *fuyu no yama* (all). Japan's mountains never lose their holy aspect, even with the onslaught of skiing. Also: **winter summit** (*fuyu santen*).

chi nagaruru	like milk
hodo no michi miyu	flowing a trail shows—
fuyu santen	winter summit

Noriko Yūki, Japan [h]

SNOW-CAPPED (all). An adjective that seems worthy of inclusion in saijiki, which already list **snowy peaks** (*setsurei*) under the topic **WINTER MOUNTAIN**. Also: **snow-covered.**

a pale glint
on her chromeplated walker . . .
snowcapped tombstones

Kenneth C. Leibman, FL [k]

a middle-aged arab
contemplates the snow-covered square
and remembers sand

Sam Yada Cannarozzi, France [k]

WITHERED FIELD, *kareno* (all). The fields of winter have lost their summer green and autumn gold, turning a pale straw color as grasses and forbs dry out and wither in the cold wind. The subtlety of that pale color, sometimes poking up through white snow, gives a touching and aesthetic beauty to the winter countryside. Also: **deserted field** (*pusto polje*—Serbian).

Sa oblakom	With a cloud
niz pusto polje.	down on the deserted field.
Senka hrasta.	Oak tree shadow.

Aleksandar Obrovski, Yugoslavia [k]

WINTER FIELD, *fuyuta* (all). The Japanese says literally "winter rice paddy". Sere and brown, unless snow-covered. Also: **snowy field** (*yuki no ta*), **white field** (*bijelo polje*—Croatian), **on the snow** (*sulla neve*—Italian). The topic **WINTER MOOR** (*fuyuno*) is also perhaps best translated "winter field". Note that while snow-related terms almost always carry the implication of late winter, the *Japan Great Almanac* includes "snowy field" in all winter under this topic. Perhaps less attention was paid to this relatively unpopular season word, which does not show up in many Japanese saijiki. Far more important to the Japanese saijiki is **WITHERED FIELD** (above), which carries with it the image of tall dried grasses gleaming pale gold in the weak sun. In the Italian poem below the **YELLOW BROOM** (*Sarothamnus scoparius*) is a wild shrub of the legume family that blooms in early summer.

Bjelinu polja	Whiteness of a field
čini stvarnom teķ dim iz	made real only by the smoke
male ķolibe.	from a small cabin.

Nada Zidar-Bogadi, Austria [k]

Ginestra gialla	Yellow broom
sulla neve di ieri	on the snow yesterday
o sto sognando?	or was I dreaming?

Livia Livi, Italy [k/s]

WITHERED GARDEN, *ķare sono* (all). In winter, when the plants have all either died down or stiffened with cold, the garden has a subdued and jagged look, with colors mostly browns and grays relieved by the occasional evergreen. Other season words associated with this topic include **winter yard** (*fuyu no niwa*), **withered yard** (*ķareniwa*), **cold garden** (*ķan-en*), and **frosted courtyard** (*patio escarchado*—Spanish).

Migas de pan	Crumbs of bread
en el patio escarchado;	in the frosted courtyard;
¡Algarabía!	gobble!

Liria Miyakawa, Argentina [k/s]

POTHOLE (late). In late winter, when roads have been subject to freezing and thawing, the pavement crumbles, often leaving these deep ragged holes which are dangerous to vehicles.

between the day moon
and the sunset
it's pothole city

Shawn Lindsay, IN [s]

WINTER BEACH, *fuyu no hama*, *winterlichen Strand*—German (all). Wind and waves take on a wilder aspect in the barrenness of a winter beach, with a cold bite to the salt spray and few people around.

Möwen und Krähen
picken zugleich am Dorschkopf
am winterlichen Strand.

Gulls and crows
pick together at a cod-head
on the wintry beach.

Christa Wächtler, Germany [k]

WINTER HARBOR (all). A cold wind whips in off the sea and leaden swells rise and fall through the wakes of ships with few people on deck because of the cold.

Winter harbor
Moonlight etches
The wake's curve

Connie Hutchison, WA [k]

FROZEN GROUND, *terre glacée*—French (late). With the freezing temperatures of late winter comes freezing ground, not just the light crusting that occurs overnight in early winter, but the deep freezing that dominates winter's latter weeks and carries over into spring.

Hiver, terre glacée
La poule hésite
à poser l'autre patte

Winter, frozen ground
The hen hesitates
to place the other foot

Bruno Hulin, France [k]

ICE, *kōri*, *ijs*—Dutch (late). Ice may form any time in winter, but indicates late winter in haikai because it seems almost omnipresent then in much of the temperate zone. Also: **iced** (*vereist*—German).*

sound of her voice
carrying eggs
across the ice

Bill Pauly, IA [k]

Twee krasse oudjes
op het ijs van de vijver
hand in hand schaatsend.

Two vigorous oldsters
on the ice of the pond
skating hand in hand.

P. A. Dietze, The Netherlands [k]

Moonlight on ice
The farmer carries heavy rocks
In his dreams

Marco Fraticelli, PQ [k]

Vereist steht sie da	standing here iced
im ersten Licht des Tages	in the first light of day
die Felswand von einst	the cliff from the past

Daniel Beck, Switzerland [k]

ICICLE, *tsurara* (late). As winter cold deepens, snow melting on roofs and trees results in icicles forming on eaves and branches, usually dripping by day but freezing hard at night.

a crow caws:
morning sun sets on fire
all the icicles

Richard Tice, UT [h]

Breaking off an icicle,
To stab it
Into snow

Masaya Saito, Japan [k]

JANUARY THAW (late). Throughout much of the north temperate zone, the deep freeze often breaks for a few days in late winter, turning the snow and ice on roads and sidewalks into slush and giving a brief sense of relief from the cold before even colder days to come. In the north this is so firmly associated with January that it is usually called the "January thaw". Another common name for the phenomenon today is **mid-winter thaw**, arising from a modern understanding of the season as beginning in December.

Observing winter from solstice to equinox has shifted the meaning of "midwinter" in popular usage, though in many contexts the word still carries its traditional meaning as the period around the solstice. (See the discussion of "midsummer" and "midwinter" in *The Haiku Seasons*, page 106.) From a traditional Japanese haiku standpoint, the poem below might be viewed as a senryu precisely because it contains a traditional term used in an unorthodox, modern sense. When translating haiku from Japanese to other languages the distinctions between traditional and colloquial diction are almost impossible to reproduce, and account in part for the difficulties non-Japanese confront when they try to understand the differences between Japanese haiku and senryu. Foreign haiku rendered into Japanese translations that do not employ traditional haiku diction may also be partly responsible for a certain Japanese hesitance in accepting non-Japanese poems as true "haiku".

midwinter thaw:
on the dented trash can lid
sparrows bathing

Carol Conti-Entin, OH [k]

WINTER—HUMANITY

LONG UNDERWEAR (all). These undergarments with long sleeves and legs, often insulated or quilted, are worn to protect one from the cold. Also called: **longjohns.**

Taking off
our longjohns: sparks
in the dark . . .

Chuck Brickley, BC [k/s]

SWEATER, *sētā* (all). A typical winter garment, usually worn over a shirt or blouse. Also: **cardigan** (*kādigan*).

after she's gone
unwinding
a long hair from my sweater

Brian Tasker, England [k]

OVERCOAT, *gaitō* (all). An outer coat, worn to protect the body and indoor clothing from the elements. Also called: **topcoat, coat.**

The delight I feel
  goes stamping up the road in
the little boy's coat.

Colin Oliver, England [k]

BLANKET, *mōfu*, *kumbal*—Urdu (all). We may need blankets before winter sets in, but they deeply characterize the season. Also: **electric blanket** (*denkimōfu*).

Thanda hai mosam	Season so cold
Ek kumbal kaise orhein	Not enough blankets
Biwi, bachchey, hum	For my family

Jamal Naqvi, Pakistan [k]

separate beds
our electric blankets ping
separately, too

Peter Duppenthaler, Japan [s]

New blanket;
the old cat
claims it first.

Helen L. Shaffer, PA [k/s]

MUFFLER, *erimaki* (all). As winter cold and winds increase, we bundle up. Note the use of "muffler" for the topic in English; it might well have been translated **SCARF**, but since scarves of one kind or another are worn at all times of the year that is an all-year topic. "Scarf" meaning **winter scarf** might best be amplified or supplied with a context that makes the winter connection clear, such as **wool scarf** or another winter season word.

erimaki ni	in the muffler
kao uzumereba	when I bury my face
waga nioi	my smell

Shigeru Ekuni, Japan [k]

HOT CEREAL (all). Hot cereal is a typical winter breakfast food in Europe, North America, and elsewhere. A cracked or rolled grain, such as wheat, oats, rye, or corn, is cooked in water until it thickens, forming a **porridge** or **mush**, to which milk, sugar, and fruit may be added. For example, **corn mush** (*žganci*—Croatian).

lonac žganaca	a pot of mush
tri puta pregrijanih	three times reheated
na staroj peči	on the old stove

Rujana Matuka, Croatia [k]

SOUP (all). Most of us think of soup as mainly a cold weather food, though of course soups may be taken at any time of year. **COLD SOUP** would be a summer topic—unless it refers to a hot soup that has become unpleasantly cool, for example because of an interruption to the meal. Also: **alphabet soup**.

eating alone
my alphabet soup
speaks to me

Brenda S. Duster, IA [s]

SEA-DEVIL STEW, *ankō nabe* (all). The fish of the family Lophidae are also called "anglers" because they have a fleshy lure at the end of a flexible spine just behind their upper lip, which they move about to attract smaller fish within range of their substantial teeth. Other names for members of the group include monkfish and goosefish. All have large, flattened heads and narrow bodies which are well-camouflaged as they lie on the bottom waiting for prey to swim by. The deep-sea varieties can reach 10' (3 m) or more in length. As Teiko Inahata puts it, "It is impossible to admire their shape, but they taste good." Not well-known in North America, they are highly appreciated in Europe and in Japan, where an **angler stew** composed of the fish's meat and liver along with tofu, onions, and other vegetables is considered a winter delicacy.

chi no hate no	on land's end
chōshi domari ya	I put up at Chōshi . . .
ankō nabe	sea-devil stew

Meiga Higashi, Japan [h]

SNOW-SHOVELING, *yukikaki* (late). This is the major outdoor household activity of late winter. The topic includes **snow broom** (*yukibōki*), **snow shovel** (*yukisuki*), **snowblower**, and the like. **BRINGING SNOW DOWN** (*yuki oroshi*)—off a roof—is a separate late-winter topic.

between shovelfuls
I covet my neighbor's
snowblower

Edward J. Rielly, ME [s]

CARDBOARD HOUSE (all). A typical winter shelter for homeless persons, consisting of one or more cardboard boxes arranged to keep off the elements and hold in one's body heat. While homeless people appear year-round, they usually adopt such makeshift shelters only when it is no longer warm enough to sleep without some covering more than clothes.

all night long
hiding from his voices . . .
in a cardboard house

David Walker, England [k]

FIREPLACE, *danro* (all). Includes Western fireplaces and heating stoves, such as the **pot-bellied stove** and **Franklin stove. BLIZZARD** is a late-winter seasonal topic, but since one is not overtly in progress in the following poem I include it here.

The pot-bellied stove—
gathering around, recalling
last year's blizzard.

Leroy Kanterman, NY [k/s]

HEARTH, *ro* (all). "Hearth" suggests the snug feeling of warmth amid the cold of winter; the Japanese *ro* means an open hearth in the center of the room.

ro ni iru ya	being at the hearth . . .
betsu no onore ga	the other self goes
kita o yuki	as the north wind

Tetsunosuke Matsuzaki, Japan [k]

FIREWOOD, *hota* (all). Wood that is cut for heating and cooking fires; includes **kindling,** finely cut wood for starting a fire. Also: **woodshed,** for protecting firewood from rain and snow.

Chopping kindling from
a knotty block . . . in each stick,
a part of its shape.

James W. Hackett, CA [k]

on the axe-head
the smell
split
out of kindling

Geoffrey Daniel, England [k]

A full desk
and empty woodshed
pull with equal force.

Steve Sanfield, CA [s]

HUNTING, *kari* (all). A traditional winter activity, whether for sport or food. **DEER** is an autumnal topic, but **deer hunting** (*shikagari*) is winter.

moss-hung trees
a deer moves into
the hunter's silence

Winona Baker, BC [k]

TRACKING (all). Following **animal tracks** or **spoor** is a hunting skill. Also: **hoofprints** (*Hufspuren*—German).

Hufspuren im Schnee—	Hoofprints in the snow—
er mußte in Eile sein,	he must have been in a hurry,
der fremde Reiter.	the unknown rider.

Richard W. Heinrich, Germany [k]

LOGGING, *marutahiki* (late). This is a traditional winter livelihood in Japan, where independent sawyers use sledges to carry timber over snow to the mills. With the advent of clearcutting (which continues through most seasons but stops in winter) as the primary technique of corporate logging worldwide, it may make sense to preserve the original meaning of "logging" in haikai, in which it implies selecting specific trees for cutting and removing them before the sap runs in spring, allowing young trees to continue their growth. Also: **felling trees.**

the old tree felled:
on its stump I show her
the year of her birth

Hal Roth, MD [k]

SNOW-VIEWING, *yukimi* (late). With **BLOSSOM-VIEWING** (*hanami*) in late spring and **MOON-VIEWING** (*tsukimi*) in mid autumn, snow-viewing is a popular pastime and occasion for parties in Japan.

With no money
I go
snow-viewing

Alan Pizzarelli, NJ [s]

CAT'S CRADLE, *ayatori* (all). A game, usually played by children. A continuous string or cord is passed over and between the fingers of both hands to form a cradlelike pattern and then transferred to the fingers of another player, forming a different figure in the process.

holding sleep at bay
catscradle
quick between small fingers

anne mckay, BC [k/s]

SNOW THROWING, *yukinage* (late). Of course the most common form of thrown snow is the **snowball** (*yukitsubute*), often involved in a **snow(ball) fight** (*yukigassen*), though sometimes in less-serious **snow-play** (*yuki-asobi*). In the American tradition we might like to add **snow fort**. The Japanese word *yukimaroge*, sometimes translated as "snow-ball", refers to a large ball of packed snow such as one might roll to form the base for a **SNOWMAN**.

A snowball
hits under my shirt
cold back.

Anna Söder, Sweden [k]

SNOWMAN, *yukidaruma* (late). The Japanese literally means "snow-Bodhidharma" (after the great Zen monk, whose mythical round shape is the basis for a good-luck doll as well as the Japanese word for snow-man); an alternative Japanese name is **snow-Buddha** (*yukibotoke*). Since they are often androgynous, one American poet has used the term **snow-person.**

little face upturned
waiting for the snowman
to talk

Michael McNierney, CO [k/s]

snowman . . . ?
only a hat
on the grass

Cathy Drinkwater Better, MD [k/s]

SKI, *sukii*, *ski*—Dutch (late). The snowy slopes of late winter provide the best opportunity to enjoy the sport of skiing. Also: **chair lift**.

sukii kata ni	shouldered skis
kawakishi machi no	go over the pavement
hodō yuku	of the dried-out town

Kayoko Hashimoto, Japan [k]

vader en zoon	father and son
staan even stil bij hun sporen	size up their tracks
skiën dan verder	ski on further

Marianne Kiauta, The Netherlands [k]

above the tree line
only the whisper
of the chair-lift wheel

Ruth Robinson, England [k]

ICE HOCKEY, *aisuhokkii* (late). Winter sport especially prominent in Canada. **Shinny** is a form of pick-up ice hockey.

under a bright moon
a friendly game of shinny
his toothless smile

Nika, AB [k/s]

SOCCER, *sakkā*, *nogomet*—Croatian (all). Also called **association football** or sometimes just **football** in England, soccer was invented there in the nineteenth century. Like **AMERICAN FOOTBALL** and **RUGBY** (which see), it is played on a large outdoor field by two teams which attempt by various means to score by carrying or kicking a ball into the opponents' end-zone or goal. All three are winter sports played by both amateur and professional teams, though their official playing seasons may overlap into autumn and spring.

Opet granate . . .	Again the shelling . . .
Dječaci igraju	The boys are playing
mali nogomet.	a little football.

Marinko Španović, Croatia [k]

RUGBY, *ragubii* (all). Otherwise known as **football**, rugby is a rough-and-tumble sport originating in the early 19th century on the fields of Rugby, England. Two teams of 15 each play on a field 160 yards (146 m) long by 75 yards (69 m) wide, and the game has elements similar to **AMERICAN FOOTBALL** and **SOCCER** (which see), both also winter sports in haikai.

hand-in-hand
a man and a boy
going to rugby

Cyril Childs, New Zealand [k/s]

BASKETBALL (all). A major winter sport in North America, though, as with baseball and football, the seasons are blurring under commercial pressure to extend them. A word like **rim** becomes a basketball-related season word in the right context.

the rim is bent
the park cold, deserted—
still I play

Patrick Frank, TN [k/s]

COMMON COLD, *kaze* (all). The minor illness characterized by upper respiratory infection. The Japanese word is a homonym for, and includes the character for, "wind" (*kaze*), in somewhat the same manner as the English suggests a feeling of coldness. The **cold and flu season**

extends into February, at least. Also: **head cold** (*hanakaze*), **cold remedy** (*kazegusuri*), **flu** (*ryūkan*), **hoarseness** (*kazagoe*), **demon of colds** (*kaze no kami*, a homonym for the "god of winds"—Aeolus). Note also the topic **SUMMER COLD** (*natsu no kaze*).

traditionalists don't forget the cold and flu season

Marlene Mountain, TN [k/s]

COUGH, *seki* (all). A typical effect of a winter respiratory infection, the cough goes along with the related winter topics **COMMON COLD** and **SNEEZE.** Also: **to cough** (*kašljati*—Croatian).

Uzdignuvši pest:
<<*Nikada neću pristati . . .*>>
—pa se zakašlja.

Raises his fist:
"No! I'll never agree . . ."
—and bursts out coughing.

Vladimir Devidé, Croatia [s]

SNEEZE, *kusame* (all). A reflex action often brought on by the chill of winter or illness. Like **COLD** and **COUGH,** an all-winter topic.

picking out his bones
from still-burning embers
—trying not to sneeze

Margaret Chula, OR [k/s]

BREATH IS WHITE, *iki shiroshi* (all). The breath condenses in chill air; in English we say we can **see the breath.** Also: **white breath** (*shiroki iki*). In the following poem the "Nenbutsu" is the name of a prayer, "Praise to Amida Buddha" (*namu amida butsu*); if repeated with complete devotion it is said to result in the devotee's rebirth in the Pure Land, a paradise preliminary to ultimate nirvana.

futomoruru
nenbutsu shiroki
iki to naru

let slip
the Nenbutsu becomes
white breath

Tansei Fuji, Japan [k]

FREEZING SHADOW, *kanei* (all). Refers always to the shadow of a person who feels cold, not to any other shadows. Also: **winter shadow** (*fuyu no kage*).

takuzō e	drawn toward
yoreba oretatsu	the crucifix—a kneeling
fuyu no kage	winter shadow

Hohsen Yokozawa, Japan [k]

BASKING IN THE SUN, *hinataboko* (all). Sunbathing is a summer activity, but basking in the sun belongs to winter. (I placed the second poem below under this topic because of its subject matter and tone, though technically it is seasonless by Japanese standards.)

hinataboko	basking in the sun—
tsui ni parii o	am I to die after all
mizu shinu ka	never seeing Paris?

Keiho Ishikura, Japan [k/s]

sunlight
covers a girl's statue
with dust

Zhu Hao, China [k]

OLD DIARY, *furunikki* (mid). Having bought a diary for the coming year, this year's diary has become old. After we get a new daybook we review—and perhaps judge—the pages of the year just past.

in a busy year's diary
one blank page
after another

David Gershator, VI [s]

finding my father
between the lines
of his old diary

Greeba Brygdes-Jones, New Zealand [k]

after her death
invading the privacy
of old diaries

Elsie O. Kolashinski, MT [s]

WINTER VACATION, *fuyu yasumi* (mid). A school vacation during the period from Christmas through the New Year holiday, which ends on 7 January in Japan. Also called: **year-end holiday** (*nenmatsu kyūka*) and **winter recess.**

winter recess
the librarian's
silent stare

Anthony J. Pupello, NY [k/s]

WINTER—OBSERVANCES

GROUNDHOG DAY (late). 2 February. Also called **Candlemas Day**. According to a European tradition, "If Candlemas Day be dry and fair,/ The half o' winter's come and mair [=more];/ If Candlemas Day be wet and foul,/ The half o' winter was gone at Youl [=Yule]."—Scotch Proverb. A German proverb has it: "The badger peeps out of his hole on Candlemas Day, and, if he finds snow, walks abroad; but if he sees the sun shining he draws back into his hole." These traditions of weather prediction have resulted in 2 February coming to be known as Groundhog Day in the United States, where, on this date in Punxsutawney, Pennsylvania, a marmot (also known as "woodchuck" or "groundhog") is encouraged to emerge from his hole. If he sees his shadow (that is, if the weather is sunny), he returns to his hole to sleep for six more weeks of winter weather; if not, then winter is over—or so they say. The Groundhog Day tradition seems to have been carried here by German immigrants, and attached to the woodchuck (*Marmot monax*), a less playful creature than the lively badger (*Meles meles*) of the custom's homeland. Candlemas Day refers to the Roman Catholic custom of blessing all the candles to be used in the church year on this day, when it is said Mary presented Jesus to be purified at the Temple in Jerusalem, forty days after his birth. While they were at the Temple, St. Simeon recognized the baby as the Christ, and declared that he would be "The Light of the Gentiles"—hence the connection with candles. (See also **MARMOT** in the all-year section.)

TV news:
Groundhog Day—
click off.

Noreen Almsdatter, IA [s]

ARMISTICE DAY (early). Whether known by its original name or as **Remembrance Day** in England or **Veterans Day** in the U.S., the holiday commemorates the date 11 November 1918, when the fighting of World War I ended. Today in the U.S. it recognizes the service of veterans of both world wars, and those of other conflicts as well. The artificial **buddy poppy**, sold as a symbol of the holiday by veterans groups, derives from the graves of combatants "In Flanders Fields" where "the poppies blow/ Between the crosses, row on row" in the famous poem written under fire by John McCrea (1872–1918), a Canadian. See also **MEMORIAL DAY**, summer.

Remembrance Day—
silently, the moving flags,
cherry tree's last leaf.

Jackie Hardy, England [k]

ELECTION DAY, U.S. (early). The first Tuesday after the first Monday in November U.S. Presidential elections take place in years divisible by four, with congressional elections held in even years, and elections for some offices every year. The day is a federal holiday. (There are local elections, such as school board elections, which take place at variable times, as do national elections in many countries.) Also: **voting booth**.

Voting booth—
I close
my eyes.

Alexis Rotella, CA [s]

THANKSGIVING DAY, *kanshasai* (early). There are many holidays called "Thanksgiving" or "Thanksgiving Day". National holidays occur on the fourth Thursday of November in the U.S. and on a Monday in early October (late autumn) in Canada. The North American holiday was originated by early English colonists who set a day aside to thank God for the harvest. Japanese Protestants observe the day on the last Sunday of November. Japan also has an indigenous Shinto **HARVEST FESTIVAL** (*niiname no matsuri*) and a national holiday **LABOR THANKSGIVING DAY** (*kinrō kansha no hi*) which both fall on 23 November. In North America the holiday is noted for **Thanksgiving dinner,** which begins with a prayer of thanks for the meal and the harvest, and often features food thought to have been eaten by the Pilgrims: **roast turkey, stuffing, cranberry sauce,** and **pumpkin pie,** all of which represent the holiday to the American reader. See also **SUKKOT** under **YOM KIPPUR** in autumn.

my youngest
saying grace on Thanksgiving—
the hush

Elisabeth Marshall, CA [k]

ADVENT, *taikōsetsu* (mid). The period including the four Sundays before Christmas up to Christmas Eve, spent in meditative preparation for the coming of the baby Jesus. Many Christians decorate homes and churches with an **advent wreath,** made of evergreen branches and set flat on a table or hung horizontally, with five candles mounted one at the center and four around the rim. The four outer candles are each lit on one of the Sundays, and the last on Christmas Eve. The **fourth candle** (*vierde kaars*—Dutch) in the poem below suggests the advent wreath, overriding the reference to "snow" in its placement here.

In de lege straat	In the empty street
lantaarnlicht op verse sneeuw—	lanterns shine on fresh snow—
de vierde kaars brandt.	lighting the fourth candle.

Karel Hellemans, Belgium [k]

HANUKKAH (mid). Also called **Feast of Lights** or **Feast of Dedication** (and sometimes spelled **Chanukah**), the holiday is celebrated for eight days. It begins on the 25th of the Jewish lunar month of Kislev (between late November and late December, Gregorian), and includes the new moon nearest the winter solstice—the darkest time of year in the northern hemisphere. Commemorates the rededication of the Temple at Jerusalem by the Maccabees after they defeated the Syrian branch of the Alexandrian empire in 165 B.C.E. Candles in a special candelabrum called a **menorah** are lit, one candle added each evening for a total of eight (plus the lighting candle) on the final night. Traditional families study Torah (scripture and law) during Hanukkah. Children receive gifts, including **gelt**, money to encourage study; and the characteristic **dreidl,** a spinning top with which they gamble for prizes. In recent times adults have also come to exchange gifts. Some associated holiday foods are cooked in oil, especially **latkes** (potato pancakes) or donuts, in memory of a miracle that occurred when the temple was rededicated: one-day's supply of lamp oil lasted a full week. As with the advent wreath's candles above, the **seven nights . . . lamps** (*zeven nachten . . . lampen*—Dutch) here suggest the lighting of the menorah.

Hanukkah candles—
from the handwoven prayer shawl
faint scent of mothballs

Muriel Ford, ON [k]

Wacht zeven nachten	Wait seven nights
dan branden alle lampen	then burn all the lamps
en de zon ontwaakt.	and the sun awakens.

Fred Bergwerff, The Netherlands [k]

CHRISTMAS, *kurisumasu* (mid). 25 December; commemorates the birthday of Jesus, the Christ. Celebrated 6 January by Eastern Orthodox Christians. Deliberately associated with the winter solstice by early Christians hoping to supplant non-Christian solstice feasts. (The actual birth date of Jesus is unknown.) Aspects of pre-Christian rites remain in the **Christmas tree** hung with **ornaments** and lights, candles, the **Yule log**, bells, evergreen decorations, and special foods. **Santa Claus,** who comes **down the chimney** to put gifts in children's **Christmas stockings,** is apparently based on **Saint Nicholas,** a kindly fourth-century bishop in Asia Minor. The **Nativity scene** or *creche* displays models of the stable where Jesus was born, the **baby in a manger,** and the parents, animals, shepherds, and **three wise men** or **magi. Christmas carols** are sung through the holiday period, especially on **Christmas Eve** (*Karácsonyest*—Magyar). One internationally famous Christmas song, "**Jingle Bells**" (*jinguru beru*), is noted as a season word in *The Japan Great Almanac*. During the weeks before the holiday, Christians send and receive **Christmas cards,** buy **Christmas presents** for others while **Christmas shopping,** and decorate homes and workplaces. Plants used include **poinsettias, Christmas cactus,** and **white narcissus,** as well as evergreens. In many English-speaking countries the period including Christmas, **HANUKKAH,** and **NEW YEAR'S DAY** (part of the separate New Year season in haikai) is often called simply **THE HOLIDAYS,** which in the U.S. may be expanded to include **THANKSGIVING DAY.***

Christmas Eve . . .
in the snowbank
a full-grown angel print

Elizabeth St Jacques, ON [k]

Christmas Eve;
hanging her ornaments
without her

Ce Rosenow, OR [k]

Karácsonyest—
Magányos anyóka az állomáson:
éjféli misére vár.

Christmas Eve—
lonely granny at the station:
shelter till midnight mass.

Pachnik Zoltán, Hungary [k]

mabatakanu	without blinking
ningyō narabi	a row of dolls—
kurisumasu	Christmas

Mitsuko Yusa, Japan [k/s]

6:30
nurse in a santa claus hat
suppository in hand

Lesley Einer, AZ [s]

BOXING DAY (mid). In England, traditionally on the first weekday after Christmas one gives boxed gifts to employees and service people, such as postal carriers, delivery people, and the like.

Boxing Day meet
one rider dressed
as Father Christmas.

Patricia V. Dawson, England [k/s]

BASHŌ'S DAY, *bashō-ki* (early). On the 12th day of the 10th lunar month of 1694 (25 November, Gregorian), Bashō, the founder of haikai and haiku as we know them today, died. He was at a stopover midway on yet another journey, in Osaka, and attended by a number of disciples. Still observed according to the lunar calendar, which varies considerably from year to year with respect to the Gregorian, the date is associated with the characteristic early **WINTER DRIZZLE**. In Japanese the name of an important figure followed by *ki* means the person's death anniversary. In English, we have sometimes used "remembered" to suggest this, as in the example for the next entry. In haikai the **Master's Day** or **Master's Anniversary** (*okina no ki*) always refers to Bashō's Day.

bashō-ki ya	Bashō's Day . . .
hanarebanare ni	spattering here and there
shigure ori	a chill shower

Shūson Katō, Japan [k]

bashō-ki ya	Bashō's Day . . .
ono ga ashi kamu	biting his own leg
kangarasu	a cold raven

Kin'ichi Sawaki, Japan [k]

koi no hi mo	love days too
owaseshinaran	he must have had—
okina no ki	the Master's Anniversary

Seijo Okamoto, Japan [k]

NICK'S DAY (mid). U.S. poet Nicholas A. Virgilio lived his entire life in Camden, New Jersey, but was one of the first non-Japanese haiku poets to become known internationally. He died 3 January 1989 in Washington, D.C., as he was preparing to appear on national television. Probably his best known haiku goes "Lily:/ out of the water,/ out of itself." Also: **Nick Remembered.**

Nick remembered—
deepening the lily
in a woodcut

vincent tripi, CA [k]

WINTER—ANIMALS

FOX, *kitsune* (all). This is the **red fox** (*Vulpes vulpes*) found throughout the northern hemisphere. The naturally occurring red fox is the most widely distributed mammal besides humans, on a par with the **WOLF** (*ōkami*), also a winter topic. (The nine other species of fox have much more restricted ranges.) Like some other Eurasian species, the fox has been introduced by humans into Australia and resulted in the destruction of native fauna there. Its success derives in part from its ability to live in a wide range of habitats, from sea level to 15,000' (4,500 m), from forest to farmland. Foxes eat a variety of smaller animals, especially rabbits, hares, rodents, and insects, as well as fruit. They have often been accused of raiding chicken coops, but their destruction of rodents probably more than makes up for any economic damage they may cause humans, wherever they live. They are active mainly at night and twilight, and their range expands in winter; this may make them more apparent then and account for their inclusion in the saijiki as a winter topic. Japanese folklore features many stories about foxes, which are said to have the ability to bewitch people. On the plus side, the fox is considered the messenger of Inari, god of rice and the harvest. This mixed heritage often finds its way into haikai verses on the fox.

mountains
blue in dawn sky—fox
cough

Thomas Fitzsimmons, NM [k]

red fox
surely denned, and dry . . .
swifter than I

Emily Romano, NJ [k]

HARE, RABBIT, *usagi*, *haas*—Dutch, *liebre*—Spanish (all). Family Leporidae. This family of wild animals found in legends and folk tales includes rabbits and hares. The two common names frequently cross over, but there are some usual distinctions between them. Hares are generally larger, with more powerful hind legs and black ear-tips; today biologists tend to see only *Lepus sp.* as hares. Confusingly, the best-known names for members of the genus are **jack rabbit**, a term often applied to all varieties of *Lepus*, and **snowshoe rabbit** or **varying hare**, referring to any of the cooler temperate-zone and arctic species that go through a color change, fur shifting from browns to near- or all-white as winter approaches. The mating season for hares usually begins in mid or late winter (early spring for *L. americanus*, a varying hare), and features fighting males boxing with forefeet and kicking with hindfeet, sometimes emitting high-pitched screams when injured. The typical American rabbits, called **cottontail rabbit** or simply **cottontail**, are members of the genus *Sylvilagus*; their native ranges include southern Canada through the rest of the Americas. Breeding times vary widely, depending on species, latitude, and elevation, but in cooler regions may begin mid winter; cottontails in warmer areas breed year-round. Despite their renowned breeding abilities, cottontails are on the decline because of habitat destruction in many areas, and are not as important a game animal as they were in the

1950s and 1960s, when millions were taken annually in eastern and plains states of the U.S. Originally based in France, Iberia, and possibly northwestern Africa, the **old world rabbit** (*Oryctolagus cuniculus*) has spread nearly worldwide through human introduction beginning during Roman times, and is the basis for the domestic rabbit. (**DOMESTIC RABBIT** should probably be considered a year-round topic; unless specified otherwise, "rabbit" or "hare" in haikai will be understood to refer to animals in the wild.) Breeding begins in mid to late winter, later in cooler areas. The widespread introduction and rapid breeding of this rabbit has led to the destruction of habitat for many native species, especially in breeding areas for some birds and marsupials of the smaller Pacific islands and Australia and New Zealand; in the latter areas they have interfered with sheep production. Introduced hares have also caused problems for native species and agriculture in many parts of the southern hemisphere. Japan has both the old world rabbit (*echigo-usagi*) and its own native **wild hare** (*no-usagi, L. brachyurus*), as well as a varying hare in Hokkaido. **RABBIT HUNTING** (*usagigari*) is also a winter topic, with associated terms **rabbit net** (*usagi-ami*) and **rabbit trap** (*usagiwana*).

onbeweeglijk	motionless
zit de haas op de helling	the hare sits on the slope
één en al oor	alone and all ears

Marcel Smets, Belgium [k]

Huye la liebre	The hare flees
huye sobre trapecios	flees over trapezoids
de hierba húmeda.	of moist grass.

Casimiro Femat Saldivar, Mexico [k]

OWL, *fukurō* (all). Many owls are most prominent in winter, when longer periods of darkness make their nocturnal activities overlap more with our waking hours. Also, their hooting calls increase with mating, mid-to-late winter and early spring for many species. The Japanese saijiki divides owls into two groups, *fukurō*, including the **snowy owl** (*shirofukurō*) and **ural owl** (*fukurō*), and *mimizuku*, including most of the horned owls, such as the **long-** and **short-eared** owls (*torafuzuku* and *komimizuku*). Additional types with similar habits include the **barred**, **great gray**, **great horned**, **saw-whet**, and **screech** owls. In haikai the word "owl" by itself indicates winter, but several other species of owl come to notice at different times of year, for example the **HAWK-OWL** of Eurasia and North America and the **brown hawk-owl** (*aobazuku*) of Japan are both commonly seen in summer, and therefore a summer topic.

northern lights shimmer
a saw-whet piping
on the distant shore

nick avis, NF [k]

NORTHERN WREN, *misosazai* (all). *Troglodytes troglodytes*. Called simply **wren** in England, this tiny bird goes by several local names, including **winter wren** in North America. This species is the sole representative of its 59-member family found outside the Americas. The wren sings almost all year, and thus has found its way into the hearts of poets of both East and West who long for birdsong in winter.

watched by the cat
the wren's tail straight up
and very still

Samantha Gates, TN [k]

SWAN, *hakuchō*, *Schwan*—German (late). *Cygnus sp.* The **whooper swan** (Japanese *ō-hakuchō, C. cygnus*), breeds in northern Europe and Asia and winters in northern Africa and parts of central and western Europe, Asia Minor, northwest India, Korea, and northern Japan. The **whistling swan** or **tundra swan** (Japanese *kohakuchō, C. columbianus*) breeds in the Asian-American arctic and winters as far south as central Honshu in Japan, Chesapeake Bay in the eastern U.S., and Baja California. The largest of these birds, the **trumpeter swan** (*C. buccinator*), grows to 6' (180 cm) long with a wingspread to 8' (250 cm). It breeds inland and near the coast of central and southern Alaska and the Yukon, and winters along the coast of British Columbia and Washington, with some colonies inland year-round. The **black swan** (*C. atratus*) at 40–50" (100–130 cm) is the smallest of the group. Native to Australia and introduced into New Zealand, it breeds in the southern part of Western Australia and throughout much of eastern Australia.

In winter black swans may be seen throughout Australia. Most swans move from inland ponds to open saltwater and brackish marshes when the freshwater freezes up in late winter, gathering in substantial flocks; this probably accounts for the traditional assignment of late winter for the topic, which includes **swans come** (*hakuchō kuru*). **SWANS DEPART** (*hakuchō kaeri*) in mid spring. The **DOMESTIC SWAN** or **mute swan** (*C. olor*) was once migratory, but today in parts of Europe and Asia and since introduction in North America, Australia, and New Zealand it has become largely sedentary, staying on or near the breeding grounds year-round—making it an all-year topic. This is the swan that points its bill downward when swimming, giving its neck the graceful curve many people associate with swans; other species hold their heads erect with the bill forward.

Schwäne im Wasser	Swans in the water
unter Hölderlins Türmchen—	below Hölderlin's turret—
spurlos wie Wolken	without a trace, as clouds

Rudolf Thiem, Germany [k]

DUCK, *kamo*, *patka*—Croatian (all). Smaller than **SWAN** (winter) or **GEESE** (late autumn), ducks share the family Anatidae with them. Since many wild ducks overwinter in Japan they have become a traditional winter topic in haikai. This topic includes many well-known species, such as **mallard** (*magamo*), **teal** (*kogamo*), **pochard** (*hoshihachiro*), **canvasback** (*ō-hoshihachiro*), **greater scaup** (*suzugamo*), **common merganser** (*kawa-aisa*), and the like. Many of these or similar species are also winter visitors in western Europe and the U.S., or move from dry-land nesting sites to marshes, bays, and estuaries in winter. Parts of the southern hemisphere observe similar migrations. The Japanese accord the striking **MANDARIN DUCK** (*oshidori*, *Aix galericulata*) its own status as a winter topic. **DEPARTING DUCKS** (*hikigamo*) is a mid-spring topic, while **REMAINING DUCKS** (*nokoru kamo*) refers to those that may not depart until late spring or even May. The following are summer topics: **SUMMER DUCKS** (*natsu no kamo*), which includes species that stay in the region year-round such as the **spot-billed duck** (*karugamo*); **LAYOVER DUCKS** (*tōshigamo*), those individuals who have stayed behind while their cohorts migrated (includes some mallards, for example); and **DUCKLINGS** (*kamo no ko*). The **FIRST DUCKS** (*hat-*

sugamo) come to their winter waterways in late autumn, and the cycle begins again.

Pustoš dvorišta	A deserted backyard
nakon kiše patka u	after the rain a duck
vrtači bombe	in a bomb crater

Duško Matas, Croatia [k/s]

GREBE, *kaitsuburi* (all). Grebes are well known for their floating nests, which they usually anchor to the bottom of inland waters by attaching them to living plants. The **little grebe** (*Podiceps ruficollis*) is the species best known in Japan.

kaitsuburi	the little grebe
ikutabi atama o	however many times it sticks
dashite mo ame	its head out—rain

Masahisa Hotta, Japan [k]

WHALE, *kujira* (all). Several kinds of whales visit Japan's coastal waters in winter, forming single-species groups for the trip from the North Pacific. These largest cetaceans, or sea-dwelling mammals, include the **baleen whale** (*semikujira*), **sperm whale** (*makkōkujira*), **humpback whale** (*zatōkujira*), **rorqual** (*nagasukujira*), and the largest animal known, the **blue whale** or **sulphur bottom** (*shironagasukujira*), which exceeds any dinosaur in size. In North America **WHALE-VIEWING** has become a common summer activity at some seaside resorts.

passing whale's eye . . .
the islands on the horizon
sink and rise again

Larry Gates, MS [k]

DOLPHIN, *iruka* (all). The dolphins and related smaller cetaceans include the **common porpoise** (*mairuka*), **pilot whale** (*gondōkujira*), and **killer whale** or **orca** (*shachi*). Some members of this group have been captured and trained for human entertainment and so are seen year-round and especially during the summer vacation season. Their placement in the saijiki derives from annual migrations of several species from the North Pacific to coastal waters off Japan for the winter; similar migrations take place along the coasts of the Americas and elsewhere.

on the lee—
a pod of orca
spouts rainbows

Darold D. Braida, HI [h]

CODFISH, *tara* (all). An important sub-family of food fish, available all winter along the northern coasts of both Atlantic and Pacific.

boning
the codfish
complicating
my life

Michael McClintock, CA [s]

WINTER BUTTERFLY, *fuyu no chō* (all). The most characteristic image of a winter butterfly is a so-called **freezing butterfly** (*itechō*)—one that has left its cocoon or come out of hibernation on an unusually warm day in winter, and now sits very still with its wings spread to soak up the sun's warmth. (Japanese saijiki have similar entries for **WINTER FLY** and other out-of-season insects.) See also entries for **BUTTERFLY** in spring (as well as the essay "Butterflies Throughout the Year" that follows it), **SUMMER** and **AUTUMN BUTTERFLY**, and **MOURNING CLOAK** (all year).

itechō no	a freezing butterfly
mijirogi mosenu	without the slightest motion
hinata nari	in the sunshine

Seigyo Imamura, Japan [k]

WINTER MOSQUITO, *fuyu no ka* (all). Occasionally a mosquito comes out into winter.

fuyu no ka ya
uteba chiisaki
tsubu to kashi

A winter mosquito . . .
slapped has become just
a little blot.

Sonō Uchida, Japan [k]

WINTER—PLANTS

EARLY PLUM BLOSSOMS, *sōbai* (late.) In Japan, people take walks hoping to find **PLUM BLOSSOMS** (an early-spring topic), even on a slim chance and often in snow. In the poem below, **first plum blossoms** is a season word under this late-winter topic. In the Humanity category we also have **LOOKING FOR PLUM BLOSSOMS** (*tanbai*) in late winter.

the first plum blossoms—
now the trail does not seem
quite so muddy

Alex Benedict, CA [h]

REMAINING WILDFLOWERS (early). In many milder parts of the temperate zones some autumn wildflowers linger on into early winter, especially those in sheltered spots formed by leaning rocks and fallen trees. Also: **leftover wildflowers** (*nokoru yakusa*).

maboroshi no
nokorite kōki
yakusa kana

this illusion
of leftover crimson
wildflowers

Ruisui Han, China [k]

BUDDHA'S-HAND ORANGE, *bushukan* (all). *Citrus japonica.* "Buddha's hand orange" is a literal translation of the Japanese name for this fruit, sometimes called a **horned orange** in English. At a certain stage of maturity it looks like a deeply ribbed, elongated yellow gourd, up to 7" (18 cm) long—somewhat like a pair of human hands palm-to-palm with the fingertips touching, as in prayer. Later, the "fingers" open up a bit, like the petals of a large, fleshy flower.

bushukan ni	imitating
nazorau waga te	the Buddha's-hand orange—
hibi mo nashi	in my palms not even a callus

Mizue Yamada, Japan [k]

WINTER'S COLORED LEAVES, *fuyu momiji* (early). The showiest time for **COLORED LEAVES** (*momiji*) is late autumn, but usually some linger into early winter to become **remaining colored leaves** (*nokoru momiji*), meaning colored leaves still on the trees. While the latter may hang on into mid winter, in most of the temperate zones the **last leaf** has gone its way before then.

On the tree top
the last leaf
and the wind

Pierre Constantin, French Polynesia [k]

COLORED LEAVES FALL, *momiji chiru* (early). In haikai **LEAVES START TO FALL** in late autumn, but the majority of leaves fall in early winter (see **LEAVES**, next entry). "Colored leaves fall"—written with the characters for **red leaves fall**—is also an early-winter topic, but note that **YELLOW LEAVES DROP** (*kōraku*) is in late autumn. Also: **late leaves fall** (*caen hojas lentas*—Spanish); in the second poem below, the word "late" takes precedence over the "yellow" shadows.

momiji chiri	colored leaves fall
omo yaya soreru	glancing off its face—
zazen ishi	zazen rock

Kajō Hara, Japan [k]

Entre penumbras	Among yellow
amarillentas caen	shadows fall
las hojas lentas	the late leaves

C. Chiesa, PR [k]

LEAVES, *konoha* (all). In Japanese this literally reads **leaves of trees** and is always taken to mean the about-to-fall, falling, or fallen leaves of deciduous trees in winter. This includes the image of **leaves falling** (*konoha chiru*) or swirling around in the **WINTER WIND** (*fuyu no kaze*). The major difference between this and other topics involving falling leaves is the absence of a specified color. So, depending on the context, one may imagine red leaves, yellow leaves, brown leaves, or a mixture. A classic topic since the *Manyōshū*, (winter) leaves represents evanescence in much the same way as (spring) **BLOSSOMS**. At the same time, the topic is highly valued in haikai because it carries a suggestion of autumn's beauty into winter. Also: **leaves fall** (*opada lišće*—Serbian), **falling leaves**. In the first poem below **hopscotch** is one of many all-year, fair-weather **GAMES.***

Hopscotch
all the squares
fill with leaves

Garry Gay, CA [k]

Opada lišće.	Leaves fall.
Izranjaju skrivena	Suddenly revealing
gnezda ptica.	birds' nests.

Vitomir Miletić, Yugoslavia [k]

falling leaves
the house comes
out of the woods

Jim Kacian, VA [k]

DRY LEAVES, *kareha, dürren Blätter*—German (all). These include the leaves of oaks or other trees, or any brown, **withered leaves**, still clinging to their branches, swirling in the wind, or lying on the ground.

windy birthday the rattle of dry leaves

Frank K. Robinson, TN [k]

kuru kuru to	round and round
kaze o wagiri no	slicing up the wind
kareha kana	these dry leaves

Kyoko Fujiki, The Netherlands [k]

Verwelkt die Blumen,	Faded the flowers,
zu dürren Haufen gewischt	swept to withered heaps
die bunten Blätter.	the colored leaves.

Mily Dür, Switzerland [k]

FALLEN LEAVES, *ochiba*, *opalo lišće*—Serbian (all). People of European culture tend to focus more on leaves as they fall, seeing the transition from colored leaves on the trees to falling leaves to fallen leaves as one continuous, autumnal process. While Japanese culture does not deny this continuity, poets of Japan have long celebrated the colored leaves of autumn and likewise the fallen leaves of winter, and have not given quite as much attention to the falling leaves as have their European colleagues. One interesting way to include this topic without using one of the preordained set phrases is to involve the leaves in a situation where they must have fallen, such as **kicking yellow leaves.**

Some translators have given "falling leaves" for *ochiba*, causing English-language haiku poets great confusion, since falling leaves have firmly autumnal associations in English. The word "fall", meaning "autumn", actually refers to "the fall of the leaves"; but, as mentioned under the entry for **AUTUMN**, fall in this sense might best be understood as referring to the period including late autumn and early winter in haikai. In haikai **falling leaves** is a season word under the winter topic **LEAVES**, above. Leaves falling in late autumn are included under the topic **LEAVES START TO FALL.**

In addition to the generic topic fallen leaves, of course there are many specific kinds of fallen leaves commonly noted in winter, including **DECAYED LEAVES** (*kuchiba*), those already subjected to rain and snow, soon to become part of the soil.

A leaf has fallen
upon my shoulder and so
I come to balance.

Cid Corman, Japan [k]

te ga miete	looking at his hands
chichi ga ochiba no	dad walks in the mountains
yama aruku	of fallen leaves

Ryūta Iida, Japan [k]

Šušti opalo lišće	Rustling fallen leaves
—ljudi vuku pse	—the boys drawn by the dogs
ili obratno?	or the opposite?

Dragan J. Ristić, Yugoslavia [k]

in her perfumed
wake I walk to class
kicking yellow leaves

John Hazelton, NM [k]

WINTER GROVE, *fuyu kodachi* (all). In winter deciduous trees stand bare, revealing the lacy shapes of their branches against the sky. **White trees** (*arbres blancs*—French) suggests the branches are snow-covered.

une ombre	a shadow
ce serait l'instant du bouvreuil	for an instant of bullfinch
encore les arbres blancs	again the white trees

Pierre Courtaud, France [k]

BARE TREE, *kareki* (all). Usually taken to mean a tree bare of leaves, the Japanese *kareki* is sometimes translated as "withered tree"—which suggests a dead tree and misses the mark. Bare or **leafless tree** is more accurate. The same may be said for **bare branch** or **barren limb** (*kare-eda*). Specific trees, such as **bare hawthorn** (*gola glogina*—Bulgarian), may also be named. The word *kare* may be taken as "withered" however in phrases such as **WITHERED CHRYSANTHEMUMS** (*karegiku*) and **WITHERED LOTUS** (*karehasu*), both also winter topics.

From a barren limb
chirps of the chickadee
twitch the old tom's ear

Timothy Happel, CA [k]

Gola glogina
stiska kičurče vulna.
Dalečni hlopki.

Bare hawthorn
some wool stuck on a spine.
Distant bells.

Dimitar Stefanov, Bulgaria [k]

NARCISSUS, *suisen* (late). *Narcissus sp.* These are the earliest bloomers in the genus, like the **paper-white narcissus** and other varieties of *N. tazetta*, usually with white petals and shallow dish-shaped coronas ranging from white to yellow-orange. Narcissus are frequently forced for **Christmas narcissus** (mid winter), but in haikai the Japanese *suisen* by itself always means the late-winter narcissus. For a fuller discussion, see the entry at **DAFFODIL**, mid spring.

A ripple of laughter
from the narcissus garden
in the convent

Ikuyo Yoshimura, Japan [k]

HELLEBORE, *kurisumasu rōzu*, *kukurijek*—Croatian (mid). *Helleborus sp.* The Japanese name derives from the English common name **Christmas rose** (refers to *H. corsicus*). The hellebores include various wild and cultivated species in Europe and western Asia with evergreen, spiny leaves; most bloom in mid winter or spring and have white or greenish-white flowers. The *H. dumetorum* subspecies *atrorubens*—native to Croatia—has purple flowers larger than other wild species. A spring-blooming species native to Greece and western Asia is known as the **LENTEN ROSE** (*H. orientalis*). All have a violent cathartic effect if eaten.

Pognute glave
tek niknuo kukurijek
raste iz snijega.

Heads bent
the hellebore just sprung up
through the snow.

Marijan Čekolj, Croatia [k]

WITHERED ROSES (all). One of many garden plants with a striking winter appearance. Also: **brown rose canes.**

hanging out clothes
  the woman's raw hands
    brush brown rose canes

Geraldine C. Little, NJ [k]

LEEK, *negi* (all). Sometimes *negi* is translated "onion", but **ONION** (*tamanegi*) is an all-summer topic. Generally leeks are harvested late and used throughout winter in soups and stews. In the following poem *boai*, which is not a season word, has been translated "misty dusk".

negi sagete	carrying leeks
rōjo boai ni	an old woman in misty dusk
hitorigoto	whispers to herself

Kayoko Hashimoto, Japan [k]

WITHERED GRASS, *kusagare* (all). Withered or **dry grasses** (*ierburi uscate*—Romanian) provide a symphony of golds and browns in graceful curves through the winter.

Ierburi uscate—	Yellow dry grasses—
sub tălpi, furnicile	under foot, ants moving
gâdilă zeii.	tickle the gods.

Mioara Gheorghe, Romania [k]

WINTER VIOLETS, *fuyu sumire* (late). As winter moves toward spring some plants may bloom early, especially if there have been a few warm days.

Hobi	At Hobi
fuyu sumire	winter violets
suna ni katamuku	bent over in the sand
tokoku no hi	Tokoku's gravestone

Meiga Higashi, Japan [k]

NEW YEAR

The following entries appear under the New Year, in the categories indicated. Note that in this section only, since there are so few entries, category titles have been omitted; they are listed below for convenience.

------- The Season -------

New Year

Last Year

New Year's Day

------- The Heavens -------

First Sun

------- Humanity -------

New Calendar

First Laughter

First Calligraphy

Toasting the New Year

Hand Ball

New Year's Resolution

------- Observances -------

New Year's Reunion

Note: An asterisk at the end of an entry's text indicates that additional poems and season words on the topic may be found in Chapter 6 of *The Haiku Seasons*.

NEW YEAR

NEW YEAR, *shinnen*, *Nova godina*—Serbian. In haikai this implies either the first day of the year or the first two weeks or so, though 7 January is usually the last day of **WINTER VACATION**, a mid-winter topic. In old Japan, before the new calendar moved the first day of the year from near the beginning of spring to 1 January, "New Year" meant a prolonged holiday comparable to the period from Christmas through **NEW YEAR'S DAY** in Christian countries. Despite the dislocation in time, some phrases including the word "spring" are still considered New Year topics. See the discussion of the names of seasons in the introduction to the saijiki, pages 32–33. Also: **beginning of the year** (*toshi no hajime*), **welcome year** (*mukauru toshi*), **young year** (*wakaki toshi*), **renewed year** (*aratama no toshi*), **year is renewed** (*toshi no aratamaru*).

saijiki o	with the saijiki
yo ni tou toshi no	questioning the world
aratamaru	the year is renewed

Teiko Inahata, Japan [k]

Nova godina—	The New Year—
koverta nekog pisma	the envelope made from
od starog kalendara.	an old calendar.

Dimitar Anakiev, Slovenia [k]

beginning the New Year—
atop the bulbless lamppost
a firefly flickers

Federico C. Peralta, Philippines [k]

LAST YEAR, *kozo*. We refer to "last year" more often during the first few days and weeks of the **NEW YEAR** than at any other time, making it a New-Year topic in haikai.

The christmas beetle
on the flyscreen finishing
death begun last year.

Norman Talbot, Australia [k]

NEW YEAR'S DAY, *ganjitsu*. In the old calendar this was about the beginning of spring, and considered a doubly auspicious day. Now moved to 1 January as a result of the new calendar, New Year's Day is still treated as the beginning of spring by some haikai poets. Note that in English the phrase **New Year's** (*Neujahr*—German) is often used as a noun, meaning "New Year's Eve" or "New Year's Day"; **NEW YEAR'S EVE** (*toshi no yo*) and **NEW YEAR'S EVE PARTY** (*toshiwasure*) are mid-winter topics.*

not even drunk on new year's
regretting this too

Karen Sohne, NY [s]

Heute ist Neujahr,	Today is New Year's,
auf meinem Schreibtisch liegen	on top of my desk lies
die alten Akten.	the old paperwork.

Richard W. Heinrich, Germany [k/s]

FIRST SUN, *hatsuhi*. The first sun or sunrise of the New Year; the Japanese may also be understood to mean the **first day** of the year.

berurin no	at the broken
kuzureshi heki ni	Berlin wall the first
hatsuhi sasu	sun strikes

Shigeru Ekuni, Japan [h]

NEW CALENDAR, *hatsugoyomi*, *nieuwe kalender*—Dutch. The annual opening and putting up of the new calendar, a small household ritual which may be performed before the New Year officially begins but still suggests the New Year period.

Een huisritueel:	A home ritual:
de nieuwe scheurkalender	the new page-a-day calendar
aan de oude haak.	on the old hook.

Bart Mesotten, Belgium [k]

FIRST LAUGHTER, *waraizome*. This refers to the first time one laughs or smiles, or sees someone laughing or smiling, in the New Year. Since long ago in Japan it has been thought that meeting the world with a smile at New Year's was a good sign for the whole year. The Japanese phrase *hatsu warai* also translates as "first laughter".

midorigo no	the infant's voice
koe towanarazu	does not come out at all—
hatsu warai	first laughter

Teiko Inahata, Japan [k]

FIRST CALLIGRAPHY, *kakizome*. The first writing of the New Year in Japan is usually devoted to formal calligraphy. One brushes a felicitous or poetic phrase as a sample of one's best hand and as a propitious act to welcome the year. Often a group of children will be brought together to do their first calligraphy, usually on the **SECOND DAY** (*futsuka*) of the year. As a private act, the first letter-writing or similar activity may also be called **first brush** (*fude hajime*) or **first ink,** and one takes pains to write something congratulatory and positive in tone. This is one of many "firsts" observed at or near the beginning of each year, including **FIRST LETTERS** (*hatsudayori*), meaning the first exchange of correspondence. In haikai the most famous is probably the **FIRST DREAM** (*hatsuyume*), on the night of **NEW YEAR'S DAY**, thought to give a portent of one's luck in the coming year. In the following example, **FIRST BLOSSOMS** (*hatsuhana*) would be recognized by Japanese haikai poets as referring to the first cherry blossoms, a mid-spring topic—though the timing here suggests **EARLY PLUM BLOSSOMS**, a late-winter topic which see. (Reason: Plum blossoms are renowned for their scent, whereas cherry blossoms have little perfume.)

first ink smells like first flowers

James Kirkup, Andorra [k]

TOASTING THE NEW YEAR. In one of the first acts of the New Year, at midnight or a moment later, the guests and hosts at a **NEW YEAR'S EVE PARTY** raise a glass for luck and happiness in the coming year.

sixth decade
we toast the New Year at breakfast
instead of midnight

Ruth Holter, OR [k/s]

HAND BALL, *temari*. I have spelled this "hand ball" as two words to distinguish it from common **HANDBALL** (a game played all year) and the ball used in that game. For this is the gaily decorated hand ball that has long been a traditional New Year toy for girls in Japan. Typical hand balls of old were made of colorful string wrapped tightly around a core in bright geometric and floral patterns; today they may be made of painted rubber. In either case, one bounces the ball on the ground while singing a **hand-ball song** (*temari-uta*).

yuki no yo no	on a snowy night
temari no kage ga	the hand ball's shadow
sankaku ni	triangular

Akiyo Hoshino, Japan [k]

NEW YEAR'S RESOLUTION. On or before New Year's Day, Europeans and Americans commonly make resolutions—promises to themselves, usually about improving some kind of behavior in the coming year. One thinks about these resolutions during the first few days of the year. **MAKING NEW YEAR'S RESOLUTIONS** is a mid-winter topic. Also called: **resolution** (*hecht*—Scots).

One resolution
this New Year's Day—not to make
one resolution.

Robert Major, WA [s]

Hogmanay splore	New Year's Eve party
bauld hechts: the morn	brave resolutions: in the morning
mair weet.	still raining.

Bruce Leeming, England [s]

NEW YEAR'S REUNION. Like **THANKSGIVING** (early winter), the New Year is a time for reunions of families or friends. Some groups of friends make a particular point of getting together annually on **NEW YEAR'S DAY** or perhaps for a **NEW YEAR'S EVE PARTY**.

New Year's reunion
old friend after a stroke searching
my face for a name

George Knox, CA [k]

ALL YEAR

The following entries appear under All Year, in the categories indicated.

----- The Year -----
Time
Days
Dawn
Evening
Night
Midnight
Year-Long
----- The Heavens -----
Sky
Cloud
Sun
Venus
Stars
Aurora Borealis
Last Light
Darkness
Wind
Tornado
Rain
----- The Earth -----
Mountain
Soil
Rock
Field
River
Lake
Sea
Wave
Road
Place Name
----- Humanity -----
Face
Eyes
Mouth
Body
Throat
Tattoo
Birthmark
Birth
Child
Elderly
Illness
Death
Baby Clothes
Western Clothes
Footwear
Laundry
Meal
Cooking
Beverage
Coffee
Roof
Porch
Wall
Door
Toilet
Furniture
Lamplight
Housewares
Pots and Pans
House Cleaning
Toiletries
Office Worker
Merchant
Prostitute
Beggar
Walking
Fishing
Amusement Park
Card Game
Billiards
Doll
Games
Visual Arts
Colors
Music
Book
Poem
Film
Travel
Vacation
Tourist
Visitor
Train
Bus
Bicycle
Parking Garage
Hotel
Traffic Signal
Ford
Talk
Mail
Laugh
Dream
---- Customs & Religion ----
Relative
Parent
Married Couple
Divorce
Love
Flirt
Kiss
Shyness
Friend
Neighbor
War
Birthday
Engagement
Funeral
Buddhism
Eid-El-Fitr
Sacred Place
---- Animals -----
Tiger
Calf
Goat
Horse
Camel
Dog
Cat
Marmot
Bird
Condor
Vulture
Gull
Crow
Pigeon
Chicken
Sparrow
Carp
Seahorse
Mourning Cloak
---- Plants----
Tree
Flamingo Plant
Sagebrush
Grass
Seaweed

Note: An asterisk at the end of an entry's text indicates that additional poems and season words on the topic may be found in Chapter 6 of *The Haiku Seasons*.

ALL YEAR—THE YEAR

TIME. Time itself may be the subject of a haikai verse. But note that specific times of day are topics, and that times of year fall under their respective seasons.

A dog barking . . .
The man making a watch
forgets the time

Esther Gress, Denmark [k]

DAYS, *rekijitsu.* **Yesterday, today, tomorrow; last week, this week, next week;** and so with months. Note that **THIS YEAR** (*kotoshi*) and **LAST YEAR** (which see) are New Year seasonal topics, since they imply a recent crossing of the barrier from one year to another.

Always tomorrow
promising that he will work—
the new hired man.

C. M. Buckaway, SA [s]

DAWN, *yoake, amanecer*—Spanish. **Daybreak** (*madrugada*—Spanish) or **break of day,** the "break of night" as the Japanese literally translates. Refers to the time between **NIGHT** and **SUNRISE,** and includes such terms as **crack of dawn,** which suggests the very beginning of **DAYLIGHT,** these being all-year topics. Note that while haikai reserves **FIRST LIGHT** (*hatsu akari*) for the dawn of the New Year's Day, most writers and readers unfamiliar with the saijiki will understand **first light** as an abbreviation for the **first light of dawn,** as it is intended in one of the poems below. (This is not the only instance of the same phrase having two different meanings in the saijiki, according to context.) In European languages **aurora,** after the Roman goddess of the same name, also means dawn.

Dawn in the city;
defective burglar alarms
shrilling.

Bruce Leeming, England [k/s]

Madrugada.	Daybreak.
Las casas salen húmedas	Houses loom moist
del sueño.	with the dream.

Humberto Senegal, Colombia [k]

first light
a bombed-out jeep smoking
in desert silence

Lenard D. Moore, NC [k]

Hoy, mar, amaneciste con más niños que olas.

Now, the sea, dawning with more children than waves.

Rafael Alberti, Spain [k]

EVENING, *yū*. **Close of day** (*higure*), **eventide** (*yūgata*), **dusk** (*tasogare*), **twilight, crepuscule** (*crepúsculo*—Spanish), names for the time when light lingers between day and night. Note that while "evening" refers only to the shift from day to night, "twilight", "crepuscule" (sometimes spelt "crepuscle"), and "dusk" may also mean the period between night and day, though dusk usually refers to evening, and is said to be the darker part of twilight.

Inmóvil, mudo	Unmoving, still
un pescador postrado	a prostrate fisherman
bebe el crepúsculo.	drinks the crepuscule.

Francisco Monterde, Colombia [k]

end of the hour—
twilight shadows obscure
the therapist's face

James Chessing, CA [k]

NIGHT, *yoru*, *noche*—Spanish. The various times of day have special qualities at different times of the year, accounting for such topics as **SPRING MORNING, SPRING NIGHT**, and so on. But night itself is a kind of season, parallel in some ways to winter, when most human activity slows down but buried fires still make heat. In some situations night may suggest a fearful **DARKNESS**, in others the passionate intimacy of **LOVE**—both also all-year topics.

La vasta noche	The vast night
no es ahora otra cosa	now there's nothing else
que una fragrancia.	but a fragrance.

Jorge Luis Borges, Argentina [k]

MIDNIGHT, *yowa*. The time when one day shifts to the next, just before the **dead of night** and the **small hours** of 1, 2, and 3 a.m. Also called the **witching hour**, because it was once believed that witches went abroad on their evil errands at this hour. See **HALLOWEEN**.

At midnight
rattling at my window
my debts

Willem Lofvers, The Netherlands [s]

a hubcap
rolls down the midnight street
into its distant sound

Alan Pizzarelli, NJ [k]

YEAR-LONG. Thoughts of **LAST YEAR** belong to the New Year period, but some phenomena have to do with the stretch of the year itself. Also: **half-year**.

down from the mountain
buying half a year's supplies
not one word

Mary Lou Bittle-DeLapa, NY [s]

ALL YEAR—THE HEAVENS

SKY, *sora*, *nebo*—Croatian. The most basic term for the fluid we go through and all above it; **the void.** The sky itself as subject: **blue sky, gray sky, lowering sky, morning sky, evening sky**. Note that many heavenly bodies and named sky conditions are seasonal. Also: **air** (*air*—French).

nakon oluje	after the storm
dječak briše nebo	a boy wipes the sky
sa stolova	from the tables

Darko Plažanin, Croatia [k]

Blanche et vide	Clear and void
Motant à toute vitesse	Rising at all speed
Une bulle d'air	A bubble of air

Abdouni Jalil, Morocco [k]

CLOUD, *kumo*. Some kinds of clouds are typical of specific times of year, for example the **BILLOWING CLOUDS** of summer, **WINTER CLOUDS**, and the like. Undifferentiated "clouds" belong here, unless some other phenomenon suggests a season.

The sun leaves
one cloud dropped
in the lake

Tadao Okazaki, Japan [k]

SUN, *taiyō*. Seen or unseen, the sun is a constant influence on all life on earth. A **solar eclipse** can occur at any time of year. The word **eclipse** is enough to specify solar if daytime is indicated by some other phenomenon in the verse. (**LUNAR ECLIPSE** is also an all-year topic, though **MOON** , of course, is autumnal.) **AFTERGLOW** (*yūyake*) is a summer topic, but **sunrise** (*kyokujitsu*), **sunshine** (*hikage*), and **sunset** (*nichibotsu*, *ocaso*—Spanish) may come any time of year. **FIRST SUN** normally refers to the first sunrise of the year, but the last poem below—though it includes the phrase **first sun** (*eerste zon*—Dutch)—does not seem appropriate to the New Year. See "Words in International Haikai" following. Also: **morning sunshine** (*asahikage*).*

sun shining
through her skirt
and she knows it

Robert Gray, PA [s]

Sparrows
quit fussing
the day of the eclipse

Eloise Barksdale, AR [k]

Hij eet zijn broodje
wat trager dan anders,
in de eerste zon.

He eats his sandwich
more slowly than usual,
in the first sun.

Ludo Haesaerts, Belgium [k]

WORDS IN INTERNATIONAL HAIKAI

In literature and in life, words and phrases acquire connotations and emotive power beyond their literal meanings. Ezra Pound calls this "logopoeia"—charging language with meaning by engaging the visual and aural imagination through words that stimulate "the associations (intellectual or emotional) that have remained in the receiver's consciousness in relation to the actual words." The tradition of season words in Japanese haikai presents a highly developed example of logopoeia. Many of the most commonly used season words have roots deep in Japanese (and

Chinese) literature. Along with a seasonal association they bring to the educated reader's consciousness the history of the way they have been used over centuries, and a sense of connection with the whole body of that literature and the people who created it.

> Aside from the fellowship of literature, how can we express our hearts? Recall the poems of old on falling plum blossoms. How do olden times and the present differ? Let us make a collection, composing poems on the plum blossoms of this garden.

mutsuki tachi	Harmony Month
haru no kitaraba	is here as spring comes
kaku shikoso	so let us
ume o okitsutsu	welcome the plum blossoms,
tanoshiki oeme	fulfilling our delight.

Thus wrote Lord Ki, secretary to a gathering in 730 C.E., in the introduction to thirty-two poems on plum blossoms produced by those present and included in the *Manyōshū*. One poet in the group wrote that should a myriad generations pass away, the plum blossoms would continue each year without ceasing. May it be so. Today's Japanese haiku poet writing on plum blossoms joins other poets of long ago, yesterday, today, and hopefully tomorrow who give attention to that sight and scent with their eyes and nose—and with their words of praise.

But the "associations in relation to the actual words" that Pound speaks of are frequently specific to a particular language or cultural group. The last poem under the topic **SUN**, above, provides a good example of a problem that arises more and more often as haikai becomes international:

Hij eet zijn broodje	He eats his sandwich
wat trager dan anders,	more slowly than usual,
in de eerste zon.	in the first sun.

Ludo Haesaerts, Belgium [k]

The Dutch words *eerste zon* literally mean "first sun"—and have been so translated. In Japanese haikai **FIRST SUN** (*hatsuhi*) has long been a seasonal topic of the New Year, and is included in this saijiki's New Year section. In the haikai tradition the phrase means sunrise on the first day of the year, and actually carries the same meaning in colloquial Japanese. The season word **first sunshine** (*hatsu hikage*) also refers to that sunrise.

When I first looked at the Dutch poem I more or less automatically classified it as a New Year poem. Reading it again later, I was not so sure. A Dutch-speaking informant advised me that the poem seemed more like summer. And, considering the unlikelihood of going outside to eat a "usual" sandwich at the dawn of the New Year in the Northern Hemisphere, I had to agree. To understand how someone less involved with the seasonal system would see the poem, I asked a colleague to read the translation and tell me what was going on. The response: It has been cloudy or rainy for several days, and the person is enjoying and prolonging his time in the welcome sunlight. When I pressed for the time of year, I was told "Oh, maybe spring or summer—could be autumn, too." On further discussion, we agreed that the poem clearly takes place at a time other than sunrise, probably lunchtime, and could happen at any time of year after a period of several cloudy or bad-weather days. After that conversation I decided to place the poem under the year-round topic **SUN**, which is not time-bound but allows readers to interpret the time of year according to their own experience, or ignore it altogether.

The way most Japanese saijiki are put together, this would not be an appropriate move. The vast majority of Japanese haiku poets share the assumption that if poets use phrases that are already understood to have seasonal meanings, the poets know the seasonal meanings of the phrases and wish those seasons to be understood by their readers.

Of course some Japanese haiku poets—a small but possibly growing percentage—ignore the season-word aspect, and when they use phrases that happen to be season words they either don't care whether the phrases are interpreted in the traditional manner or may not recognize them as such. Still, even the works of these poets often contain phrases which are, in fact, traditional season words. I have found poems by Santōka and Hōsai in the *Japan Great Saijiki*, dutifully listed under the appropriate phrases in their poems, regardless of whether the authors intended the poems to have a seasonal context.

As of this writing, most non-Japanese haiku poets know little about the traditional seasonal system. Does it make sense to give their poems seasonal contexts on the basis of the chance occurrence of phrases which, when translated, duplicate season words in the Japanese tradition?

There seem to be three possible situations here. One, a poem may indicate the time of year by means of the phenomena named in it, even if the author took no particular notice of this fact at the time of composition. Clearly, such a poem belongs in the appropriate season for the phenomena, which may include an already recognized seasonal topic.

Two, even if the season seems ambiguous, we may know the author's intent. If the author feels strongly that a poem has a connection with a particular time of year that is not immediatly obvious to the reader or accounted for in the saijiki, it would be a courtesy to the author to accept the season the author feels is appropriate. However, if the author's understanding of the poem's seasonal connection is purely personal and the poem itself does not reveal even a hint of the season to the reader, or clearly could apply to three or more seasons, I would suggest that the poem be treated as ambiguous—the third case. (Note that season words for phenomena that occur through spring and summer, or autumn and winter, are often considered appropriate to the season in which the phenomena first become prominent.)

Third, a poem may be quite ambiguous regarding the time of year, even if it includes some apparently obvious season word. Judging by the opinions of my colleagues, the poem above on the "first sun" fits this case exactly. I believe that readers of such a poem will not be well served if the poem is forced unnaturally into a season based solely on its semantics. It seems more reasonable to recognize the poem as appropriate to many different times of year by including it in a non-seasonal section of the saijiki—along with a note indicating that such-and-such a phrase is usually understood to indicate a season. Thus the placement of the poem does not mislead the reader, who will also learn the traditional season of the phrase in question.

Sensitivity to this and similar issues will become more and more important as global contact among contemporary haiku poets increases. The Japanese will have to recognize the validity of seasonal perceptions other than their own. And those of us less familiar with the seasonal aspects of haikai should respect their paramount place in the tradition by learning more. By doing so, we will participate more fully in that tradition, creating and sharing poems that will be more easily understood and better appreciated by others worldwide.

VENUS. The brightest planet in our solar system, Venus is especially radiant when it appears—virtually alone in the twilight sky—as the **evening star** or **morning star**. Note that "the curve of Venus" in the following poem has at least a double meaning.

in space
the curve of Venus
my son's crown at birth

Lequita Vance, CA [k]

STARS, *hoshi*, *zvijezde*—Croatian, *estrellas*—Spanish. Certain stars will be more apparent at one time of year or another, but "stars" can be seen on any clear night. Note, however, the autumn topic **STARLIT NIGHT**, which see.

rust speckles the new saw
left by the carpenter
under the stars

Randal Johnson, WA [k/s]

Zvijezde	Stars
nad selom. Pokoja	above the village. Some
u obližnjoj lokvi.	in a nearby pool.

Ivan I. Ivančan, Croatia [k]

El tanque	The reservoir
se pasa la noche entera	passes its whole night
haciendo gágaras de estrellas.	gargling stars.

Francisco Mendez, Guatemala [k/s]

AURORA BOREALIS. The **northern lights** appear as a luminous glow in the northern night sky. Forms vary from a stationary white arc or band to colorful curtains or rays. Caused by high-energy particles from the sun interacting with molecules of the earth's atmosphere, auroras occur most frequently within a few weeks of the equinoxes, in March and April and again in September and October. The chance of seeing them increases as one moves further toward the pole. Since they are caused by electromagnetic activity, auroras may interfere with electrical and broadcast transmission. The identical phenomenon in the southern hemisphere is called the **aurora australis.** Note that the word "aurora" by itself may refer to this phenomenon, but will usually be understood as meaning **DAWN**, after the Greek goddess Aurora.

almost asleep
a breeze wakes me—
northern lights

Tom Lynch, CA [k]

LAST LIGHT. Refers to the last moments of light sky in the west before night fully descends.

last light
pouring up the slope
—and higher still

Richard Bodner, NM [k]

DARKNESS, *yami, tiniebla*—Spanish. The condition of very little light or none, which may or may not imply **NIGHT**. It always indicates low visibility, and may imply an inability to understand, as in the phrase **in the dark** which may be interpreted both literally and figuratively. Also: **dark,** usually as "the dark".

coming from behind
a silent jogger passes
too close in the dark

Annie Bachini, England [s]

Balanceaban	Balancing
cráneos, muela usada	skulls, worn millstones
de la tiniebla.	of darkness.

Salvador Espriu, Spain [k]

WIND, *kaze, vântul*—Romanian, *vent*—French, *viento*—Spanish, *vyatur*—Bulgarian. Many specific kinds of wind have their seasons, such as the mild **EAST WIND** (*kochi*) of spring and cold **NORTH WIND** (which see) of winter, but "wind" by itself is a year-round phenomenon.

yanked from the clothesline
the sound of the sheet
becoming wind

Christopher Herold, CA [k]

vântul plimbă	the wind blows a bag
o pungă prin oraş—	through the town—
sete de tine	hunger for you

Ana-Olimpia Sima, Romania [k/s]

lourd	heavy
le vent	the wind
dans les poussières	in the dust

marie mas-pointereau, France [k]

Knothole:
wind in
my eye

Ty Hadman, Peru [k/s]

¡Qué silencio!	That silence!
Despues el viento	After the wind
ha abierto la puerta . . .	has opened the door . . .

Luis Rosales, Spain [k/s]

Desde un balcon	From a balcony
cortinas al viento	curtains in the wind
diciendo adios.	saying good-bye.

V. M. Crespo, Venezuela [k/s]

Žena i kniga	Woman and book
na pyasuka, vyatur	on the sand; the wind
prelistva vulnite.	turns over the waves.

Dimitar Stefanov, Bulgaria [k]

TORNADO. "Tornado" would probably qualify as a seasonal topic for a specific region, but tornadoes peak in different seasons according to locale, ranging from March through June in parts of the southeastern U.S., April through July in the northern plains states, July and August in parts of Canada, and reappearing in November in Lousiana and Mississippi. They can occur at any time of year, with January being the least tornado-prone month. Tornadoes consist of a rotating column of air reaching from a turbulent cloud to the ground, achieve winds of 100–250 mph (160–400 kph), and are the most violent storms on our planet. An incipient tornado that has not yet reached the ground is called a **funnel cloud**. A **WHIRLWIND** or **twister** is a small, local rotating air column typical of summer that may lift leaves, papers, and other loose debris but does little damage; a **DUST DEVIL** or **sand devil** is similar. Both are produced by local ground heating; neither involves the violently turbulent cloud caused by clashing warm and cold air masses that characterizes a tornado.

Tornado:
the elephant stands
against it

Juris Krumins, ON [k]

RAIN, *ame*, *reën*—Afrikaans. Despite many seasonal topics relating to rain, sometimes rain seems a season unto itself. Also: **night rain.**

Teen die berghange	On the mountain slopes
sif Xhosa-liedjies en reën	sift Xhosa songs and rain
saam neer	gently together

Hélène Kesting, South Africa [k]

the sound of night rain
falling on so many
different things

Doris Heitmeyer, NY [k]

ALL YEAR—THE EARTH

MOUNTAIN, *yama*. Mountains have many seasonal characteristics (see **AUTUMN MOUNTAINS**, for example), but their main characteristic, altitude above surrounding terrain, has little to do with seasons. Also: **precipice.**

At the edge of the precipice I grow logical

George Swede, ON [s]

SOIL. The soil of the earth, **dirt, earth,** is a basic element with many manifestations: **dust** (*prašina*—Serbian), **mud, loam,** and so on. Note that dust and mud may be associated with specific seasons in some areas, but that either can occur in any season. **SPRING MUD** (*shundei*) is a seasonal topic. Also: **dusty track, muddy road** (*blatni put*—Croatian).

the mailman's dust
passes him
at the mailbox

Randy Brooks, IL [k/s]

dusty track
with a few good
kickable stones

Chris Mulhern, England [k]

U mojoj sobi	In my room
prašina je jedini	dust is the only
deo prirode.	part of nature.

Olivera Shijacki, Yugoslavia [k]

Pognute glave	With head down
žurno gazi blatni put	hastily tread the muddy road
rijeka ljudi.	streaming people.

Sunčica Šamec, Croatia [k]

ROCK, *pietra*—Italian. Rock and **stone** are almost but not quite equivalents; rock suggests unmanipulated raw material, stone suggests pieces, sometimes cut or dressed.

Nessuna pianta	No plant
qui, nessun animale	here, no animal
ma pietra e luce.	but rock and light.

Margherita Guidacci, Japan [k]

FIELD, *heiya*, *Feld*—German. This includes open ground that may or may not have been cultivated, but that is not covered with plants higher than shrubs and usually suggests shorter vegetation, such as grasses or other low-growing plants. Often one specifies a type of field, for example **FIELD OF DAISIES**, which would be a spring topic; this topic is reserved for poems in which the field is the main subject, but the season cannot be determined.

Im Licht der Sonne
des stillen Feldes kehrt mir
die Kindheit wieder.

In the sunlight
of quiet fields returns
my childhood again.

Gaby G. Blattl, Austria [k]

RIVER, *kawa*. Rivers vary in size from **streams** one can throw a stone across to great **water-courses** like the Mississippi, Nile, or Amazon. They provide both barriers to land travel and convenient transport routes. River flooding can be a substantial economic asset, or a major disaster. A river is a symbol of power, as well as a source of food, recreation, and music.

the river
with day's closing
becomes sky

Dwight L. Wilson, NJ [k]

LAKE, *koshō*, *jezero*—Serbian. Includes **marshes**, **swamps**, **ponds**, and **pools** (natural), as well as **reservoirs**. **SWIMMING POOL** is a summer topic in the Humanity category.

old pond
throwing a stone at it
watching it bounce

Kenneth C. Hurm, KY [k/s]

Imam tajni ključ
dodirnuću sunce
u dubini jezera.

I have the secret key
that will touch the sun
in the depths of the lake.

Petar Kavgić, Yugoslavia [k]

SEA, *umi*, *mar*—Spanish. The sea covers most of the earth, both separating and connecting the landmasses. While best known as a food source and a medium for summer recreation, the **ocean** rewards attention at all times of the year. It also suggests the origin of life.

walks down to the sea
and with a sudden movement
bends to wet her wrists

Bernard Lionel Einbond, NY [k]

Ah, el mar de Cuba a lo lejos	Ah, the sea of Cuba in the distance
Aquí, cerca, las olas	Here, nearby, the waves
Se rompen como espejos.	Break like mirrors.

Ana Rosa Núñez, FL [k]

WAVE, *ola*—Spanish. The waves of the sea are only its most obvious motion, created by a combination of winds, tides, and currents. In the poetry of all peoples who live near the ocean, waves represent constant motion, constant change, and both the connection and the distance between objects touched by the waves.

Todavía	Still
en esta orilla.	on this shore.
Las olas siguen llagando.	The waves keep on coming.

Berta G. Montalvo, FL [k/s]

ROAD, *michi*. Road and its variations—**highway** (*kaidō*), **street** (*dōro*), **alley** (*roji*), **trail, path** (*michi*)—all suggest movement, travel, transport. Our feelings about a particular road will vary according to the surroundings and materials under foot or wheel: **cobblestone, yellow brick, asphalt** (*asfalt*—Catalan) or **macadam** (with its undertones of "MacAdam"—son of Adam), or **concrete.**

"Road" and "path" in particular will also bring to mind "the **way**", both as a practical means of getting from one place to another and as a spiritual or aesthetic discipline—the way to accomplish a task, the way to self-realization. In haikai it is almost impossible to think of "road" or "way" without hearing Bashō's verse, "this road . . . / no one goes along in/ the autumn dusk" (*kono michi ya yuku hito nashi ni aki no kure*), so the topic may have a touch of autumnal feeling, though of course it specifies no season.

en l'asfalt gris	on grey asphalt
un petit cor escarlata	a little scarlet heart
rebotant	bounces

Josep Maria Junoy, Spain [k]

PLACE NAME, *chishi*. Many poems with place names also contain season words. But a place name that replaces a seasonal topic in a poem should create an equally powerful image; the name must be well recognized by readers for its physical or emotional resonance. For example: **Diamond Head**, a well-known scenic spot in Hawaii; **Mirogoj**, a famous cemetery in Zagreb, and **Subothan** (*Subotchan*—Polish) is a stream in Poland.

rain on Diamond Head
small ponds
in the lava flow

Tony Quagliano, HI [k]

na mirogoju	at Mirogoj
zračna uzbuna: svi su	an air-raid siren: they're all,
u skloništima	all in their shelters

Visnja McMaster, Croatia [k]

cicho tak cicho	quiet so quiet
nanizałem na palce	I threaded on my fingers
szmer Subotchanu	murmurs of Subothan

Robert Szybiak, Poland [k]

ALL YEAR—HUMANITY

FACE, *kao*. The first thing that everyone looks at in photographs of people (or animals). We communicate a great deal with our facial expressions. Also: **blush** (*kleur*—Dutch).

Expressionless
as she puts on
  her face

Tom Tico, CA [s]

burned as a child
living with this face
and others'

Mary Lou Bittle-DeLapa, NY [s]

De jonge boswachter	The young forester
vraagt met hoogrode kleur	asks with a bright red blush
wat wij daar deden.	what we were up to.

Servaas Goddijn, The Netherlands [s]

EYES, *me.* **Eyebrows, eyelashes** (*wimpers*—Dutch), and **eyelids** each serve physiological functions and are also involved in communication. The opening, narrowing, and other movements of eyes form a significant part of communication, and have a great deal to do with our sense of who a person is. A **blink** may be simply a reflex action when something gets in an eye; a **wink** bespeaks shared confidence or amusement at the least, and may be part of **FLIRTING**, which see later in this category.

Haar lange wimpers	Her long lashes
strijken zo'n parkeerdeukje	should easily smooth away
moeiteloos glad.	such a parking-dent.

Ton Koelman, The Netherlands [s]

MOUTH, *kuchi.* The mouth serves as the source of verbal and other communication, and as the conduit for food passing into the body. The mouth and eyes are our primary means of interacting with the world and other people.

sharing a sandwich:
my mouth   your mouth

Ross Clark, Australia [s]

BODY, *shintai*. The human body and its parts; **FACE** and **HANDS** are separate topics. Also: **back**. Many of us are concerned about our size or **body weight**, as evidenced in the poem below with the phrase **i'm not . . . big**.

Loading my toolbox
to begin work
my back goes out.

Steve Sanfield, CA [s]

walking behind thinking i'm not that big in my dress

Janice M. Bostok, Australia [s]

THROAT, *nodo*. The throat carries food from mouth to digestive organs, air from atmosphere to lungs and back, and is involved in speech. The throat and **neck** may also be considered erogenous and have aesthetic qualities.

listening to
the blue veins at
her throat

John Knight, Australia [k/s]

TATTOO. This and other added body marks, such as a **scar** (*colm ort*—Irish), are historical artifacts.

I love you
the tattoo beneath
her waist

Marian Olson, NM [s]

an colm ort	that scar
nár thaitin riamh liom	i never liked
lig dom é a fheiceáil	let me see it

Gabriel Rosenstock, Ireland [s]

BIRTHMARK. Or **birth mark** in the poet's more careful enunciation —a blemish present on the skin at birth, usually pink, red, brown, or bluish in color. Some may be seriously disfiguring; others may be like a **BEAUTY MARK** in effect or located on the body in an area not usually seen. They are often used as means of identification.

birth mark
on her cheek—a rain cloud
at nightfall

John O'Connor, New Zealand [k]

BIRTH, *sei*. This topic is devoted to the fact of human birth itself, to babies, and to their legend and lore. Related terms such as **newborn** (*sanji*), **umbilical cord, baby** (*akanbō*) (all referring to humans), **midwife, obstetrician, first bath,** and the like may be included here. Note that name-giving ceremonies, such as **CHRISTENING,** come under the following category, Customs and Religion; **BABY CLOTHES** is a separate topic grouped with other clothing. Animal births are treated in the appropriate seasons, or under the year-round Animals category if they are not associated with a particular season.

hoping the shape
of the navel will be good
father cuts the cord

Shōkan Kondō, Japan [k]

CHILD, *yōji*, *enfant*—French. From **infant** (*eiji*) to **toddler,** to **young boy** (*dōji*) or **young girl** (*dōjo*). The last poem in this group ably demonstrates an implied topic; though we are not directly told the age of the person given attention in this poem, it seems clear that "he" refers to a child.

suddenly we see
what our child has been collecting:
surveyor stakes!

Tom Clausen, NY [k/s]

deux livres dans mon sac	two books in my bag
mais dans le parc	but in the park
les enfants et leur jeux	children and their games

marie mas-pointereau, France [k/s]

Laughing children
fan the air as bubbles rise
in their bathwater . . .

Adam Stanton, Australia [s]

he won't go to sleep
unless we play him the tune
that keeps him awake

Alvaro Cardona-Hine, NM [s]

ELDERLY, *oi*. **To age** (*oiru*), **maturity** (*rōsei*), **get up in years** (*toshiyori*), **growing old** (*toshi toru*), **old man** (*rōya*), **old woman** (*rōjo*), **senior citizen, golden age.** In haikai these last two phrases may have a deliberate ironic twist. "Grandfather" and "grandmother" are sometimes used to refer to elderly persons, but are normally **RELATIVES**. Note that **my old man** is a pet term for husband or father; see **MARRIED COUPLE**. Also: **old folks' home.**

Growing older
I have further to return from
when awakening

Willem Lofvers, The Netherlands [s]

old woman shaping
a grapevine wreath—
veins in her hands

Mildred Williams Boggs, KY [k]

old folks' home—
the square of light
crosses the room

Michael Dylan Welch, CA [k]

ILLNESS, *yamai.* Illnesses of many kinds, and the professionals and apparatuses related to them. **COUGH** and **SNEEZE** belong to winter, but **choking** has no season. Also: **cancer patient, clinic, hospital** (*gasthuis*—Dutch), **dentist, therapy.***

deciding to go out
the cancer patient
reaches for her wig

Peter Duppenthaler, Japan [k/s]

Choking,
he keeps explaining
how he choked.

Anita Virgil, VA [s]

the dentist—
all his ten fingers
and thumbs in my mouth

Laura Bell, CA [s]

in hospital
knowing which day
by the food

John F. Turner, Australia [s]

after therapy
at lunch the waitress asks
have you been helped?

Michael McNierney, CO [s]

DEATH, *shi*, *smrt*—Croatian. The end of a human life on this plane of existence, perhaps the doorway to another. Relevant ceremonies and burial customs are treated under the category Customs and Religion, which follows this category. Also: **deathbed** (*sterfbed*—Dutch), **gone, gone many years, death poem.**

smrt prijatelja—	dead friend—
zrnca fine prašine	fine grains of dust
na šahovskoj tabli	on the chessboard

Robert Bebek, Croatia [k]

Een ogenblikje	A moment
zijn sterfbed verlatend,	left his deathbed,
geeft ze	to give his
de bloemen water.	flowers water.

Willem Lofvers, The Netherlands [k]

friend gone
the silence
of untouched water

Charles H. Easter, NJ [k]

gone these many years
the scent of lavender still
in her dresser drawer

Herb Barrett, ON [k]

these death poems—
grandson hearing Bashō's
asks for mine

H. F. Noyes, Greece [k/s]

BABY CLOTHES. As well as the term "baby clothes" itself, this topic includes all special clothes and related items for babies: **swaddling clothes** (*pelene*—Croatian), **receiving blanket, diapers, booties,** along with phrases that add the word "baby" to the names of adult articles, such as **baby cap, baby shoes, baby blanket,** and so on. (But **BLANKET** is a winter topic.) Specialized clothing for toddlers, such as **training pants,** also belongs under this topic. Note that ceremonial garb, such as a **christening gown,** properly belongs with the topic for the relevant ceremony, for example **CHRISTENING.**

zabijelili se	whitening
balkoni pelenama	swaddling clothes on the balconies
grad je tako mlad	the town is so young

Boris Nazansky, Croatia [h]

WESTERN CLOTHES, *yōfuku*. This topic includes all the typical western business and casual clothes, such as **dress shirt** or **sport shirt, slacks** or **pants, blouse, skirt, jacket,** and **dress.** In haikai dress usually refers to the women's garment, though in certain contexts it may mean clothes in a more general sense.

at the party
someone older than I
wearing a dress like mine

Naomi Y. Brown, TX [s]

FOOTWEAR, *hakimono*. Includes all manner of **shoes** (*shūzu*, *schoenen*—Dutch), **boots** (*būtsu*), **socks** (*kutsushita*), **slippers,** and so on. Note that some footwear is seasonal, for example **SNOW SHOES** (*kanjiki*) and Japanese-style split-toed socks—*tabi*—both belong in winter. Also: **shoe laces** (*veter*—Dutch).

night comes—
picking up your shoes
still warm

Gary Hotham, MD [k]

Met een zakdoekje	With a handkerchief
veegt hij zijn schoenen schoon	he shines up his shoes
de ondernemer.	the entrepreneur.

Servaas Goddijn, The Netherlands [s]

shoes so dear to me
they all but take a few steps
in my direction

Alvaro Cardona-Hine, NM [k]

Mijn veter knopend	Tying my laces
zie ik opeens de wereld	I suddenly see the world
op hondjeshoogte.	from a dog's height.

Agnes Verhulst, Belgium [s]

nothing to do
putting on
loud socks

Michael McClintock, CA [s]

Grandfather's old boots
I take them
for a walk

George Swede, ON [k]

HANDBAG. The sturdy bag used to carry personal necessities such as **money**, cosmetics, medications, **identification** or a **driver's license**, and other objects needed when one is outside the home. The word **purse** may be used instead, or may refer to a **wallet** that might be carried inside a handbag to hold **ID, cash, credit cards,** and **wallet photos.** Note that a handbag is considered an accessory to clothing, which may become more obvious when one encounters an **evening bag**—usually quite small and appropriate to an **evening gown** or other **FORMAL ATTIRE.** With today's **CASUAL WEAR** one might substitute a **fanny**

pack for a handbag; the latter usually suggests that the bearer is a woman, while the former may be worn by either sex.

about this punk girl
someone saw on a train
using a kettle for a handbag

Eve T. Pilcher, Ireland [s]

LAUNDRY. Doing the laundry, an activity that goes on week after week, year after year. Also: **folding sheets** (*vouwen laken*—Dutch).

Een man en een vrouw—	A man and a woman—
elk laken dat ze vouwen	each sheet they fold
brengt hen bij elkaar.	brings them together.

Nanneke Huizinga, Denmark [k]

MEAL, *shokuji*. Everything from **breakfast** (*chōshoku*) to **dinner** (*seisan*). Like its midday counterpart, **luncheon,** "dinner" implies a social event as well as eating, while **lunch** (*ranchi*) and **supper** (*yashoku*) are simple meals intended mainly to sustain the body.

at dinner
biting into the roast beef . . .
the butcher's thumb nail

Mary Thomas Eulberg, OSF, IA [s]

COOKING. Many foods are seasonal; this topic includes any kind of **food preparation, recipe, cook** and so on, that is not specific to a particular season or holiday.

His turn to cook
again he can't find
the thyme

Carolyn G. Banks, MN [s]

Pasta shell—
the little cook holds it
to her ear.

Alexis Rotella, CA [k/s]

puckering the breeze
  smell of the new recipe
    my wife concocted

Federico C. Peralta, Philippines [k/s]

BEVERAGE, *inryō*. This topic includes all non-alcoholic drinks that do not have strong seasonal associations, from **drinking water** (*beau apă*—Romanian) to **milk shake**. Note, however, that **ICE WATER** suggests summer.

Beau apă din palmă.	Drinking water from my palm.
pe linea vieţii,	on the life line,
nisipul . . .	the sand . . .

Valentin Busuioc, Romania [k]

COFFEE, *kōhii*, *koffie*—Dutch, *café*—French. As with most addictive substances, a whole collection of paraphernalia and specialized equipment surrounds the production and serving of coffee as a beverage. From roasting **coffee beans** and sending them through a **coffee mill** on to the **coffee pot, coffee maker,** or **espresso machine** to **coffee cup** or **mug,** whether **drip grind, perk,** or **instant coffee,** hot or **ICED COFFEE** (a summer topic), **coffee lovers** will have their coffee year-round. If not at breakfast, then at the factory or office during the **coffee break** which came into vogue during World War II—to increase production—perhaps with a piece of **coffee cake,** a pastry made to serve with coffee. And if not at home or work, then at a **coffee shop** or **coffee house,** the former designed for short snacks, the latter for leisure and perhaps called a **café.** Neighbors may indulge in a **coffee klatch** in someone's kitchen, or in the living room around the **coffee table** (properly under the topic **FURNITURE**). Newly arrived college students or new members of clubs may take their coffee at a **coffee** (under the topic **PARTY**) where they will expect to meet other members of their institutions. From **java** and **café au lait** to **Turkish coffee** and Italian **espresso,** the names and specialty varieties of coffee suggest exoticism. Finally, with **Irish coffee** we move to the joining of two intoxicants, adding **Irish whiskey** (see the topic **WHISKEY**) and whipped cream to coffee.

dans son café	in his coffee
cherchant obstinément	searching obstinately
l'éternité	for eternity

Jean Antonini, France [k]

Een plastic beker	A plastic cup
en een plastic lepeltje.	and a plastic spoon.
Hoe smaakt de koffie?	How does the coffee taste?

Karel Hellemans, Belgium [s]

ROOF. One of the major components of a **HOUSE** (*ie*) or **BUILDING** (tatemono), which are also year-round topics.

three-pot harmony
sings me to sleep—
my leaky roof

Christopher Schendel, CA [s]

PORCH, *pōchi*. Any roofed but otherwise open shelter that is part of a building. One might also classify the following poem under the year-round topics **EXERCISE** or **MARTIAL ARTS**, but its focus does seems to be on the porch. Note that the words **BALCONY** (*rōdai*) and **veranda** (*beranda*) comprise a traditional summer topic.

Practicing T'ai Chi
on the porch . . .
knowing which boards shift

Donna Gallagher, CA [k/s]

WALL, *muro*—Spanish. Permanent partitions separating the interior from the outside, or one space from another in a house or building. Walls protect us from others while they limit our view.

Sueño llanuras,	I dream prairies,
mientras indiferentes	while the indifferent
muros me oprimen.	walls oppress me.

Ertore José Palmero, Argentina [k/s]

DOOR, *monḳo*. A door as a physical object, part of a house or other building. Types include **front door**—the main entrance to a house, **wood door, glass door**, and the doors to various rooms or spaces. Note also **SCREEN DOOR**, a summer topic, and **STORM DOOR**, a winter topic.

he packs a crate
too big to go
through the door

Margaret Schultz, TX [s]

TOILET. In haikai the most common household objects may be fit for poetry. The toilet or **W.C.** is one of them.

flushing the toilet
the sound   of darkness
sucked down

Janice M. Bostok, Australia [k]

FURNITURE, *ḳagu*. Includes all kinds likely to be found in a house, office, or waiting room, such as **bed** (*beddo*), **dresser** (*tansu*), **desk** (*tsuḳue*), **table** (*tēburu*), **couch** (*sofa*).

sure you can sleep here
she says
pointing to the couch

Mykel Board, NY [s]

my new
secondhand dresser
smells old

Ronan, OR [k/s]

LAMPLIGHT, *tōka*. This topic includes all kinds of **artificial light** (*shōmei*) used in and around the home and other spaces. Also: **lightbulb** (*denkyū*), **floorlamp, flourescent light, fishing light** (*isaribi*) such as one uses in night-fishing, **paper lantern** (*chōchin*), and **candle** (*rōsoku*).

switching off the lights
switching off the shadows

Ruby Spriggs, ON [k]

HOUSEWARES, *nichōhin*. Small appliances and other household furnishings, cleaning tools and materials, such as **broom** (*hōki*) and **vacuum cleaner** (*sōjiki*), **iron** (*airon*) and **scissors** (*hasami*), **clock** (*tokei*) and **tissues** (*tisshu*), **mousetrap** (*muizenval*—Dutch).

Ik zet een muizenval	I set a mousetrap
met gemengde gevoelens	with mixed feelings
en vang mijn vinger.	and catch my finger.

Wiel Claus, The Netherlands [s]

POTS AND PANS. This topic includes the various containers used in **COOKING**, such as **sauce pan** and **skillet, roasting pan** and **cake pan, kettle.**

Where does happiness
come from—swapping poems
for a kettle

Bill Wyatt, England [s]

HOUSE CLEANING. The topic includes the activities involved in cleaning house, such as **cleaning windows, scrubbing floors**, and the like.

Note that cleaning tools and supplies are included under **HOUSE-WARES.**

that woman's not waving
she's cleaning her windows

Fred Schofield, England [s]

TOILETRIES, *keshōdōgu*. This includes all the soaps, cosmetics, and implements used in daily ablutions, personal grooming, and so on. For example: **shaving brush** (*scheerkwast*—Dutch).

Mijn nieuwe scheerkwast:	My new shaving brush:
na drie maanden is hij	now after three months
zijn wilde haren kwijt.	its wild hairs gone.

Bart Mesotten, Belgium [k]

OFFICE WORKER, *sarariiman*. This topic includes a number of terms related to the office environment, which is certainly a "season" unto itself: **white-collar worker** (*tsutomenin*), **capitalist** (*shihonka*), **company employee** (*sha-in*, with the overtones of **company man**), **transfer** (*tenkin*), **unemployment** (*shitsugyō*), **career change** (*tenshoku*), **promotion** (*shōshin*), **meeting** or **conference** (*kaigi*), **engineer** (*gijutsusha*), **government official** (*yakunin*), and so on. Similar lists have been assembled for other work situations, such as **FARMER** (*nōfu*), **LABORER** (*rōdōsha*), **WORKER** (*shokkō*), and others.

kaigi go ni	after the meeting
pon-pon tobikau	popping out all over—
shinkikaku	new plans

Hebiisumōkā ("Heavy Smoker"), Japan [s]

MERCHANT, *shōnin*. Includes all persons who buy and sell merchandise, as well as their places of business, such as **supermarket, store,** and many other retail enterprises, along with words like **price** and **sale.** Note that some are seasonal, such as **FLEA MARKET** (summer), **WHITE SALE** (late winter), and the like. Also: **craft fair, florist, plant shop, jewelry sale.**

a craft fair
we sit among the pots
price hidden

Sara Hong, MD [k/s]

with his clippers
the florist prunes
his cigar

Evan S. Mahl, NY [k/s]

Jewelry sale—
 the shop aglitter
  with eyes

Virginia Egermeier, CA [s]

The plant shop shutter
half up: smell of night jungle
on the city street.

Padraig Rooney, Japan [k]

PROSTITUTE. No livelihood is exempt from observation in haikai. Associated terms include **streetwalker, call girl, pimp, john, trick**. Also called: **hooker**. Note that in the following poem **street girl** might properly belong under **BEGGAR**, below.

passing the dolls hospital
the hooker walks
more slowly

John O'Connor, New Zealand [k/s]

street girl approaches
man buying newspaper
hands her the want-ads

George Knox, CA [k/s]

BEGGAR, *prosi*—Croatian. Begging has become the profession of an increasing number of people in the developed countries as well as the "developing", and knows no season. Also: **beg.**

The beggar limps up
and skips away
with her money

John Brandi, NM [s]

downcast eyes
hiding behind his dreads . . .
local boy begs

David Walker, England [k/s]

Pružajući ruku	Extending a hand
kojom prosi, skriva drugu	the beggar hides the other
koje nema.	he hasn't got.

Marinko Španović, Croatia [k/s]

WALKING, *aruku*. A popular form of exercise and recreation.

walking the dirt road
she in her rut
I in mine

Christopher Herold, CA [k/s]

walking downhill
the little stones
run ahead

M. M. Nichols, NY [k]

FISHING, *chōgyo*. Many specific types of sport fishing have their seasons, but by itself the term can refer to any time of year. Note that the legally acknowledged **fishing season** which requires a **fishing license**

usually begins in spring and runs through autumn, but that legal seasons for specific types of fish—such as trout—may be limited to a few weeks. **FLY-FISHING** may start in mid-to-late spring and carry over into autumn, but is mainly a summer sport, related to **MAYFLIES** and similar insects. **ICE FISHING** (*kanzuri*) relates to winter. Also: **fisherman, night fishermen** (*nachtvissers*—Dutch), **rod and reel, tackle box, creel,** and so on.

calm river
fisherman leaving
a fish jumps

Jean Campbell Simmonds, WA [s]

fisherman
pulling the lake closer
with each cast

Lawrence Rungren, MA [k]

Het vuurtorenlicht	The lighthouse beam
werpt lijnen naar nachtvissers	casts a line to the night fishermen
telkens maar even.	every now and then.

Wanda Reumer, The Netherlands [k]

AMUSEMENT PARK. Many amusements formerly associated with a **SUMMER CARNIVAL** are now part of amusement parks that operate all year. Also: **funhouse, ferris wheel, roller coaster,** and so on.

funhouse mirror
a startled child's
cranky image

Gloria H. Procsal, CA [k/s]

CARD GAME, *toranpu*. Includes all games played with cards other than the famous **POETRY CARDS** (*karuta*), which are especially associated with the New Year, and various kinds of cards used in

FORTUNE-TELLING, an all-year topic. Also: **bridge** (*burijji*), **gin-rummy, poker** (*pōkā*), **solitaire, whist** (*oisuto*), and so on.

a game of solitaire—
sun off the cards
slashes at the walls

Rod Willmot, PQ [k/s]

BILLIARDS, *tamatsuki*. This game of **cuestick**, balls, and table—often, but not always with pockets, as in **pocket billiards**—is a pastime for rich and poor which has become a popular family amusement. Found in rural bars in many parts of North America, in most cities pocket billiards goes by the name **pool** and has echoes of **pool halls**, gambling, and the underworld. Wherever played, one wishes to avoid finding the **cue-ball** "behind the eightball"—**eightball** itself being another name for the game. Related games include **three-cushion billiards, snooker,** and **bumper pool.**

Riverside tavern—
eighty, she still shoots pool
—smoking a cigar

Robert Spiess, WI [k/s]

DOLL, *ningyō*. Indoors, outdoors, year-round, dolls provide children with companions and opportunities to express their images of the world. Dolls may have **doll clothes**, a **dollhouse** and various other accessories. Note that the Japanese word *hina*, usually translated as simply "doll", specifically refers to the decorative dolls of the March **DOLL FESTIVAL** (*hinamatsuri*) held in Japan on 3 March; *ningyō* is the Japanese word for ordinary toy dolls.

After falling down,
she asks for a bandaid
for her doll too

Garry Gay, CA [s]

In the dollhouse
On the tiny table, a miniature
Divorce agreement.

Cat Thompson, NJ [s]

GAMES, *gēmu*. Many games and toys have seasonal associations. In haikai we have **SWING** (spring), **CAT'S CRADLE** (winter), and so on. But others know no season: board games such as **mah-jongg, chess,** and **checkers,** and various gambling **CARD GAMES** (see above) appear any time of year. People are as likely to assemble a **jig-saw puzzle** during a summer vacation afternoon as on a winter evening. And various hand games such as **shadow play,** requiring little or no equipment other than one's fingers, go anywhere, any time of year. Also: **checkerboard, chess-board** (*tablero de ajedrez*—Spanish).

on my wall
two monsters fight—
shadow play

Penny Harter, NM [k/s]

winning too much,
the retarded brother glares
over the checkerboard

Frank Higgins, MO [k/s]

Desde aquel día	Since that day
no he movido las piezas	I have not moved the pieces
en el tablero.	on the board.

Jorge Luis Borges, Argentina [k]

VISUAL ARTS, *bijutsu*. This topic includes **painting** (*yōga*), **drawing** (*senga*), **landscape** (*sansui*), **sculpture** (*chōkoku*), **figure drawing,** and the appreciation of these arts in **galleries** and **art museums,** public buildings, parks, homes.

figure drawing class—
in the model's deepest shadows
a stark white string

Lee Gurga, IL [k/s]

COLORS, *shikisai*. Obviously, there are many colors, and many uses. In Chinese and Japanese several names of colors have direct connections with fabric and dyes. Various colors have subtle associations with seasons and moods. And any **primary color** (*genshoku*), such as **blue** (*plavetnilo*—Serbian), has several varieties: **pale blue** (*asagi*), **light blue** (*hanada-iro*), **deep blue** (*koniro*), **dark blue** (*konpeki*), **navy blue** (*konjō*), **indigo** (*ranshoku*), **peacock blue** (*kujaku-aoi*), **lapis lazuli** (*ruri-iro*), **ultramarine** (*gunjō-iro*), and more.

In haikai color names frequently are not needed, especially when speaking of an object whose colors are well-known. If an object has only one color, naming the object is usually sufficient, just as one does not have to mention "water" in the same verse with "boat"—the one immediately suggests the other. But occasional use of a more specific color word can also be quite effective. Also: **pigment** (*shikissō*), **cool color** (*kanshoku*), **warm color** (*danshoku*), **lustre** (*kōtaku*), and so on.

Plavetnilo neba	The blue of the sky
s plavetnilom mora	and the blue of the sea
gdje se susreću?	where do they meet?

Nada Zlatić-Kavgić, Yugoslavia [k]

MUSIC, *ongaku*. Includes traditional and **classical music** (*kurashikku*) and **jazz** (*jazu*), **folk music** and **blues,** and popular music of all kinds and cultures, plus instruments from **wind instruments** (*suisō*) to **percussion,** and performance locations—from **concert halls** (*ongaku kaijō*) to **blues clubs,** composers from **Bach** to the **Beatles.**

in the spotlight
the bluesman tips the brim
to shade his eyes

Jeffrey Winke, IL [k]

"Jesu, Joy
of Man's Desiring"—the pure line
in a child's mouth

Geraldine C. Little, NJ [k]

BOOK, *shomotsu*. The topic focuses mainly on literary works, such as **stories, novels, biographies, belles lettres**, and so on. **Textbooks** relate to the year-round topic **SCHOOL**; **POEM** has its own topic, below.

closing the book
already homesick
for paths never walked

Addie Adam, FL [k/s]

POEM. Includes all kinds of **poetry**, from **doggerel** and **light verse** to **epic poem**; **verse** and **stanza**, **quatrain** and **sonnet**; **rimed verse** (or **rhymed**—but why perpetuate the spelling error of some medieval scribe who confused the word with "rhythm"?), **blank verse**, and **vers libre** or **free verse**; even **prose poem**. Of course the varieties of **haikai** would be included here: **hokku, haiku** (*haiku*—Croatian), **senryu**, and **renku**.

Napisatću	I shall write
haiku—možda me	a haiku—perhaps rage
mine bijes!	will pass me by!

Marijan Čekolj, Croatia [s]

FILM. The topic includes **movie, motion picture, movie theater, movie star, actor** (a gender-neutral term), such phrases as "**lights—action—camera**", and so on.

in the silent movie
a bird I think extinct
is singing

LeRoy Gorman, ON [k/s]

TRAVEL, *tabi*. A great theme of classical renga, travel is still prominent in renku. A number of more focused topics relate to specific kinds of travel, from **COMMUTING** and **BUSINESS TRIP** to **VACATION** and **FOREIGN TRAVEL** (*gaiyū*). Also, all manner of conveyances have their own status as topics. Note that some travel-related seasonal topics occur in other seasons, such as **PILGRIMAGE** in spring. A related year-round topic, **WANDERING** (*hyōhaku*), is separate because it includes the notions of **homeless** (*ryūbō*), **drifting** (*tadayou*), **hobo** (*rurōsha*), and being **on the road**. Also: **flyer.**

alone on the road
the one distant light
turns off

Lequita Vance, CA [k]

Forgetting his underwear—
the one with so many
frequent flyer miles

Donna Claire Gallagher, CA [s]

VACATION. **On vacation** one generally travels away from home and work for recreation, which may consist of simply **sight-seeing** (see **TOURIST**, next entry), or may have other more specific objectives, such as **FISHING** (year-round) or **CAMPING** (*kyanpingu*, summer). The military has its own terms, such as **leave; R and R,** an abbreviation for **rest and recuperation,** suggests one has been in battle. Of course the topics **SUMMER VACATION** and **WINTER VACATION** are seasonal, but people take vacations at all times of the year.

on vacation—
mind, the old nemesis
tagging along

Mitzi Hughes Trout, GA [s]

TOURIST. A tourist or **sightseer** travels to see notable sights, and perhaps to be able to talk of having been to such places. On **VACATION**

people rest and engage in recreational activities for their own sake and to take a break from work, often returning to the same area or even the same house or resort for the purpose at a set time each year. But the tourist tends to be a voyeur, attempting to observe the life of a place without fully taking part in it or forming a bond with its people. As such, tourists often provide a humorous topic in haikai.

cliff-dweller ruins—
tourists' voices
echo faintly

Tom Lynch, CA [k]

VISITOR. The visitor does not stay permanently, and often is a welcomed **guest**. However welcomed even a blood **RELATIVE** or **FRIEND** may be, whether the **visit** is for an hour or a month or more, a visitor also changes the routines of a household. The following poem implies this topic without overtly stating it.

tyres on the gravel:
we prepare
our cries of great delight

Geoffrey Daniel, England [s]

TRAIN, *ressha*. All kinds of trains except underground, which has its own category: **electrified train** (*densha*), **diesel locomotive** (*dezeru*), **steam train** (*kisha*), **express train** (*kyūkō*), **passenger train, commuter train; freight car** (*kasha*), **dining car** (*shokudōsha*), **sleeping car** (*shindaisha*), and so on.

the aged elbow
of someone sleeping . . .
train at dusk

Kim Dorman, India [k]

"All Change!"
on the next train
the same faces

John F. Turner, Australia [k/s]

BUS. The most common form of public transportation in many cities, the bus has replaced the **trolley car** or **trolley** which dominated the field in the early twentieth century. In many regions busses also supply an important means of transportation between cities, especially in areas where people typically commute to work from one town to another.

on the crowded bus
standing straighter
when offered a seat

Laura Bell, CA [s]

BICYCLE, *jitensha*. For some the bicycle is a year-round means of transportation; a toy **tricycle** (*tricicleta*—Romanian) will be more common from spring to autumn, but either may also be a gift at **CHRISTMAS.**

Copilul fuge pe tricicletă	The child rides the tricycle
Să nu-l întreacă	Competing with
Umbra-i	His shadow

Elena Manta Ciubotariu, Romania [k/s]

his bicycle
on hers—path
by the meadow

John O'Connor, New Zealand [k/s]

PARKING GARAGE, (*parkeergarage*—Dutch). This refers to a garage attached to or associated with a public building, apartment house, shopping complex, downtown, and so on. We have also the one- or two-car **garage** associated with a single-family **HOUSE.**

Het betonnen paaltje	The concrete pole
in de parkeergarage—	in the parking garage—
ik hoorde het staan.	I heard it stand.

Ferre Denis, Belgium [s]

HOTEL. A place where one stays while away from home, or a temporary residence; other keywords for this topic include **inn, motel, rooming house, boarding house, flophouse, fleabag.** In contrast, the topic **HOUSE** implies permanent residence, and includes **apartment building** and **residential hotel** as well as **dwelling** and **home.**

in the motel room
someone else's
stale smoke

Ruby Spriggs, ON [s]

TRAFFIC SIGNAL, *kōtsū shingō*. Intimately related to the topic **ROAD** under "The Earth" category, a traffic signal will be most noticed when its **red light** (*akashingō*) stops us on our way.

akashingō	red light
minna de watareba	if all cross together
kowakunai	we won't go astray

anonymous, Japan [s]

FORD, (*vad*—Romanian). The need to cross a river or stream knows no season. While many have never seen a ford because of the modern prevalence of bridges, fords still function in rural areas and on private land. Also called: **shallows.**

Trecând prin vad—	Crossing the ford—
ce greu eşti, chicotesc	how heavy you are, giggle
pietrele.	the stones.

Dan Doman, Romania [k/s]

TALK. From **argument** to **sweet nothings** and **confession.** Some talk **makes a point,** some doesn't. Also: **what you said.**

deathbed confession
the charming rogue smiles
and tells his last lie

Addie Adam, FL [s]

he makes his point—
all the water glasses
tremble

Paul O. Williams, CA [s]

hearing what you said
thirty years
after you said it

Charles H. Easter, NJ [k/s]

MAIL, *yūbin*. All sorts of paper and package communications sent by mail or courier services, and related paraphernalia—**stamps, registered mail,** and so on—fall under this topic. (Careful writers avoid using the names of delivery services and other trade names.) **FACSIMILE** or **fax** and **ELECTRONIC MAIL** or **e-mail** are also year-round topics. Note that if the subject or type of mail is specified, it may come under another topic, such as **CHRISTMAS** (mid winter) or **BIRTHDAY** (year-round).

Not knowing what to say
he mails
only the envelope

John Brandi, NM [s]

LAUGH, *warai*. The haikai topic includes **smile** and **grin,** all expressions of pleasure or amusement made with the mouth and eyes. **Laughter** suggests open amusement, as does a **broad smile** or grin, but the latter two may also express appreciation or friendship.

missed it the moment to join in the laugh

George Marsh, England [s]

DREAM, *yume*. Dreams provide another "life", one associated with myth and the subconscious. Some people believe they can help us understand the future. Note that **FIRST DREAM** is a New Year topic. Also: **nightmare.**

restless dream
a game of hide and seek
in the graveyard

Joanne Morcom, AB [k]

ALL YEAR—CUSTOMS AND RELIGION

RELATIVE, *nikushin*. Includes blood kindred and relations by marriage, such as **nephew.**

my nephew
pumping gas
tankful of dreams

Jocelyne Villeneuve, ON [k/s]

PARENT, *oya*. We begin by depending on our parents for our very existence. If lucky, we will have to care for them in their declining years. Also: **mother, father.**

Mother & daughter,
each aware of the other
writing poetry.

Norman Talbot, Australia [s]

MARRIED COUPLE, *fūfu*. In addition to the couple as **husband and wife,** this also includes all the individual terms for married persons—grand, sweet, or demeaning—from **lord of the manner** to **my old man, my lady** to the **little woman** and **better half.**

spellbound husband
his wife's version
of their courtship

Francine Porad, WA [s]

Her back turned,
the husband zaps his wife
with the TV remote

Katrina Middleton, CA [s]

Methodical husband:
On his list of chores, she finds
Her name

Anita Krumins, ON [s]

DIVORCE. The permanent end of a marriage that once bound a **MARRIED COUPLE** together. The topic includes divorce itself as a fact, **divorcee**, the legal documents involved, such as a **divorce decree** or **property settlement**, and the continuing aftermath in the form of **alimony** or **child support** payments. See also the related poem under **DOLL**, above.

after the divorce
she sleeps on his side
of the bed

Stuart Quine, England [s]

at the antique sale
smiling at bargains she'd like
and won't know about

Frank Higgins, MO [s]

LOVE, *koi*, (*luat*—Romanian). A classic subject, love is second only to the seasons in linked poetry. In renga and renku the theme of love usually centers on the sadness of being apart from one's **lover, waiting in vain**, or **love lost**. The English pun on the word "pine", as in "pine tree" and **pining for a lover,** is nearly duplicated by the Japanese pun on "pine tree" (*matsu*) and "to wait" (*matsu*)—and frequently occurs in the love stanzas of renku. See also **KISS** and **FLIRT**.

Cameră goală	The deserted room—
iubirea a luat cu ea	love took with it
chiar şi pereţii.	even the walls.

Dumitru D. Ifrim, Romania [k]

from my lover's lips . . .
a phrase
my ex-husband used

Valorie Broadhurst Woerdehoff, IA [s]

FLIRT, *koketiranje*—Croatian. Flirting is behavior that suggests sexual attraction. It may be simply an enjoyable part of everyday communication between two people who know one another, or perhaps a prelude to getting to know someone better. Flirting may be quite unwelcome, in which case the **flirt**—a person who flirts—might be best advised to drop such behavior, as it can only drive the other person away. But some flirts are quite insensitive to the way they appear to others. A **leer** or a **wink** may include a **SMILE** or grin, but suggests more involvement of the **EYES** in a look that conveys a sly, sinister, or lustful suggestion. As with most matters pertaining to sex, flirting is an obvious target for humor.

Sudska rasprava	Court debate
koketira koketa	the flirt flirts
čeka presudu	awaiting the verdict

Duško Matas, Croatia [s]

androgynous stranger
winks at me

Karen Sohne, NY [s]

KISS, *phili*—Greek. Whether a perfunctory **peck on the cheek** or a deep **tongue kiss,** a kiss expresses relationship.

cemetery
our first feared
kiss

Christopher W. Howell, IA [k/s]

Ksypno me thlipse	I wake up sad
psykhos kai photia mazi	cold and fire together
phili se brakho	a kiss on a rock

Tota Sakellariou, Austria [k/s]

SHYNESS. A **bashful** or **timid** person may have a hard time making friends, but sometimes it is best to act **shyly** (*scheu*—German).

Er lächelt dich an,	He smiles at you,
blickt scheu in deine Augen—	looks shyly into your eyes—
und sieht doch nur sich.	and sees only himself.

Kurt F. Svatek, Austria [s]

FRIEND, *kōyū*. One of the most important and diverse relationships experienced by humans, **friendship** normally involves shared interests and experience and does not imply a sexual relationship, though the word "friend" may occasionally be a euphemism for **lover** (see **LOVE**, above). A **close friend** or **bosom buddy** may be someone more important than a **BLOOD RELATIVE**. An **acquaintance** is a person one knows but does not consider a friend. An **old friend** is someone who has been a friend for a long time, not necessarily an elderly person.

More interruptions.
Seething, I open the door—
to my oldest friend.

D. C. Trent, England [s]

NEIGHBOR. Sometimes a neighbor is a **FRIEND**, sometimes barely an acquaintance. Nonetheless our neighbor's welfare and our own are intertwined.

across the canyon
the neighbor hammers
on an echo

Jane Reichhold, CA [k]

My neighbor—
He borrowed too much, I know,
Still, the moving van . . .

Patrick Worth Gray, NE [s]

WAR, *sensō*. Fighting between nations or major groups of people within nations, as in **civil war**. The topic includes the names of various **weapons**, from **fighter plane** to **battle ship** to **land mine**, and language appropriate to fighting, such as **salvo** and **shot** (in appropriate contexts—"shot" may also suggest **HUNTING**, a winter topic). Note that many of the human situations and results of war may show up in other topics. The Croatian Haiku Association has published an anthology entitled *Haiku Iz Rata / War Haiku* containing poems illustrating their recent experience, from which some of the poems in this saijiki are drawn.

Sarajevo walk
Serb and Muslim united
shot from front and back

Ruth Robinson, England [s]

BIRTHDAY, *tanjōbi*. Includes **birthday party, birthday present, blowing out the candles** on the **birthday cake**, and so on.

my birthday cake—
jumping back
from the blaze

Jerry A. Judge, OH [s]

all the candles
with one breath
the flame in her eyes

nick avis, NF [k]

ENGAGEMENT. Usually before entering the permanent relationship of a **MARRIED COUPLE**, a man and a woman **plight their troth** or **get engaged**. The act of **betrothal** is often symbolized by the man giving an **engagement ring** to the woman, and the ring itself gives some indication of the man's wealth or status and warns that the woman is not available to others as a prospective mate.

supermarket—
checked out with each purchase
her engagement ring

David Cobb, England [s]

FUNERAL, *sō*. All societies have ritualized ways of acknowledging that a person has died. Such rituals may include **burial** or **cremation**; most include prayers or meditations either to help the departed one into the next world or next life, or to assist those still living with accepting the loss. In some religious groups **last rites** are administered while a person is dying or immediately after death; a funeral usually takes place within a day or a few days after the death. When many of those who might otherwise attend a funeral are prevented from doing so by time or distance, a **memorial service** may be arranged to accommodate their needs. Also: **coffin.***

this letter
after your funeral
wishing me well

Jacqui Murray, Australia [k]

after the funeral
they talk about
who has his nose

Evan S. Mahl, NY [s]

BUDDHISM, *bukkyō*. One of the two religions which have most deeply influenced haikai, the other being **SHINTO**. However, haikai has a strong worldly bias, and, while some authors may feel a spiritual influence in their work, others may not. That said, everything is subject matter for haikai, regardless of one's religious persuasion, and something to do with religion is normally included in a linked poem. Also: **non-attachment.**

i buy
another book about
non-attachment

Chris Gordon, CA [s]

EID-EL-FITR (abbreviated **Eid**). Islamic holy day, ends the month of Ramadan (ninth in the Moslem calendar). Throughout Ramadan, one fasts during daylight hours, in honor of the first revelation of the Koran. At the end of four weeks, on Eid-el-Fitr, one must have new clothes. Since the Moslem calendar is strictly lunar, a year in it is shorter than a solar year, so this and all Islamic holidays progress 10 or 11 days earlier in the Gregorian calendar year-by-year, and do not correspond to solar seasons. Ramadan began on 11 February in 1994.

close to Eid
no-one sweeps the floor
in the tailor's shop

Dick Pettit, Sultanate of Oman [k/s]

SACRED PLACE. Sacred places include **houses of worship, consecrated ground**, and a **graveyard** or **cemetery**. A **final resting place** may be a simple **grave** (*grobovi*—Croatian, *morminte*—Romanian) or **grave plot** with a **gravestone** or **headstone** to identify the deceased; a structure that houses the remains of a human body, a **mausoleum**; or one where the ashes of the dead may be kept, a **columbarium**. People in different cultures pay formal visits to graves at different special times of the year, making such visits seasonal. In Japan **GRAVE VISITING** takes place during preparations for the early autumn **BON FESTIVAL**. In the U.S. one decorates the graves of veterans on **MEMORIAL DAY** in early summer. Of course one may visit a grave for a **FUNERAL** at any time of year. Note that a specific **PLACE NAME**, even for a sacred place, is included under that topic in Geography.

U pečinama	In the caves
grobovi prošlog rata.	the graves of the past war.
Vani bombardiranje!	Outside, a bombardment!

Nediljko Boban, Croatia [k]

Flori pe morminte—	Flowers on graves—
miresmele lor poartă	their fragrance carries
visul oaselor.	the bones' dream.

Florin Vasiliu, Romania [k]

ALL YEAR—ANIMALS

TIGER, *tora. Panthera tigris*. While most of us do not live near tigers, the image of the large orange and black striped cat is easily conjured with but the word. Exclusive to mainland Asia and Indonesia, it still finds its ways into the dreams of people worldwide. Prized by hunters and feared by humans living on the ever-diminishing frontier of its habitat, the tiger has in effect been a cornered species for most of recorded human history. Today a majority of tigers in the wild inhabit reserves where they are supposed to be able to live in balance with the other animals in their range and without human interference. Like the frog, the tiger may be an indicator species for the general health of the planet, and needs us mainly to avoid developing the areas where it lives.

Sweating, we pass
the sleeping tiger
wrinkles his nose.

William B. Rozier, MA [k]

CALF. The young of a cow. Domestic cattle mate and bear young throughout the year.

Feeding a calf
warm breath and big eyes
make me innocent

Keiko Shiraki, Japan [k]

GOAT, *yagi*, *caprei*—Romanian. The domestic goat (*Capra hircus*) differs from the **DOMESTIC SHEEP** (*hitsuji, Ovis aries*, also an all-year topic) mainly in its pungent smell, its pugnacious disposition, and its function—usually providing milk and meat rather than wool, though some breeds are used for wool production. Goats have been domesticated for 8–9,000 years.

Nemisçcat, cerul	Still, the sky
din ochiul caprei.	in a goat's eye.
Sângerândă tăcerea.	Bleeding, quietness.

Nicolae Stefanescu, Romania [k]

HORSE, *uma*, *calul*—Romanian. While **COLTS** and **foals** belong to spring, horses know all seasons.

none of the horses in the western poops

Marlene Mountain, TN [s]

Adăpând calul	Watering the horse
refac drumul	I remember a journey
început în noapte.	begun at night.

Ana-Olimpia Sima, Romania [k]

CAMEL *rakuda*. Native to the steppes and semideserts of central Asia are **Bactrian camels** (two-humped), and to the Arabian peninsula, **dromedaries** (one-humped); domesticated camels are now found from North Africa to China. Today the only wild camels are feral (that is, domesticated animals gone wild or the wild offspring of animals once domesticated).

shifting sand—
feral camels race
a tank

Darold D. Braida, HI [k]

DOG, *inu*, *perro*—Spanish. Unlike cats—**CAT'S LOVE** in early spring and **KITTENS** in late spring—dogs will do most anything at any time of the year, including **dogs mating,** so that **puppy** (*psić*—Croatian) is also an all-year season word.

peanut butter   the speed of the dog's tongue

Frederick Gasser, OH [k/s]

feuding neighbors:
their dogs
mate anyway

Barbara Ressler, IA [s]

U svakom oku
djeteta—dva oka
psića.

In each eye
of the child—two eyes
of a puppy.

Vladimir Devidé, Croatia [k]

Yace el soldado.
Un perro sólo
ladra por él furiosamente.

There lies the soldier.
Only a dog
barks for him furiously.

Rafael Alberti, Spain [k]

CAT, *neko. Felis domestica* or *F. catus.* Since being domesticated and worshipped in Egypt some 4,000 years ago, cats have retained an air of mystery. A cat may seem totally devoted to a human who feeds, grooms, or pets it one minute, and turn into a spitting, clawing demon the next, given the provocation of an unfamiliar animal or other threat. One of the best examples of behavioral variety is the mating behavior of otherwise genteel domestic cats, celebrated in the early-spring haikai topic **CAT'S LOVE**. The **house cat** has been bred into some thirty distinct varieties, from short-haired **tabby** to long-haired **angora**. The **Japanese bobtail** is highly prized for its friendly disposition and striking white fur with distinctive markings in black or "red" (actually, orange or ginger-colored); a cat with all three colors is called *mi-ke* (pronounced mee-keh), meaning three-colored but not to be confused with the Western **calico**. An abandoned domestic quickly becomes a **feral cat**, scavenging a living in almost any circumstances. Domestic and feral cats are a primary enemy of songbirds (see **TWITTERING** in spring).

cloud passing
the cat jumps
on its shadow

George Ralph, USA [k/s]

after feeding the cat
she scolds it for having
bulging sides

Kam Holifield, NY [s]

MARMOT, *morumotto*. *Marmota sp.* A North American and Eurasian cat-sized rodent; different species live in slightly overlapping ranges and have a variety of common names. In North America we have *M. monax*, known as **groundhog**, **woodchuck**, and **marmot** (trans-Canada and northeastern and midwestern U.S.); *M. flaviventris*, **yellow-bellied** or **yellow-footed marmot** (western U.S. and British Columbia); *M. caligata* and related species, called **whistler** (western Canada, northwestern U.S., and Alaska). Western species are also called **rockchuck** and **mountain marmot**. Marmots are often seen sunning or eating grasses and other herbage in fields and meadows during spring and summer, and hibernate in their underground burrows from mid autumn to early spring. They are noted for their sharp whistling cry of alarm, after which they normally run for their burrows. In the U.S. the marmot is the "groundhog" of **GROUNDHOG DAY** (see winter Observances).

a marmot's whistle
pierces the mountain—
first star

Ruth Yarrow, NY [k]

BIRD, *tori*. While most birds are associated with specific seasons in haikai because of their annual appearances and departures during migrations or their distinctive mating behavior and so on, the generic "bird" has no seasonal association. It is hard to find a place or a time with no birds.

lady crying over
  a dead bird
the plume in her hat

Laura Bell, CA [s]

CONDOR. The **California condor** (*Gymnogyps californianus*), one of the largest flying birds known in historical times, became extinct in the wild during the 1980s. Small populations at two California zoos are involved in breeding programs, and there is hope for their eventual reintroduction to their natural habitat. Though fossil records show they once spread across North America to Florida, by the time Europeans arrived the condor population had greatly decreased, and their range had become limited to the Pacific coast of the U.S. and inland to Utah. Their recent range had been somewhat taken over by turkey vultures (wingspread less than 6'/2 m), and their numbers depleted by humans. California condors have a wingspan of close to 10' (3 m), and feed on large carrion. Like other vultures, condors do not build nests as such, but lay eggs in high, inaccessible crevices. (Their egg-laying and tending is still called "nesting".) Mating pairs may produce one surviving offspring every two years, the low reproductive rate being another factor in their decline. Some **Andean condors** (*Vultur gryphus*) of similar size and habits have been released in the former range of the California condor with hopes that they will accommodate to the environment and breed successfully.

cloud shadows
on silent cliffs
where condors nested

Jerry Kilbride, CA [k]

VULTURE. Built like the **CONDOR** (see previous entry) but roughly one-half to two-thirds the size of a condor, vultures include the **turkey vulture** or **turkey buzzard** (*Cathartes aura*), **black vulture** (*C. atratus*), and **king vulture** (*Sarcoramphus papa*) in the Americas; there are also a number of species in Eurasia and Africa, including the **Egyptian vulture** (*Neophron percnopterus*) and **griffon vulture** (*Gyps fulvus*). The **white-backed vultures** of southern Africa (*G. africanus*) and India (*G. bengalensis*) are closer in size to condors than most other vultures, and are fairly common in their areas. Vultures have a bald or partially bald head and neck and are mainly black-feathered with some species white or brown. All are year-round residents in their areas and eat carrion. Note: The word **BUZZARD** has long been associated with North American vultures, but elsewhere applies to a group of falcon-like birds, *Buteo sp.*, which do not have bare skin on their heads (a winter topic).

turkey buzzards
riding the valley thermals:
I whistle a waltz

Muriel Ford, ON [k]

GULL, *kamome*, *maw*—Scots. Family Laridae. Because of the mistranslation "sea-gull" (*kamome* in Japanese) for "duck" (*kamo*, a winter topic) in R. H. Blyth's *Haiku*, "sea gull" was once erroneously thought of as a winter season word in English. Several species nest inland, and **sea gull** is simply a common name for any gulls seen along shores or over oceans. Many areas have gulls of one kind or another all the time. The gull most widely seen in Japan, the **BLACK-TAILED GULL** (*umineko*, literally sea-cat), is not frequently noted in winter, and consequently is a seasonal topic for summer and appears in topics for spring and autumn. Meanwhile, the **BLACK-HEADED GULL** (*yurikamome*) does winter in Japan and is a winter seasonal topic. Many other gulls migrate in for winter or summer, or stay year-round. Much the same situation occurs in large areas of the temperate zones in both hemispheres.

Flesh of the sky—
two gulls against the wind.
Your white shirt, drying.

Norma Voorhees Sheard, NJ [k]

a nazi swastika
which the gull swoops over
in complete ignorance

Barry Edgar Pilcher, Ireland [k/s]

I' the smirr	In the light rain
heich abune the hotchin toun	high above the busy town
ane maw wimplin.	one gull meandering.

Bruce Leeming, England [k]

CROW, *karasu. Corvus sp.* The Japanese refers equally to **raven** and crow. Ravens tend to be larger than crows, typically 25" (63 cm) long, while crows average about 18" (45 cm). Ravens have noticeably heavier beaks, a wedge-shaped tail in flight—crow's is rounded—and a deeper call and more oral variety than the crow's typical "caw-caw-caw". The English translation "crow" probably stems from the relative absence of ravens in Britain and the more urban areas of North America. In Japan ravens are often kept in city parks and hotel grounds, so they may be as familiar as crows. **BABY CROW** (*karasu no ko*) is a summer topic.

a raven
that dark guttural sound
his shadow

Elizabeth Searle Lamb, NM [k]

PIGEON, DOVE, *hato*, *duif*—Afrikaans, *golub*—Croatian. *Columbidae*, a family of some 300 species world-wide, includes the **rock pigeon** or **rock dove** from which the common pigeon apparently descended. Other members: the **turtle dove, mourning dove,** and **woodpigeon** of old and new worlds. Almost all areas have native or introduced species, several of which do not migrate, and so they are seen year-round in many habitats.

In die enigste gleuf	In the only hollow
van die druppende rotswand—	of the dripping rock-face—
die blou duif	the blue dove

Deon Kesting, South Africa [k]

Sred prazna grada	In the deserted town
gladne žrtve rata	hungry war victims
hrane golubove.	feed the pigeons.

Mile Stamenković, Croatia [k]

CHICKEN, *niwatori*. **Hens** (*găinile*—Romanian) and **roosters** naturally begin mating in late winter, but the laying hen is not allowed much time off from her year-round job of producing eggs. While "egg" could be that of any bird, in the following poem the context seems to make clear that the subject is a **hen's egg** (*jaje*—Croatian).*

Kokodakanje!	Great cackling!
Vječna slava i hvala!	Eternal glory and praise!
Ovom jajetu!	To this egg!

Dubravko Marijanović, Croatia [k/s]

Recesiune.	Recession.
Chiar şi găinile fac	Even the hens are laying
ouăle mai mici.	smaller eggs.

Manuela Miga, Romania [s]

SPARROW, *suzume*, *pardais*—Portuguese. Sparrows of many kinds are noted year round. The **house sparrow** (*Passer domesticus*), originally from Eurasia and Africa and formerly called the **English sparrow** in the U.S., is probably the world's most common bird. It lives near people, and is now found in large numbers on every continent inhabited by humans. Pugnacious, its flocks take over other birds' habitats and may be partially responsible for the decline of the American **BLUEBIRD** (spring). Japan's **tree sparrow** (*P. montanus*) is a close look-alike of the house sparrow with similar habits. There are also a number of other, more local "sparrows"—smallish finch-like birds, their usual colors mainly brown, russet, and gray, often with some white markings. Since many of these other sparrows are migratory, they may have seasonal associations in their locales, but the word "sparrow" in English will usually be understood to mean the house sparrow.

mura suzume	gathered sparrows
ichiban hoshi ni	raise up a clamor
tachisawagu	to the first star

Tohta Kaneko, Japan [k]

fim de tarde: os pardais	evening: the sparrows
(canto abafado	(song drowned out
pelo rodar dos carros)	by passing cars)

Yvette Kace Centeno, Portugal [k/s]

CARP, *koi*. In Japan this refers to the large "goldfish" bred to decorate ponds and pools (colors usually gold or silver, patches of gold and silver on white, or all black). Today we find these attractive fish in garden ponds worldwide. The managed varieties derive from the common carp (*Cyprinus carpio*), which originated in Asia and has been introduced as a game and food fish in most freshwaters of the world.

swimming away
the carp carries daylight
on its back

Wilma M. Erwin, OR [k]

SEAHORSE, *tatsu-no-otoshigo*, *căluţul de mare*—Romanian. *Hippocamus sp.* Several species of this small cousin of the pipefish inhabit warm ocean waters. The seahorse carries its head perpendicular to the body, which is normally oriented vertically in the water, and typically ranges from 2" to 6" (5–15 cm) long. The body is encased in bony rings, and has a relatively long prehensile tail. The female seahorse deposits her eggs in a brood pouch of the male, where they incubate for two weeks or so. Seahorses live among ocean vegetation such as eelgrass and sargassum, where their coloration changes with the background to make them inconspicuous.

printre alge şi scoici	among weed and shells
căluţul de mare	the seahorse
aşteaptă valul	waiting for a wave

Olga Duţu, Romania [k]

MOURNING CLOAK. *Nymphalis antiopa.* This butterfly is known as the "Camberwell beauty" in England, where it is an autumn season word (see **AUTUMN BUTTERFLY**), and is found spring through summer or autumn in much of Eurasia, making it a spring season word in those locales. But in most of its range in North America—where it is called the "mourning cloak"—the same species appears sporadically throughout the year, and therefore I include it here under its North American name as an example of a mid-temperate butterfly that has no seasonal limits. Of course many butterflies appear year-round in the tropics, and several of their ranges extend into Texas and Florida, such as the **giant sulphur** (*Phoebis sp.*), to cite only an instance from the Americas. In North America, at least, one must include a governing season word with any of these to make a poem seasonal. For example, **WITHERED GRASS** would have placed the following poem in winter. See also the entry for **BUTTERFLY** (spring) and the essay which follows it, and entries for **SUMMER**, **AUTUMN**, and **WINTER BUTTERFLY**.

that shadow
over the pale grasses—
a mourning cloak

Ursula Sandlee, PA [k]

ALL YEAR—PLANTS

TREE, *jumoku.* The names of many trees suggest their blossoms or fruit, which are often seasonal. But the evergreens, such as **pine** (*matsu, pinheiros*—Portuguese) and **cedar** (*sugi*), and the names alone of many deciduous trees, such as **oak** (*kashi*) and **birch** (*kaba*), do not have particular seasonal associations. (Note, however, that **MAPLE** [*kaede*] is a late-autumn topic for its colorful leaves, and **WILLOW** [*yanagi*] represents late spring with its bright green foliage.) This topic also includes such collective terms as **grove** (*kodachi*), **woods** (*mori*), and **forest** (*shinrin*).

A tree described
in five different languages
is only a tree.

Barbara Lindner, Germany [s]

as copas dos pinheiros	the tops of the pines
outro mar	another sea
outra respiração	another breathing

Yvette Kace Centeno, Portugal [k]

FLAMINGO PLANT. *Anthurium sp.* Also called **anthurium** or **painter's palette**, the flamingo plant provides an example of a houseplant that may bloom for a period in spring, summer, or autumn. This one has a flower composed of a broad leaflike spathe, usually bright red, with a protruding white or yellow spadix. Like many houseplants, it is native to the tropics, in this case Colombia and Guatemala. Some houseplants, such as the popular **AFRICAN VIOLET** (*Saintpauli ioanantha*), can bloom at any time of year. Note also the winter topic **HOT-HOUSE BLOOMING** (*murozaki*).

first light
cancer patient died
anthurium by the bed

Naomi Y. Brown, TX [k]

SAGEBRUSH. Usually refers to **big sagebrush** (*Artemisia tridentata*), also known as **wormwood** or **mugwort**. Evergreen and aromatic, the gray-green shrub, 2–10' (to 3 m) tall, is found on valley floors of the southwestern U.S. **SAGEBRUSH IN BLOOM**, with thin spikes of inconspicuous white flowers, would be a seasonal topic for mid-to-late autumn.

wind in the sagebrush—
the same dusty color
the smell of it

Elizabeth Searle Lamb, NM [k]

GRASS, *kusa*. **GRASS GREENING** (*kusa aomu*, early spring), **LUXURIANT GRASS** (*kusa shigeru*, summer), **GRASS SEEDS** (*kusa no mi*, autumn), and **WITHERED GRASS** (which see in winter) are all seasonal topics, but just plain grass is with us all year. Note that the Japanese term *kusa* includes many broad-leafed plants that would be called "forbs" or "wildflowers" in English.

one blade of grass—
the circle it makes
in the sand

Leatrice Lifshitz, NY [k]

SEAWEED, *kaisō*, *iarbe de mare*—Romanian. Many seaweeds appear in Japanese seasonword guides: *arame* and *nori* (also known as **laver** in English), spring; *konbu* (a **kelp**), summer; *hondawara* (**sea-grape** or **gulfweed**, another kelp) with the New Year. Seaweeds, as flavorings, the basis for soup-broths, and the black *nori* used to wrap *sushi*, form a staple part of the Japanese diet. **CUTTING KELP** (*konbu kari*), and **GATHERING AGAR-AGAR** (*tengusa tori*) are economically important activities all summer in Japan, as is **CUTTING DUCKWEED** (*mo kari*) in late summer. The generic "seaweed" is relevant all year.

In zorii zilei	At dawn
Se unduieşte sub val	Floating under the waves
Iarba de mare.	Seaweed.

Florina Dobrescu, Romania [k]

ACKNOWLEDGEMENTS

Many of the poems in this book were previously published in one of the following periodicals and books. I am very grateful to the authors or publishers for permission to reprint the work here. All copyrights remain with the authors and publishers.

Periodicals (by title): _Albatross/Albatros_ (Constanţa Haiku Society) * _Amelia_ * _Artillelres, revista cultural_ * _Azami: Haiku in English Newsletter_ * _Blithe Spirit_ * _Blue Jacket_ * _Brussels Sprout_ * _Cicada_ (Toronto) * _The Daily Yomiuri_ ("International Haiku") * _Dragonfly_ * _Frogpond_ * _Geppo_ * _Haiku_ (Poland) * _Haiku Časopis Vrabac/Sparrow Haiku Magazine_ (Croatian Haiku Association) * _Haiku Canada Newsletter_ * _Haiku Headlines_ * _Haiku Magazine_ * _Haiku Quarterly_ * _Haiku Southwest_ * _Haiku Zasshi Zo_ * _Heisei Haidan Kadan_ (Asahi Gurafu) * _Heisei Joryū Haijin_ (Mainichi Gurafu) * _HI_ * _Hoshi_ * _Hummingbird_ * _Inkstone_ * _Kaze_ (Nara Prefectural Government) * _Kennebec: A Portfolio of Maine Writing_ * _Kō_ (Kō Poetry Association) * _Lienzo_ * _Mainichi Daily News_ ("Haiku in English") * _Mayfly_ * _Mirrors_ * _Modern Haiku_ * _Neblina_ (Haiku Association of Colombia) * _New Cicada_ * _Newsweek Japan_ * _Nindō_ * _Northeast_ * _Pacific Friend_ * _Persimmon Tree_ * _Phoenix_ * _The Plaza_ * _Point Judith Light_ * _Raw Nervz Haiku_ * _Red Pagoda_ * _Spin_ * _Suimei_ * _The Alchemist_ * _The Windless Orchard_ * _US 1 Worksheets_ * _Vuursteen_ (Haiku Circle of the Netherlands and Haiku Center of Flanders) * _Windchimes_ * _Woodnotes_ (Haiku Poets of Northern California).

Books (by author or editor): Alberti, Rafael, _Antología poética_, Editorial Losada, 1942 * Andreyev, Alexey V., _Moyayama_, A Small Garlic Press, 1996 * Antonini, Jean, _Exercices sensationnels_, Editions Elaine Vernay, 1987 * Arima, Akito, _Ten-i_, Fujimi Shobō, 1987 * Associazione Italiana Amici del Haiku, _Premio Nazionale Poesia Haiku_, 1989 * avis, nick, _bending with the wind_, Breakwater, 1993 * Baker, Winona, _Beyond the Lighthouse_, Oolichan Books, 1992 * Ball, Jerry, Garry Gay, and Tom Tico, eds., _The San Francisco Haiku Anthology_, Smythe-Waithe Press, 1992 * Blanche, Patrick, _Jours ordinaires_, 1994 * Blanche, Patrick, _Rien de spécial_, 1992 * Bodner, Richard, _Like Water: Poems and Photographs_, Land of Enchantment Poetry Theater, 1994 * Borges, Jorge Luis,

La Cifra, Alianza Editorial, 1981 * Braida, Darold D., *Hawaii Education Association Fifth Annual Contest*, 1982 * Brandi, John, *Poems from the Green Parade: Haiku from a Journey to Nepal and Thailand*, Tooth of Time Books, 1990 * Brandi, John, *Weeding the Cosmos*, La Alameda Press, 1994 * birch, brian, ed., *Silenced Spring: 1991 Haiku Canada Members' Anthology*, Haiku Canada, 1991 * Brooks, Randy, *The Last Quarter Mile*, Grey Whale Press, 1981 * Brooks, Randy, and Lee Gurga, eds., *Midwest Haiku Anthology*, Brooks Books, 1992 * Brown, Naomi Y., *Seasons' Enigma*, Yucca Books, 1989 * Burleigh, David, *Winter Sunlight*, 1992 * Čekolj, Marijan, ed., *Haiku iz Rata*, 1992 * Cardona-Hine, Alvaro, *When I Was a Father*, New Rivers Press, 1982 * Childs, Cyril, ed., *New Zealand Haiku Anthology*, New Zealand Poetry Society, 1993 * Codrescu, Ion, ed., *Antologie de haiku*, 1994 * Codrescu, Ion, ed., *Constanţa Antologie de Haiku*, Editura Muntenia, 1992 * Davidson, L. A., *The Shape of the Tree*, Wind Chimes, 1982 * Desai, Jhinabhai "Sneharashmi", *Sunrise on Snowpeaks*, Gujarat Sahitya Akademi, 1986 * Dickson, Charles B., *A Moon in Each Eye*, AHA Books, 1993 * Donegan, Patricia, *Without Warning*, Parallax Press, 1990 * Donegan, Patricia, ed., *A Poppy Blooms*, Two Autumns Press, 1991 * Dunlap, Hank, *Daffodils & Dragonflies*, Poligion Publications, 1992 * Ehime Prefecture, *1990 International Haiku Contest Anthology*, 1990 * Einbond, Bernard Lionel, *The Tree As It Is*, in press * Einer, Lesley, *Way Station: on the edge of tomorrow*, Sage Shadow Press, 1993 * Ekuni, Shigeru, *Haiku Made in Japan*, [1990] * Espriu, Salvador, *Obras completas*, Edicions 62, 1989 * Evetts, Dee, curator, *Haiku on Forty-Second Street*, 1994 * Evetts, Dee, ed., *The Parakeet's Mirror*, Spring Street Haiku Group, 1993 * Evetts, Dee, ed., *Woodshavings*, Spring Street Haiku Group, 1994 * Ford, Muriel, *Mya Pasek*, 1985 * Fraticelli, Marco, *Night Coach*, Guernica Editions, 1983 * Frost, Palle Seiersen, *Haikai*, Impresos Laguna, 1976 * Fukuda, Shinkū, *Amanogawa*, Shinseyosha, 1994 * Furuta, Sōichi, *a man never becoming a line*, Edition Heliodor, 1979 * Gadd, Bernard, *Poetry NZ 7*, Brick Row, 1993 * Garb, Ivor, *Haiku: Some with an African Flavour*, 1991 * Gerits, Anton, *Alleen wanneer ik kijk*, In de Fazantenhof, 1984 * Ginsberg, Allen, *White Shroud: Poems 1980-1985*, Harper & Row, copyright © 1986 by Allen Ginsberg, by permission of Harper and Row * Gorman, LeRoy, *only shadflies have come*, Swamp Press, 1979 * Guidacci, Margherita, *Una Breve Misura*, 1991 * Hackett, James W., *The Zen Haiku and Other Zen Poems of J. W. Hackett*, Japan Publications, 1983 * Hadman, Ty, *Dong Ha Haiku*, Smythe-Waithe Press, 1982 * Hadman, Ty, *The Poor Part of Town*, Smythe-Waithe Press, 1982 * Haiku International Association, *Haiku International 1992*, 1992 * Haiku International Association, *Haiku International 1995*, 1995 * Haiku Society of America, *A Haiku Path: The*

Haiku Society of America 1968–1988, 1994 * Hao, Zhu, *First Frost*, AHA Books, 1990 * Harr, Lorraine E., *The Red Barn: Variations on a Pastoral Theme in Haiku*, J & C Transcripts, 1975 * Harter, Penny, *Shadow Play*, Simon & Schuster, 1994 * Harter, Penny, *Stages and Views*, Katydid Books, 1994 * Hashimoto, Kayoko, *Requiem*, 1988 * Heinrich, Peggy, *Patch of Grass*, High/Coo Press, 1984 * Hellemans, Karel, *De Heuvels Rondom*, 1981 * Hesse, Harvey, *Skipped Stones: Faces in Time*, Eight Pound Tiger Press, 1994 * Higashi, Meiga, *Nekominoan Hokkushū*, Nagata Shobō, 1994 * Higgins, Frank, *Eating Blowfish*, Raindust Press, 1996 * Higginson, William J., ed., *Wind in the Long Grass: A Collection of Haiku*, Simon & Schuster, 1991 * Higginson, William J., *Haiku Compass: Directions in the Poetical Map of the United States of America*, Haiku International Association, 1994 * Higginson, William J., *Met on the Road: A Transcontinental Haiku Journal*, Press Here, 1993 * Holmes, Dick, *The Red in the Rose*, Frog Pond Press, 1991 * Hotham, Gary, *As Far as the Light Goes*, Juniper Press, 1990 * Hotham, Gary, *Against the Linoleum*, Yiqralo Press, 1979 * Houwink, Roel, *Door het open raam*, De Beuk, 1992 * Howard, Dorothy, and André Duhaime, eds., *Haiku: Antologie canadienne/Canadian Anthology*, Les éditions Asticou enrg., 1985 * Hryciuk, Marshall, *Singed Leaves: A Book of Haiku Poetry*, Simon & Pierre, 1989 * Huizinga, Nanneke, *Pijltjes in de sneeuw*, 1988 * Inahata, Teiko, *Inahata Teiko: Haiku Bunko*, Shunyōdo Shoten, 1991 * Ishihara, Yatsuka, *Aki Fūkin*, Shoshi Yuriika, 1955 * Ishihara, Yatsuka, *Yuki Ryōsen*, Aki Hakkōsho, 1964 * Ivančan, Dubravko, *Life in the Country*, 1975 * Japan Air Lines, *Out of the Mouths . . . An anthology of English haiku by elementary schoolchildren of British Columbia*, 1987 * Jorgensen, Jean, *New Kid on the Block: Haiku and Senryu*, 1990 * Junoy, Josep Maria, *Obras poética*, Edicions dels Quaterns Crema, 1984 * Kagyūsha, eds., *Kagyū Shin Kiyose*, 1995 * Kakami, Keiko, ed., *Rainbow*, Rainbow English Haiku Society, 1992 * Kamegaya, Chie, *Seasons in New Denver: Haiku*, Laughing Raven Press, 1993 * Kaneko, Tohta, *Minna no*, Tachikaze Shobō, 1986 * Kanterman, Leroy, *The Ram's Horn*, n.d. * Katō, Kōko, *A First Bird Singing*, Hub Editions, 1993 * Katō, Kōko, ed., *Four Seasons: Haiku Anthology Classified by Season Words*, Kō Poetry Association, 1991 * Kenny, Adele, *Castles and Dragons*, Yorkshire House Books/Muse-Pie Press, 1990 * Kilbride, Jerry, ed., *Playing Tag Among Buddhas: 1992 Haiku Anthology*, Haiku Poets of Northern California, 1992 * Kirkup, James, *dengoban messages*, kyoto editions, 1981 * Kirkup, James, ed., *The Haiku Hundred*, Iron Press, 1992 * Klinge, Günther, *Day into Night: A Haiku Journey*, Charles E. Tuttle Co., 1980 (new translations by WJH) * Knox, George, *Tendrils of the Eye*, Haiku Moments Press, 1993 * Kondo, Kris, *You and I*, Toyo Junior College, 1987 * Kuroda Momoko, *Kachō Haiku Saijiki*, Heibonsha,

1987–88 * Kusama, Tokihiko, *Sixteen Haiku*, 1992 (new translations by WJH) * Lamb, Elizabeth Searle, *Casting into a Cloud: Southwest Haiku*, From Here Press, 1985 * Lamb, Elizabeth Searle, *in this blaze of sun*, From Here Press, 1975 * Leeming, Bruce, *Poems: In the haiku manner*, 1991 * Leveroni, Rosa, *Poesia*, Edicions 62, 1981 * Little, Geraldine C., *Star-Mapped*, Silver Apples Press, 1989 * Loperfido, Galilea, *Rubando Le Ore Agli dei*, 1990 * Lucas, Martin, *bluegrey: 121 haiku*, 1994 * Lyles, Peggy Willis, *Red Leaves in the Air*, High/Coo, 1979 * Lynch, Tom, *Rain Drips from the Trees: Haibun along the Trans-Canadian Highway*, 1992 * Lynch, Tom ed., *Summer River*, Two Atumns Press, 1992 * Mainone, Robert, *High on the Wind: Haiku*, 1975 * Matas, Duško, *Water Reeds*, 1991 * McClintock, Michael, *Maya: Poems 1969–1975*, Seer Ox, 1975 * mckay, anne, *from the upper room*, Wind Chimes Press, 1990 * Mesotten, Bart, ed., *Duizend kolibries: Haikoe van hier en elders*, Uitgeverij Sintjoris, 1993 * Miller, Florence, *Eleven Renga*, Jade Mountain Press, 1992 * Mizuhara, Shūōshi, et al. eds., *Nippon Dai Saijiki*, Kōdansha 1981–83 * Mizuhara, Shūōshi, *Gendai Haiku Saijiki*, Ohizumi Shoten, 1978 * Modern Haiku Association, *The International Haiku Contest: Work Collection*, 1987 * Montalvo, Berta G., *Gotas de Rocio*, 1992 * Moore, Lenard D., *Desert Storm: A Brief History*, Los Hombres Press, 1993 * Murray, Jacqui, Ross Clark, John Knight, et al., *Wattle Winds: An Australian Haiku Sequence*, Paper Wasp, 1994 * Nakamura, Teijo, et al. eds., *Gendai Joryū Haiku Zenshū*, Kōdansha, 1980–1981 * Neubauer, Patricia, ed., *Morning Snow*, Two Autumns Press, 1993 * New Zealand Poetry Society, *Annual Anthology*, 1990 * New Zealand Poetry Society, *Black Before the Sun*, 1993 * New Zealand Poetry Society, *Ginger Stardust*, 1992 * Núñez, Ana Rosa, *Escamas del Caribe: Haikus de Cuba,* 1971 * Oliver, Colin, *Ploughing at Nightfall*, Downstream Press, 1993 * Olson, Marian, *Songs of the Chicken Yard*, Honeybrook Press, 1992 * Pizzarelli, Alan, *a Silver hubcap: 1975–6*, Pizzazz Publications, 1976 * Pizzarelli, Alan, *Karma Poems: Haiku/Senryu, 1970–1973*, 1974 * Porad, Francine, *Without Haste*, Amelia, 1990 * Priebe, Renge / David, *Timepieces: Haiku Week-at-a-Glance*, Cloverleaf Books, 1993 * Reichhold, Jane, *A Dictionary of Haiku: Classified by Season Words with Traditional and Modern Methods*, AHA Books, 1992 * Reumer, Wanda, *Samen Oud Worden*, n.d. * Rodríguez Lodoño, Gloria Inés, *Libeluna*, 1990 * Rosenstock, Gabriel, *Cold Moon: The Erotic Haiku*, Branden Book Publishers, 1993 * Ross, Bruce, ed., *Haiku Moment*, Charles E. Tuttle Co., 1993 * Rotella, Alexis, *Yes*, Jade Mountain Press, 1994 * Roth, Hal, *Her Daughter's Eyes*, Wind Chimes, 1990 * Saito, Masaya, *Ash*, TELS Press, 1988 * Sanders, Lewis, ed., *Ship of the Moon*, The Red Pagoda, 1990 * Sanfield, Steve, *A New Way*, Tooth of Time, 1993 * Sanfield, Steve, *He Smiled to Himself*, Shakti Press, 1990 * Satō, Kazuo, *Neko* *mo mata*, Nagata Shobō, 1988 * Schultz, Margaret, *Happiness Is . . . A Book of Poems*, 1993 * Shapiro, Steve, *In a Borrowed Tent*, 1995 * Sherry, Helen J., *Colors of Haiku*, Chōchō Books, 1991 * Shiffert, Edith Marcombe, *Forest House With Cat*, 1991 * Sologuren, Javier, *Flores del Perú*, Lienzo 11, 1991 * Spiess, Robert, *The Turtle's Ears*, Wells Printing Co., 1971 * Stamm, Jack, *My Haiku Journey*, Kawade Shobō, 1993 * Story, Ebba, *The Shortest Distance*, Press Here, 1993 * Suzuki, Mitsu, *Temple Dusk: Zen Haiku*, Kazuaki Tanahashi and Gregory A. Wood, translators, Parallax Press, 1992 * Swede, George, ed., *Canadian Haiku Anthology*, Three Trees Press, 1979 * Swede, George, ed., *Cicada Voices: Selected Haiku of Eric Amann 1966–1979*, High/Coo Press, 1983 * Swede, George, *The Modern English Haiku*, Columbine Editions, 1981 * Swede, George, *Holes in My Cage: Poems for Young Adults*, Three Trees Press, 1989 * Szybiak, Robert, *Haiku Krymskie*, 1993 * Takada, Sakuzō, trans., *Toranomon Haiku Group 105 Haiku*, 1995 (new translations by WJH) * Takaha, Shugyō, *One Year of Haiku*, [1989] (new translations by WJH) * Takeshita, Ryūsai, *Zoku Minato*, Kadokawa Shoten, 1992 * Talbot, Norman, *Where Two Rivers Meet*, Nimrod Publications, 1980 * Tanemura, Kenneth, *No Love Poems*, Small Poetry Press, 1994 * Tasker, Brian, *Notes from a Humdrum*, 1992 * Theodoru, Stefan, *Traista cu Stele*, Editura Haiku şi Editura Tempus, 1995 * Thompson, John, ed., *Two Autumns*, Two Autumns Press, 1990 * Thorsen, Christopher, *Gnarled Grasses*, Rau Painu Press, 1968 * Tice, Richard, *Station Stop: A Collection of Haiku and Related Forms*, Middlewood Press, 1986 * Tokizane, Shinko, *Yufuren*, Asahi Shinbun, 1987 * Tulloss, Rod, *December 1975*, From Here Press, 1978 * Ueno City Master Bashō Museum, *Bashō Festival Dedicatory Haiku Anthology* (annuals), 1989, 1990, 1995 * Vakar, Anna, *Haiku*, postcard, n.d. * van den Heuvel, Cor, *The Geese Have Gone*, King's Road Press, 1992 * van den Heuvel, Cor, et al. eds., *An Anthology of Haiku by People of the United States and Canada*, Japan Air Lines, 1988 * Villeneuve, Jocelyne, *Marigolds in Snow*, Penumbra Press, 1993 * Virgil, Anita, *One Potato Two Potato Etc*, Peaks Press, 1991 * Virgilio, Nicholas A., *Selected Haiku*, Burnt Lake Press, 1985 * Vizenor, Gerald Robert, *Raising the Moon Vines*, Nodin Press, 1964 * Vizenor, Gerald Robert, *Seventeen Chirps*, Nodin Press, 1964 * Vučetić, Dragan, *Table-land*, 1992 * Walsh, Phyllis, *center stillness*, 1989 * Weiss, Brigitta, *Gib allem ein bisschen Zeit*, Wolfgang Hager, 1994 * Welch, Michael Dylan, ed., *Fig Newtons: Senryu to Go*, Press Here, 1993 * Welch, Michael Dylan, ed., *Harvest: An Anthology of Haiku Commemorating Haiku North America*, Press Here, 1991 * Willmot, Rod, *Sayings for the Invisible*, Black Moss Press, 1988 * Willmot, Rod, *The Ribs of Dragonfly*, Black Moss Press, 1984 * Wills, John, *Reed Shadows*, Burnt Lake Press, 1987 * Yamada, Mizue, *Yamada Mizue: Haiku Bunko*,

Shunyōdo Shoten, 1993 * Yarrow, Ruth, *Down Marble Canyon*, Wind Chimes, 1984 * Yarrow, Ruth, *No One Sees the Stems*, High/Coo, 1981 * Yoshimura, Ikuyo, *At The Riverside*, Kō-no-nai, 1990 * Yoshino, Yoshiko, *Haiku Sakura*, Hoshi Publisher, 1993 * Young, Virginia Brady, *warming a snowflake*, Sleeping Giant Associates, 1990 * Young, Virginia Brady, *Waterfall*, Timberline Press, 1982 * Zandboer, Piet, *Samen Oud Worden*, n.d.

AUTHOR INDEX

SAIJIKI INDEX

Page references are to the beginnings of entries. All capital letters indicates a topic; lower case letters a season word or keyword. Seasons are abbreviated (sp = spring; su = summer; au = autumn; wi = winter; yr = year). Note that not all references are to the appropriate seasonal section, since many topics, season words, and keywords are discussed under other, related entries. There are many homonyms, so several entries appear to be duplicates; they are not.